IMAGES
of America

Around
STEMLEY BRIDGE

Somewhere Around Stemley Bridge

Caverns holding unearthed steps once trodden by the Creek Tribe
Became the military bunker for explosives and secret mines.
More extreme than the winter solstice these chambers have survived
Like an eternal carcass with a luminescence of spirits alive.

Rustic barns and weedy pastures standing post along the roads
Speak an unknown voice of mules, plows, and ghostly growth.
Chicken-coops, out-houses, kerosene lamps, and pot-bellied stoves
Are some of the forgotten necessities from the days of old.

The long-winded train whistle brought with it an exasperating moan
Along its tracks that once laid in what became the Coosa River's home.
Wagons, mules, and Model T Fords on the dirt roads would roam
Soluble into the dust that black top is now upon.

The Little Rock Store, Camp Pleasure, and old cotton gins
Are establishments that created the foundation for prosperity back then.
As families struggled with bill collectors to make amends,
They worked the gins, mills, and fields until the sunset brought them in.

The Little Rock Church still stands today as it has yawned and tired away
Once it served as a one-room school and a house of worship and praise.
Now this building, like a wilted rose, limps of being fragile, orphaned, and grieving of age.
Generations who have yet to pass must listen to its story and still see its anointed grace.

There remains a structure that joins a great divide to this day.
It once crossed a river that has now become the Logan Martin Lake.
The community shares the name of what machines and man have made.
The Stemley Bridge proudly stands today as a remarkable stake.

Generations who reside here today carry a heritage that has upon them been bestowed.
Untarnished legends, folk tales, and historical information lie within their souls.
When they too travel beyond the rim of time where parting and sorrow are never told,
Their spirit will remain somewhere around Stemley Bridge—forever gold.

—Wendy Renae Gurley
July 28, 2005

On the Cover: Hendrix Martin posed on the old Stemley Bridge in the early 1960s with two of his sons, Harvey, left, and Michael. (Courtesy of Norman Martin.)

IMAGES
of America

Around
STEMLEY BRIDGE

Mildred J. Stathelson

ARCADIA

ISBN 0-7385-4215-6

Published by Arcadia Publishing
Charleston SC, Chicago IL, Portsmouth NH, San Francisco CA

Printed in Great Britain

Library of Congress Catalog Card Number: 2005933414

For all general information contact Arcadia Publishing at:
Telephone 843-853-2070
Fax 843-853-0044
E-mail sales@arcadiapublishing.com
For customer service and orders:
Toll-Free 1-888-313-2665

Visit us on the Internet at www.arcadiapublishing.com

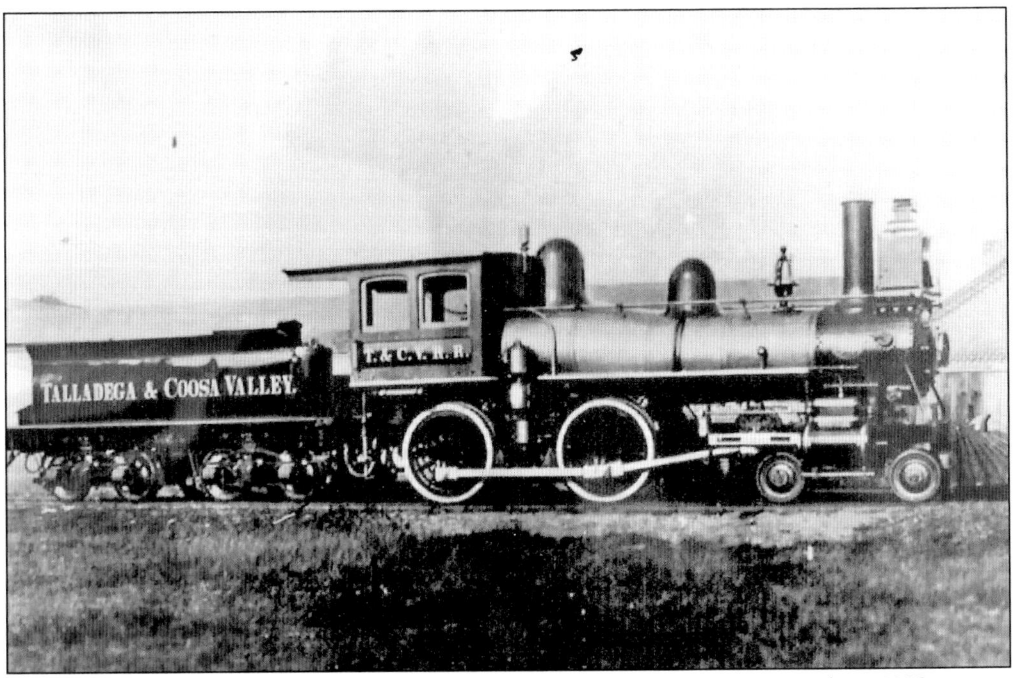

A charter for a railway between Murphy and the Coosa River was granted in 1883 to two brothers, D. W. and D. M. Rogers, who had moved their lumber milling business from Georgia to Renfroe. They named the railroad Talladega & Coosa Valley Railroad Company. It began operating in 1886, and by 1889, it was extended to 26.9 miles, from Talladega to Pell City, with a wooden bridge across the Coosa River. The name was changed to Birmingham & Atlantic Railroad in 1890. (Courtesy of Rob Strickland.)

Contents

ACKNOWLEDGMENTS

My heartfelt thanks go to all who have contributed to the compilation of this book. I cannot list everyone, but it goes without saying I could not have done it alone. First I thank my aspiring author, Sarah Stathelson, who helped put the idea into my head and on paper. Without Sarah, the first word would not have been written. Dot Wesson, JoAnn Gauldin, Derrell Hann, and Virginia Gurley got us started by collecting old photographs from family and friends. Their dedication and encouragement was indispensable. My grandsons, Nik, Landon, and Ben Cordes, installed my scanner and taught me to operate it. Wendy Gurley's cheerfulness sustained us, and her contributions spanned all areas, including writing, scanning, and typing. Laura Schmidt put her energy and heart into writing, editing, and proofreading. Calvin Sanders was our expert on the history around Stemley Bridge. Most of all I thank my 91-year-old angel, Muriel Goldberg, who watched over us all and kept us plied with cappuccino. I cannot give enough praise to these people and to all the others who gave so much of their time and effort to make this book a worthwhile work.

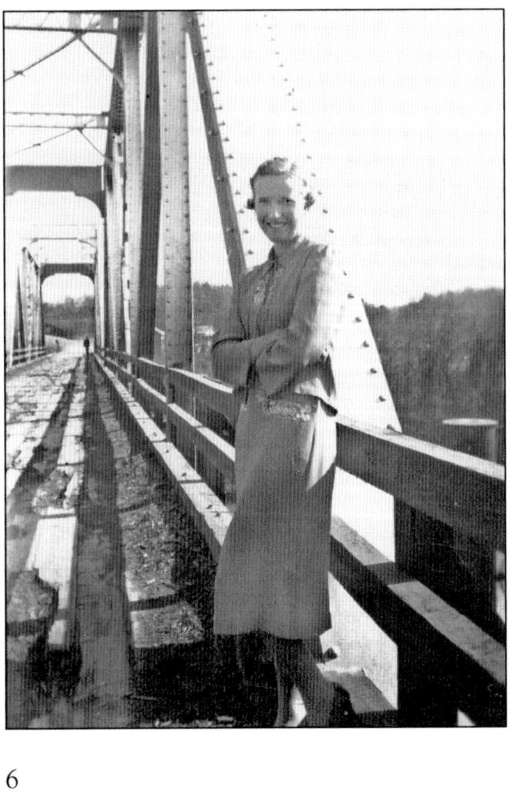

The old Stemley Bridge is a landmark of the area. Thelma Daffron poses on the bridge in 1939. The bridge was in operation until 1963 when the Logan Martin Dam was being constructed. Then the bridge was torn down in preparation for the backwater from the dam, and a new, modern bridge was constructed about a quarter of a mile upstream. (Courtesy of JoAnn Gauldin.)

INTRODUCTION

Jackson's defeat of the American Indians in the Battle of Talladega in 1813 was well publicized and celebrated and had people all over the country wanting to settle in the area to trade, farm, or practice their profession.

There were American Indian trails connecting villages all across the country. These evolved naturally into roads, several of which ran through northern Talladega County when white settlers began arriving. Wider roads and more ferries were built. Planters arrived to farm the rich, fertile Coosa land with its abundant supply of water.

The Creek Indians loved their land and were reluctant to leave their home, but after years of negotiations, a treaty was made. In 1832, the Creeks ceded to the United States all their land east of the Mississippi River. Each Creek family was allowed to select a section of land for their use for five years before selling it and going west. They didn't have to rush to sell the property cheaply, and they didn't have to sell at all if they didn't want to. And a few American Indians did remain.

When the Coosa Land Division Land Sales put American Indian lands on sale in 1835, there were still many Creek Indians living in the territory. In the latter part of 1836, about 3,490 American Indians were assembled at Howell's Cove to begin the infamous Trail of Tears, and by 1837, most of the tribe had left the area headed for lands in Oklahoma.

By 1840, there was a large population of settlers in this area. There were blacksmiths and millers every few miles where waterpower was available. The area was mainly agricultural. There were small farmers and some large planters. The planters began bringing in slaves to help cultivate the fields, and by 1860, there were 54 large slaveholders in north Talladega County with more than 3,160 slaves.

The Civil War changed everything.

Near the end of the war, Union general John T. Croxton and his brigade were moving eastward and camped near the ferries of Truss and Collins. (The Collins ferry crossed the Coosa River where Stemley Bridge was later built.) They seized both ferries and crossed the river on April 21, 1865. Unaware that Confederate general Joseph E. Johnston and Union general William Sherman had signed an armistice to stop hostile activity, they proceeded with their devastating activities, burning and destroying property and removing valuables from residences and businesses along the way.

When the war ended, slave families were each given a parcel of land. Some of them were devoted to their white families and stayed on to work for them. But many, through mismanagement, were not able to hold on to their land and began selling it. It was just a matter of time before they found themselves at the poverty level. It was also a hard time for the planters who found themselves without sufficient labor to work their fields. It was a struggle for all who remained in the community, and prosperity was slow in coming.

But timber was plentiful, and new lumber mills began coming into the area. It was not long (1886) before a railroad was built to haul lumber, iron ore, and other commodities. A railroad bridge was built across the Coosa River at Collins Ferry, and the surrounding community was named Stemley.

Stemley was named for Emily Ware, sister-in-law of D. M. Rogers, sawmill owner and village founder. Sister Emily became "Sist Emly," which was shortened further to "Stemly" or "Stemley."

The New Deal (1933–1937) was set up during Roosevelt's administration in an effort to recover the economy. Several work programs were implemented in the county to improve road conditions and give jobs to unemployed people.

During the Great Depression, the economy was unstable and supply was greater than demand. As prices went up, people could not afford to buy, farmers could not make a profit, and prosperity was so uneven that recovery was most difficult. Some men around Stemley Bridge became ill and were unable to work because of poor diet and inadequate medical care. Women had to go to work to help put food on the table. In one family, when the mother was hospitalized in a mental institution for several months at a time, the father would go off horse-trading and leave their five children without making any provisions for their care. One of the older children begged food from a neighboring black family until asked not to come back as they had trouble feeding their own children. It was not unusual for the children to go days with only gravy and an occasional biscuit to eat.

Nationwide food rationing was instituted in the spring of 1942. Each member of the family was issued ration books, and ration stamps became a type of currency. The homemaker had to pool the stamps and plan the family's meals within the set limits. Sugar, butter, coffee, lard, and beefsteak were some of the items that were scarce. When the rationing ended, many mothers in the area fed their children biscuits with sugar and butter as a special treat. In addition to a scarcity of food during the rationing, the area was plagued by shortages in housing and clothing. The Stemley area was hit hard. Many children had only one set of clothes to wear to school, and some were even unable to attend school because of the lack of clothes, shoes, and the necessary supplies. Reconstruction and eventually prosperity followed World War II.

For the past 40 years, Logan Martin Lake has been the biggest single boost to the economy around Stemley Bridge.

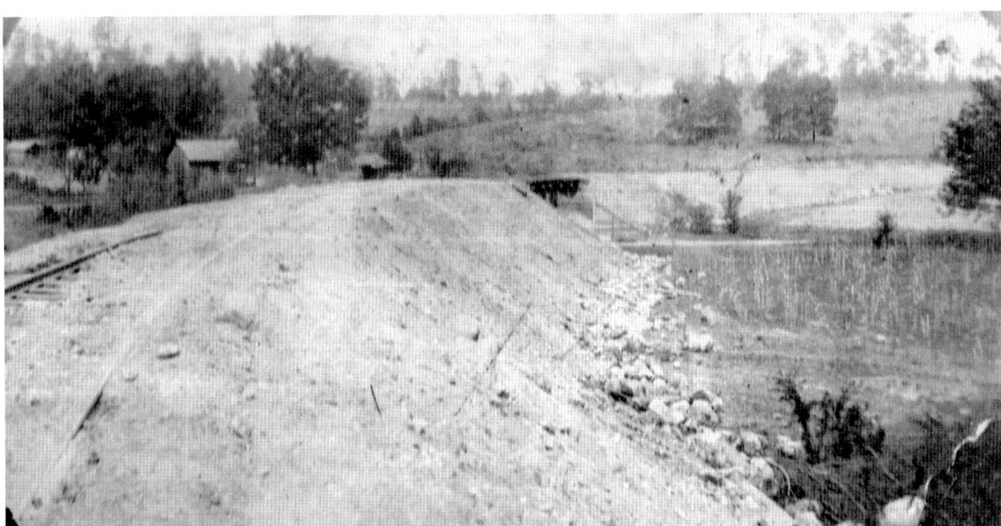

This is a picture of the first railroad bridge across the Coosa River at Stemley. It was a trestle bridge built in 1889 by the Talladega & Coosa Valley Railroad.

One

PLACES

Triple Lye Cave, located near Stemley Station, was a source of rich deposits of guano (bat droppings), which, when mixed with charcoal and sulphur, was used for making explosives during the latter part of the Civil War.

One Sunday afternoon in the early 1900s, Thomas and Marshall Rich, Henderson Brown, Troy Lee, Turner Jones, and Jim Funderburg entered the cave using a trotline for a guide rope and flashlights. There was no ladder, just an old tree with limb stumps for steps. Jim Funderburg, the only one of the group still living, says there were American Indian drawings and symbols on the lime rock walls of "men with bows and arrows" and the writing was in a language they couldn't understand. A three-foot-square opening on one side led into another area with a creek running through it. They made plans to return the following Sunday with better lighting and lines, but before they could do so, the large room collapsed.

Among other places of interest around Stemley Bridge are the old houses. A popular early style was the "dog trot"—one or two rooms on each side of an open breezeway. Examples from this area include the Sisson house on Stemley Road and the Thomas house that has been moved from the old Stemley Bridge Road to Renfroe Road and is being remodeled.

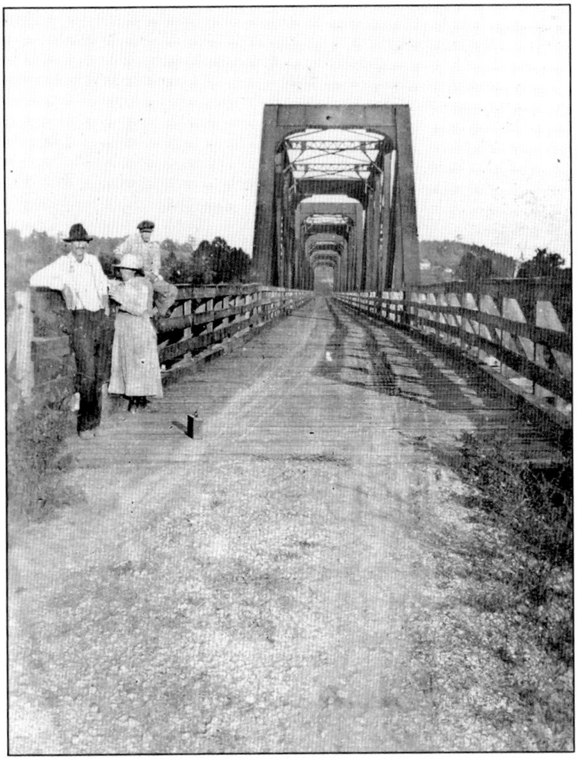

From left to right, Leslie K. Johnson, Caty Johnson, and an unidentified man are shown *c.* 1923 standing on the old one-way bridge spanning the Coosa River at Stemley. This bridge was used as a railroad bridge from 1889 to 1919. It was floored and turned into a highway bridge *c.* 1922. It was a toll bridge until sometime in the 1930s. (Courtesy of Martha Jean Freeman.)

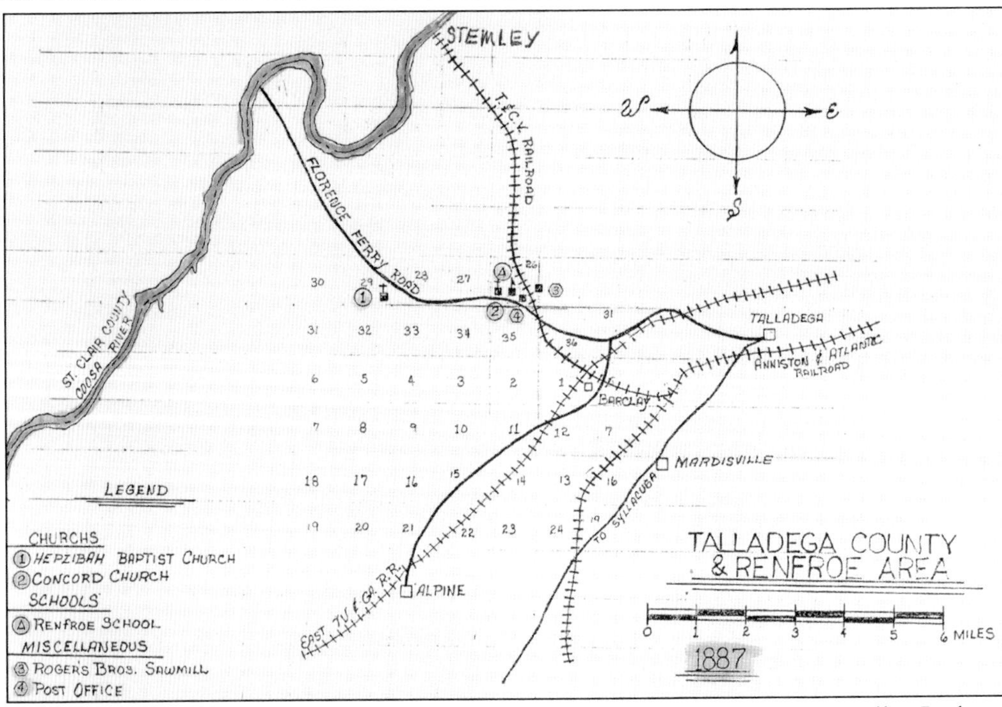

This 1887 map is a drawing of area railroads. It shows the Talladega & Coosa Valley Railroad from Stemley to Renfroe. Also shown are Hepzibah and Concord churches, Rogers Brothers Sawmill, and the Renfroe Post Office. (Courtesy of Evelyn Roach.)

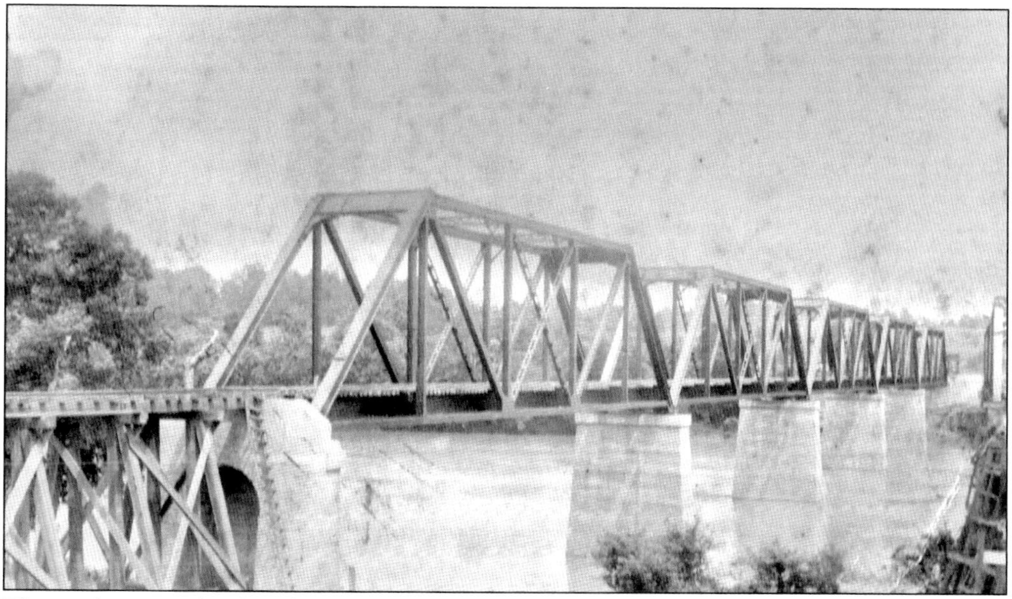

This is the second railroad bridge that spanned the Coosa River at Stemley. The bridge was replaced or repaired several times. The first bridge was built in 1889, and the second bridge was still in operation in 1919 when the Birmingham & Atlantic Railroad Company train made its last run. (Courtesy of JoAnn Gauldin.)

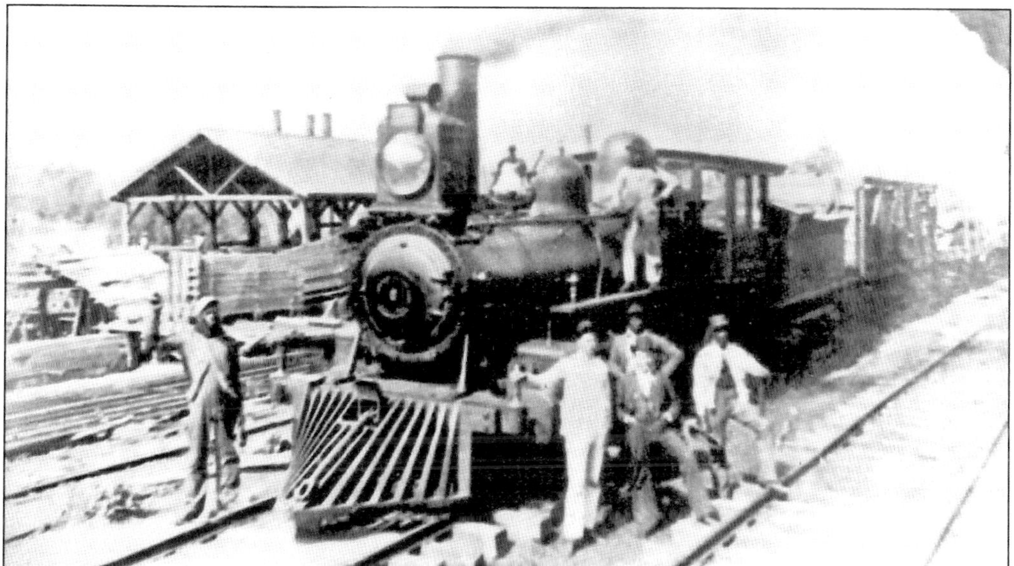

Stemley Bridge, over which the Birmingham & Atlantic Railroad ran, was deemed dangerous in 1894. Passengers were asked to detrain and walk across the bridge. On October 11, the bridge collapsed, and a train fell into the Coosa River. Passengers were rescued by train hands; one passenger, C. H. Simons, drowned. The train crew was treated for minor injuries. The bridge had been scheduled for repairs in two weeks. In 1897, Stemley Bridge was again condemned. A new bridge was constructed c. 1904. The B&A continued to run until May 11, 1919. Mr. Waide later bought the bridge, had it floored, and it became a highway toll bridge. (Courtesy of Thelma Daffron.)

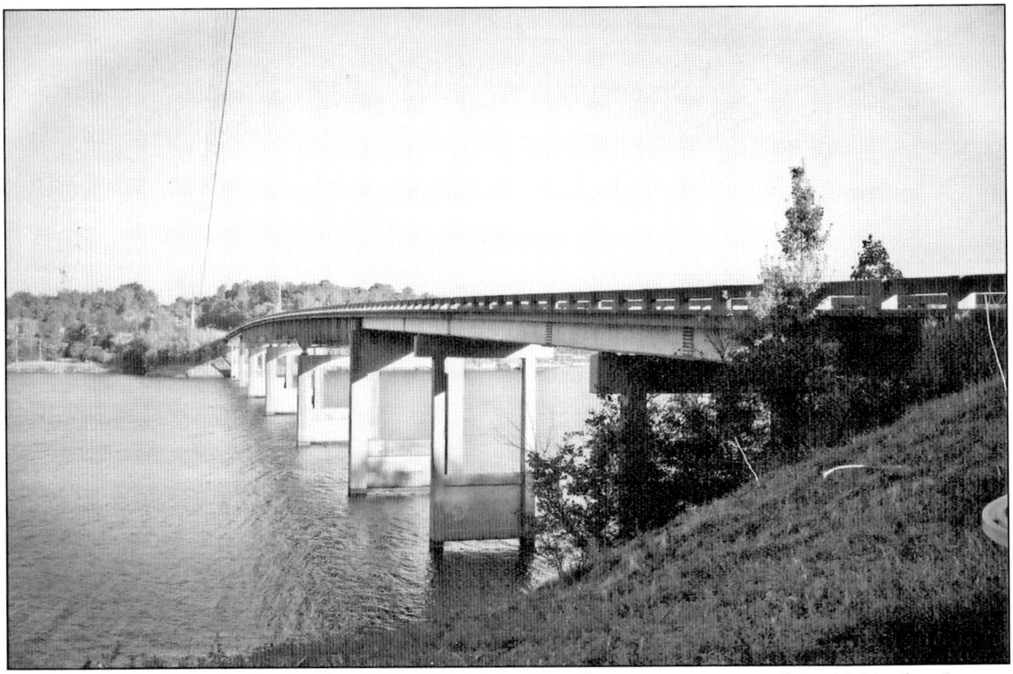

The present bridge spanning the Coosa River at Stemley was constructed in 1964 after Logan Martin Dam was put into operation. It is upstream about a quarter mile from the site of the old one-way Stemley Bridge that was in use for 42 years. (Courtesy of Laura Schmidt.)

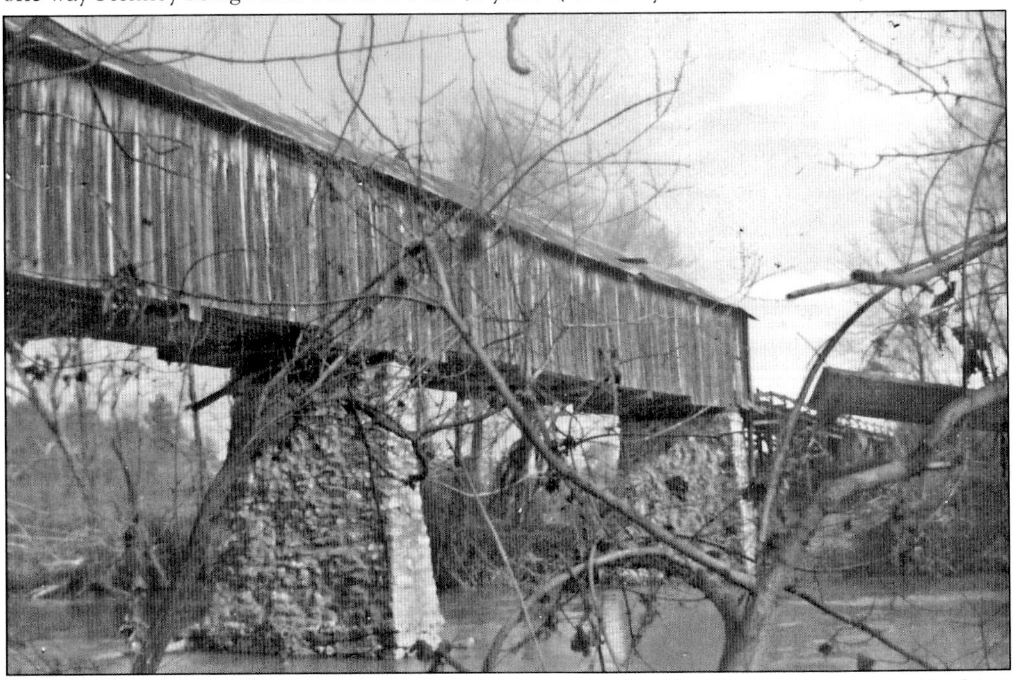

Eureka Bridge spanned Choccolocco Creek connecting the Stemley community to Rushing Springs, Embry's Crossroads, and Lincoln. This picture was taken in March 1963, about a year before it burned. The backwater of Logan Martin Dam covered the remains of the bridge. (Courtesy of Calvin Sanders.)

The first bridge across Choccolocco Creek just below Schmidt's Mill was a flat bridge built sometime after 1835. Because it flooded during high water, it was replaced in 1906 by this higher steel truss bridge. The steel truss bridge was torn down when the first of the present-day bridges was built *c.* 1937. A second, southbound, bridge was built around 1975. Pictured from left to right on the steel truss bridge are G. L. Schmidt; his wife, Inez; her brother Jim Cofield; and an unidentified man. (Courtesy of Laura Schmidt.)

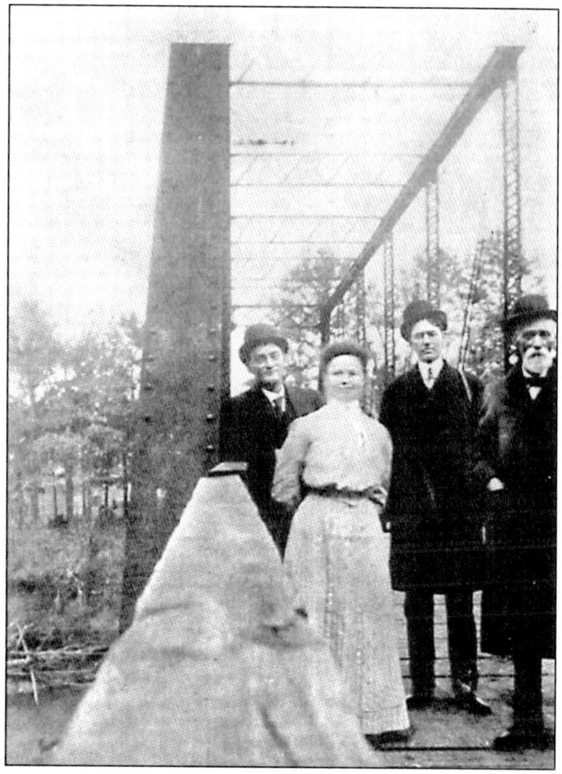

Hendrix Martin posed on the old steel truss bridge spanning the Coosa River at Stemley in the early 1960s with two of his sons, Harvey (left) and Michael. (Courtesy of Norman Martin.)

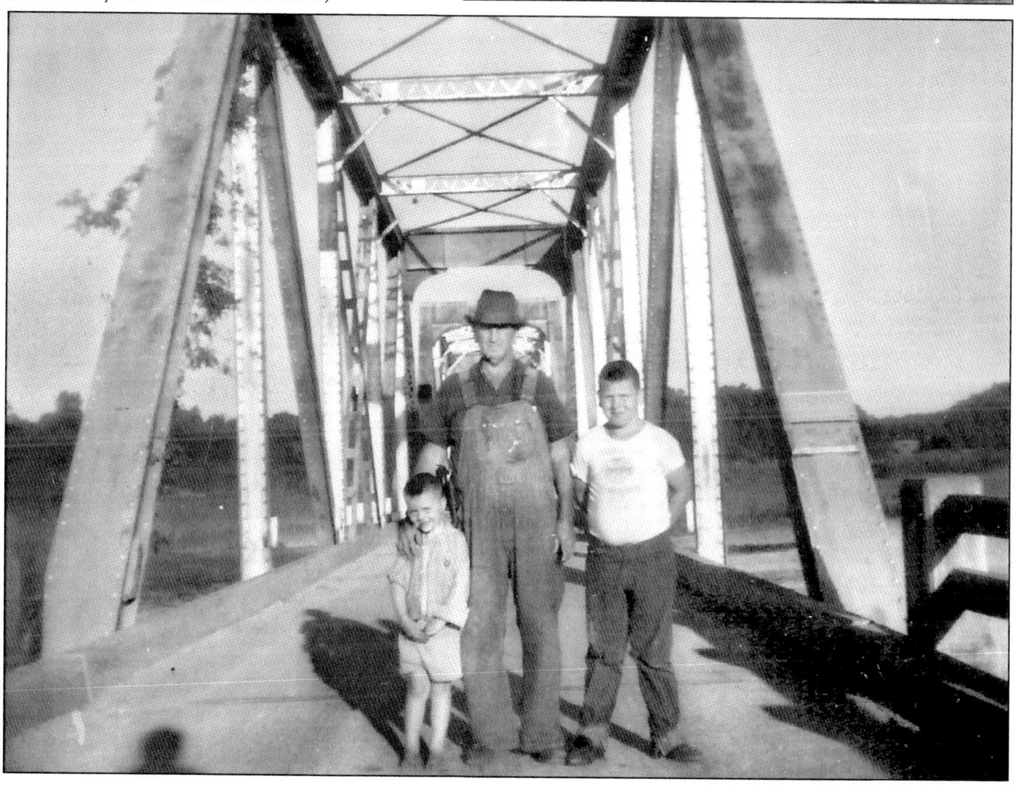

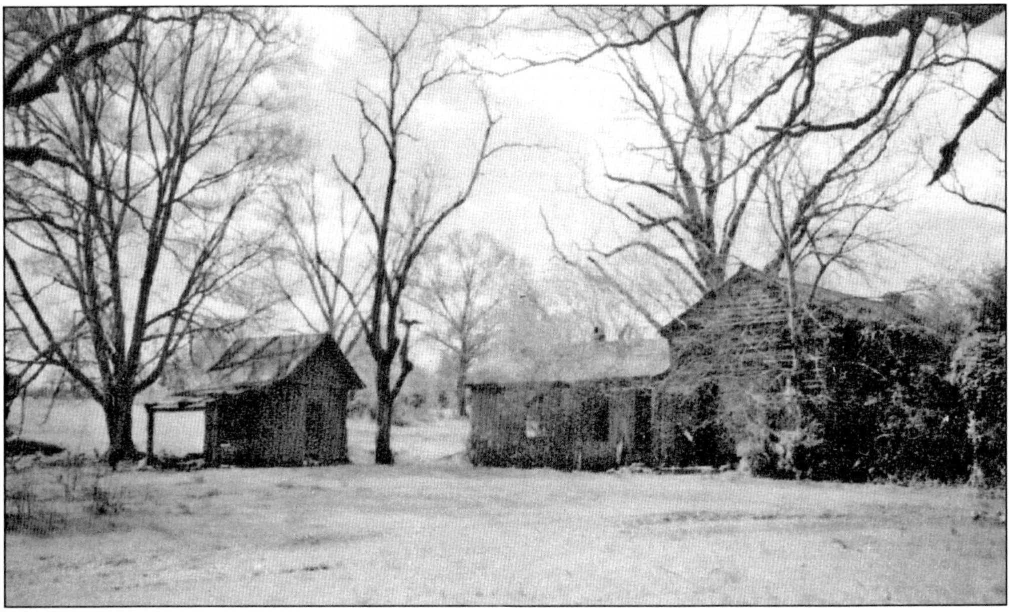

Jacob Harmon (*c.* 1806–1884) and his wife, Lucinda Gann (*c.* 1810–1892), were born in Washington County, Tennessee. Jacob and Lucinda were pioneers who traveled to Alabama by flatboat with their three children and settled in Talladega County *c.* 1832, across the creek from where Jacob and his son-in-law, Bernhard Schmidt, built a gristmill after the war. Jacob's house, shown here, has almost fallen in. (Courtesy of Laura Schmidt.)

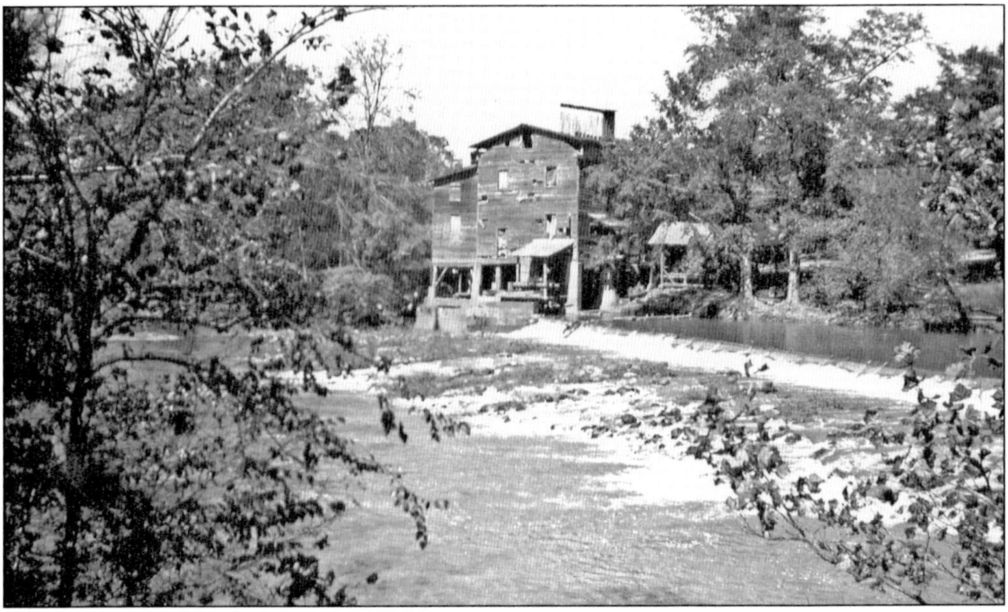

Bernhard Schmidt (1831–1901) came from Germany in 1853. He fought in the Civil War and afterward dammed the Choccolocco Creek and built a gristmill with his father-in-law, later adding cotton gins and an oil mill. From 1890, the mill was owned and operated by B. Schmidt and Son, and from 1945, it was owned and operated by G. L. Schmidt and Son. Alabama Power purchased the mill from Bernard Schmidt, Bernhard's grandson, in the early 1960s and tore it down. (Courtesy of Laura Schmidt.)

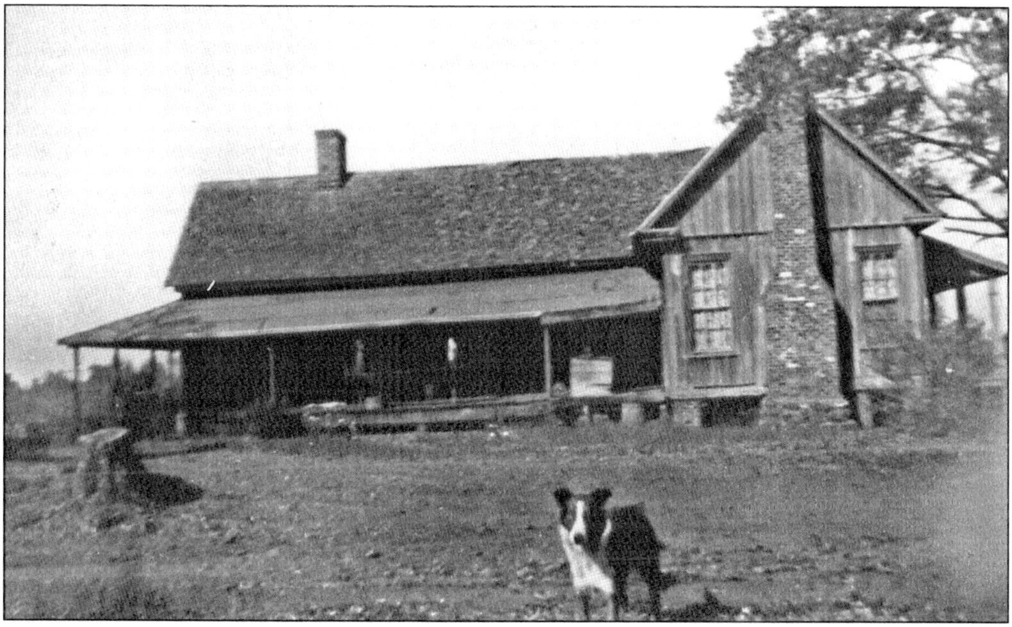

This early-1930s photograph is of the old Linder Place on Stemley Bridge Road just off Highway 77. The Ahten family came from Ostfriesland, Germany, and ran a dairy here from 1929 until 1936, when they returned to Germany. In the 1940s, Johnnie Barnes purchased the property and, with his sons, also ran a large dairy here. Daniel and Mary Barnes now own the farm and have renovated the old home. (Courtesy of Laura Schmidt.)

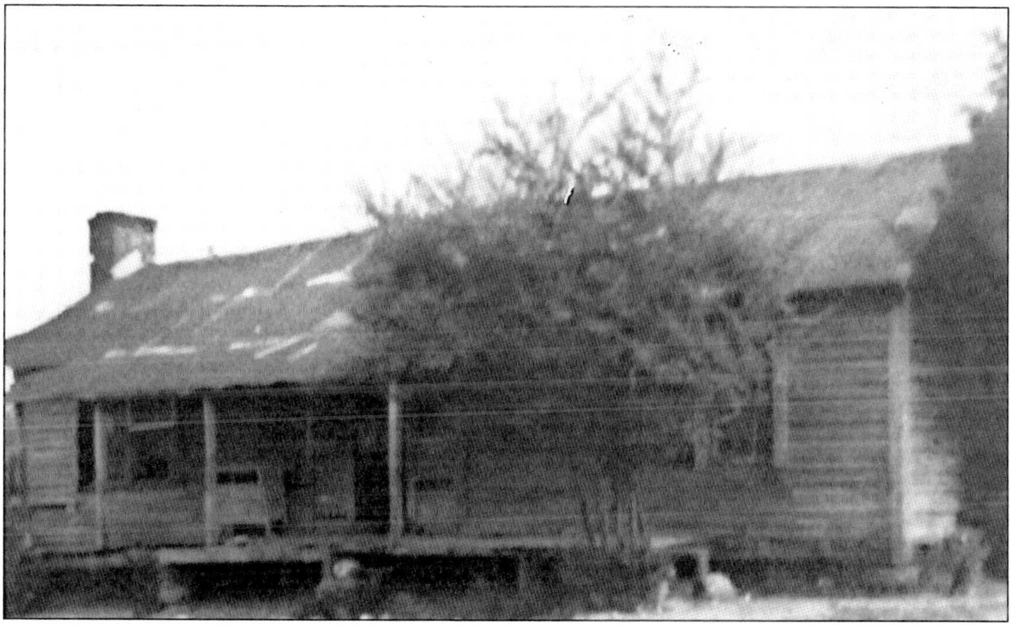

This is the old Thomas place that stood on Stemley Bridge Road next to where the volunteer fire department is now. In the 1990s, owner Herbert Sims moved it to Renfroe Road, where he is in the process of remodeling it. The Germans who built this house used a unique method of cutting the logs. The logs are double cut, cut in two different directions, so they will not slip either way. (Courtesy of Herbert Sims.)

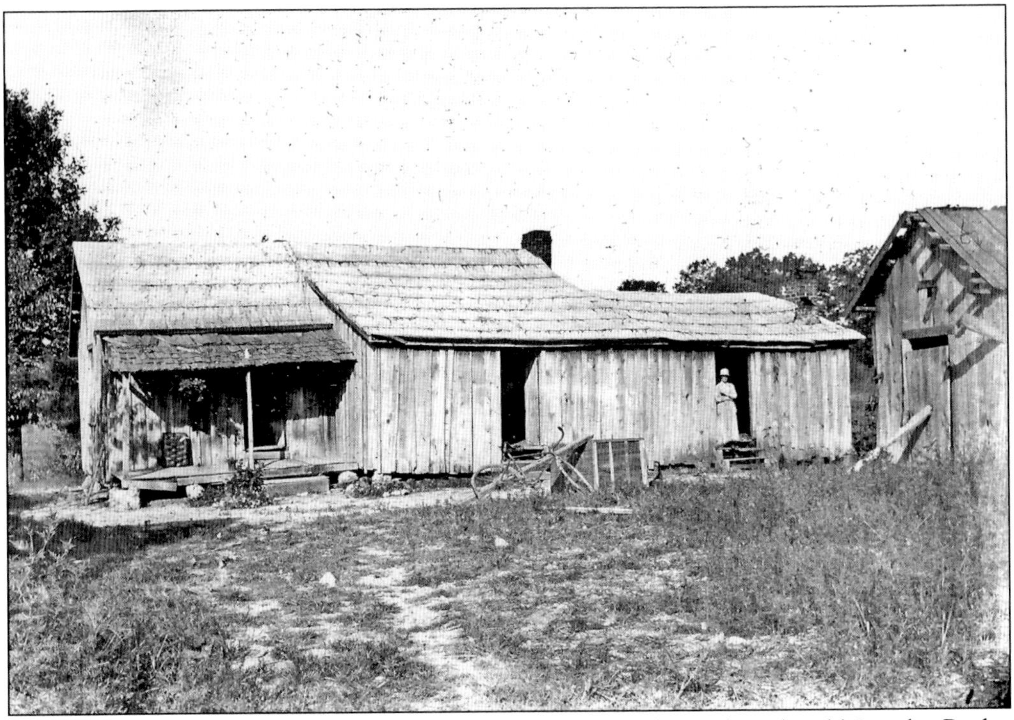

This was Leslie and Caty Johnson's first home, c. 1915. It was located on the old Stemley Bridge Road on property that is now covered by Logan Martin Dam backwater. The lady standing in the doorway is probably Caty. (Courtesy of Martha Jean Freeman.)

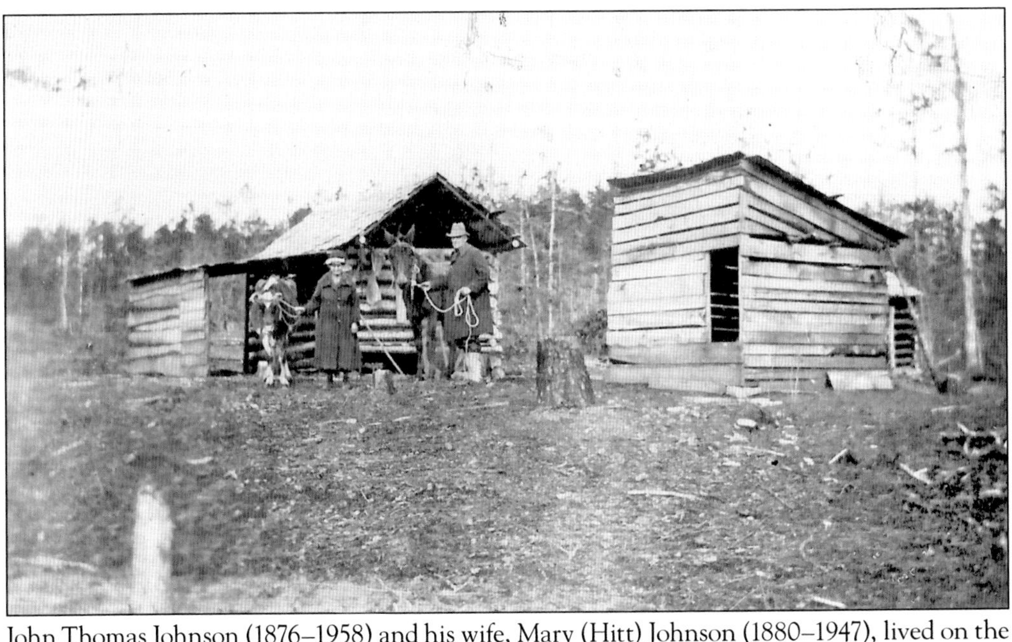

John Thomas Johnson (1876–1958) and his wife, Mary (Hitt) Johnson (1880–1947), lived on the Thomas place. John was a farmer and horse trader and worked at a dairy for a while. Mary had the reputation of being a very kind person, never saying a bad word about anybody. (Courtesy of Jeanette Zachero.)

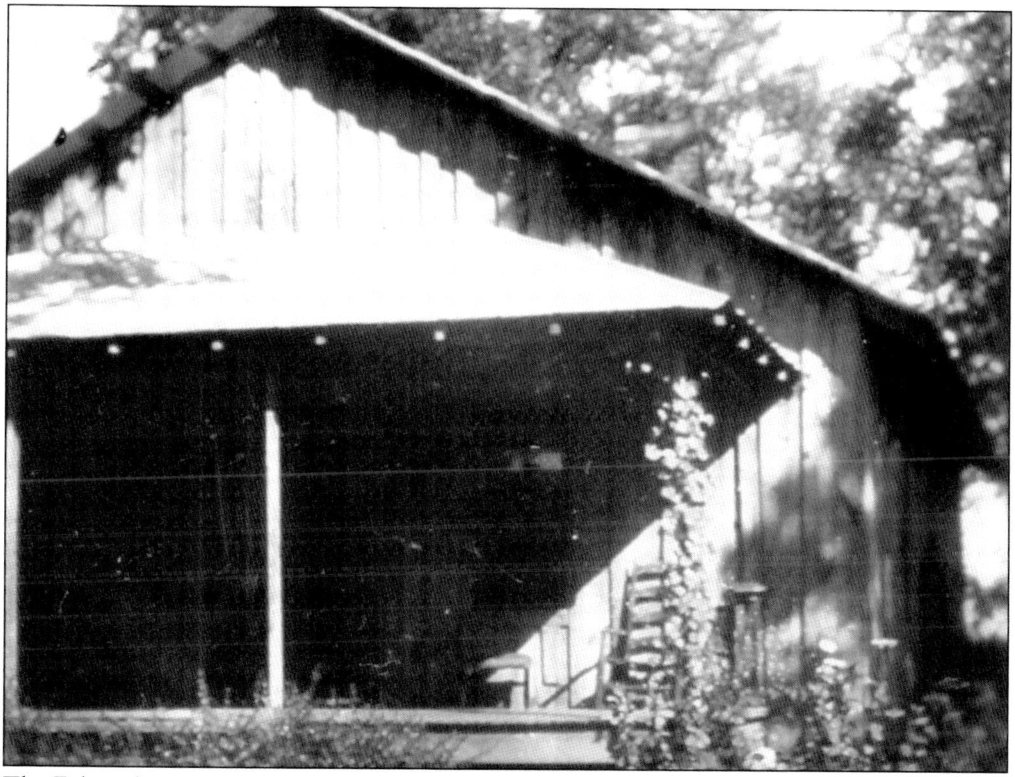

The Fulmer house on Stemley Road, located on the hill above their old home that burned, was built in 1933 by Claude Fulmer for his family. Claude and his wife, Josie, lived here until their deaths. It is now occupied by Calvin Sanders. This photograph was made in 1942. (Courtesy of the Sanders family.)

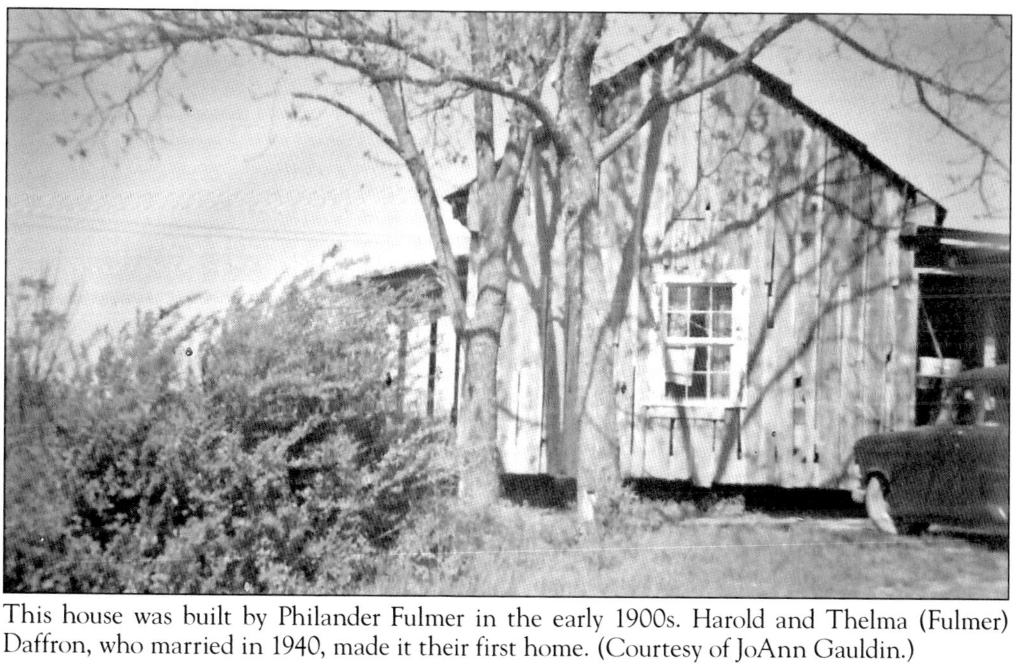

This house was built by Philander Fulmer in the early 1900s. Harold and Thelma (Fulmer) Daffron, who married in 1940, made it their first home. (Courtesy of JoAnn Gauldin.)

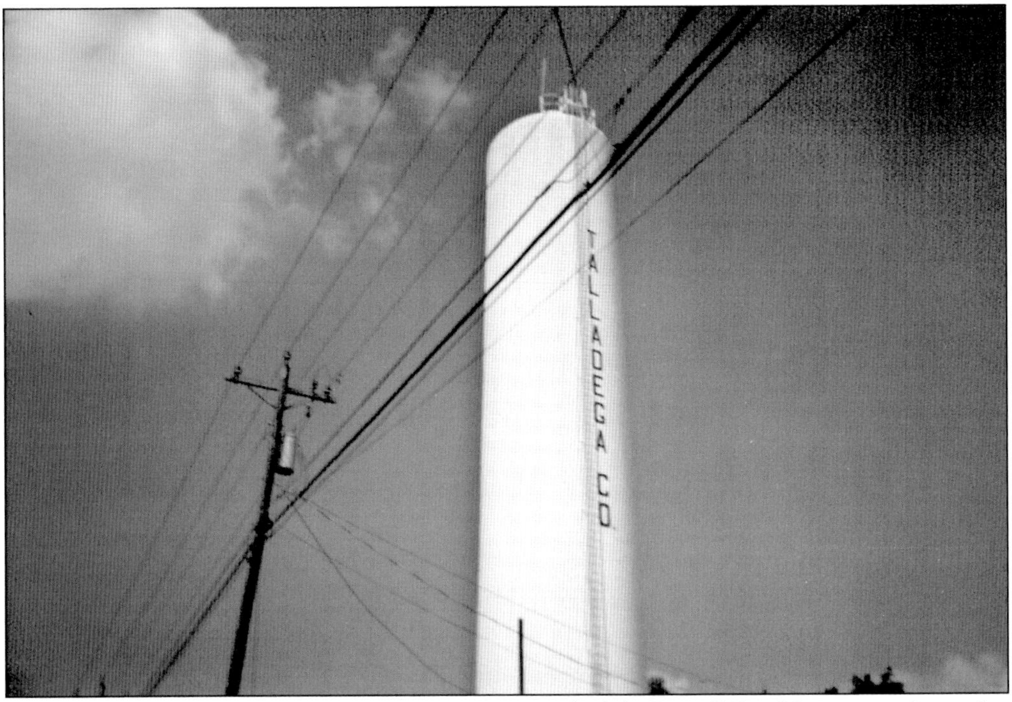

A water system for Talladega County was constructed while Derrell Ray Hann served as judge of probate and was able to get grants to fund the project. The highest point of land in the area that was suitable for this system belonged to the Jones family, and this is where the water tower was built in the 1990s. (Courtesy of Laura Schmidt.)

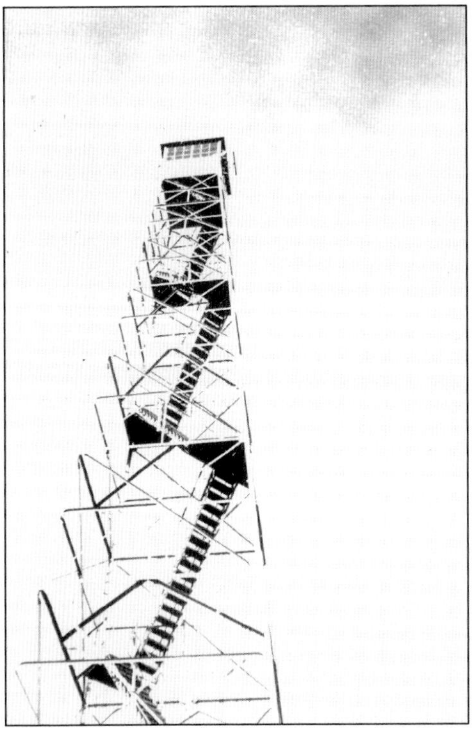

The Renfroe Tower on Sleeping Giant Mountain was one of a triangle of towers built by the Alabama Forestry Commission primarily to locate and get to forest fires before they burned out of control. One of the three towers would see smoke and would confer with the other two to determine exactly where the fire was and how to proceed. With the coming of the use of television antennas and airplanes, the towers were no longer needed. The Renfroe Tower was torn down and replaced with television antennas by the 1990s. (Courtesy of Adrienne Fuller.)

Two

CHURCHES

Early churches provided a refuge from the hardships and isolation of the settlers' lives as well as an opportunity for spiritual growth. Like the schoolhouses, they were built by the community on donated land. Many early churches also served as schoolhouses, just as the schools were used for church and social functions.

Bethel Methodist is the oldest church in the area, 173 years old, and is in its fourth building. Hepzibah Baptist is the next oldest, having its beginning in 1837. Concord Baptist began in 1855, Pleasant Grove Baptist in 1856, Antioch Missionary Baptist in 1872, Macedonia Baptist in 1875, and Cave Springs Baptist around 1892. Wesley Chapel was built in 1900, Shiloh Methodist in 1903, Mount Cleveland in 1914, and Stemley Methodist "Little Rock Church" in 1922.

Other churches of the area include Cumberland Presbyterian, Concord Methodist, Eureka Baptist, Eureka Methodist, Howard Chapel, Howell Cove Methodist, Lebanon Baptist, Limbaugh Chapel, Renfroe Baptist, Rushing Springs Baptist, Stemley Bible Baptist, Stemley Baptist, Sycamore, and Fair Park.

Church buildings have succumbed to floods, tornados, fires, and decay. Many have been relocated several times, renamed, remodeled, or rebuilt. But their spirit continues uninterrupted.

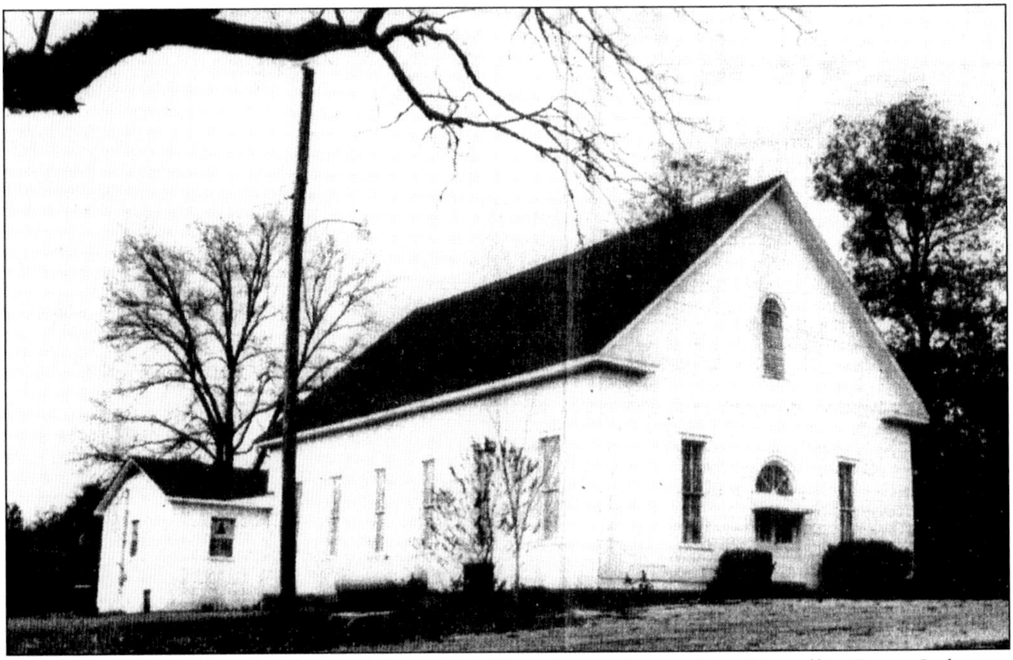

The original building for Bethel Methodist Church was located in Howell's Cove. It began as Talladega Mission in December 1832 with Rev. Jesse Ellis as the pastor. In December 1982, Bethel Church celebrated its 150th anniversary in its third building (pictured). Nineteen years later, Bethel Church built their fourth building on Stemley Bridge Road within sight of the original building. (Courtesy of Laura Schmidt.)

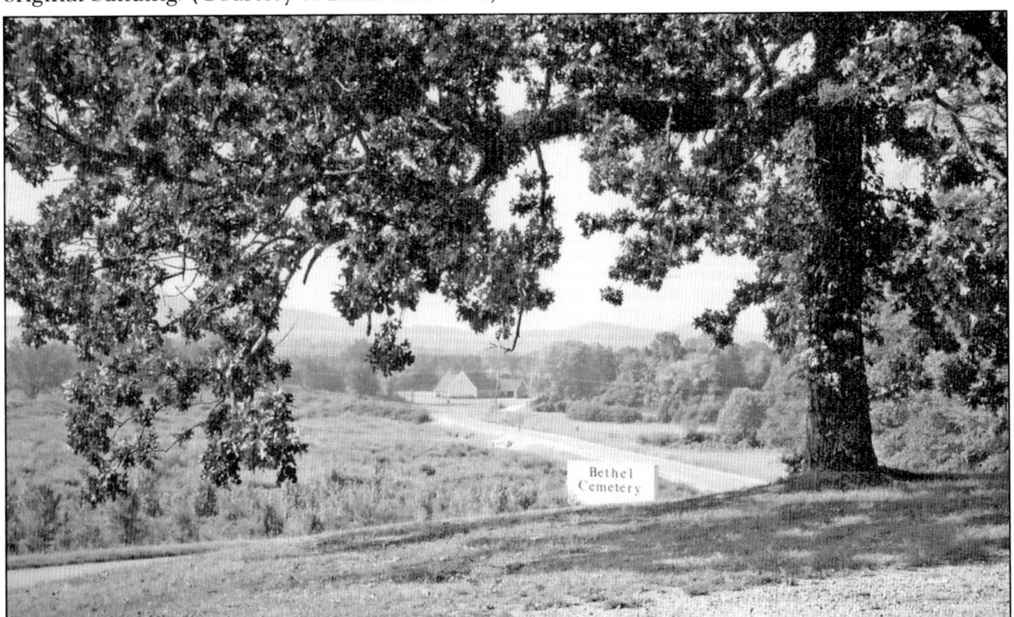

This recent photograph shows the new Bethel United Methodist Church in the distance, as seen from the site of the old church building. The new church was consecrated in April 2001. (Courtesy of Laura Schmidt.)

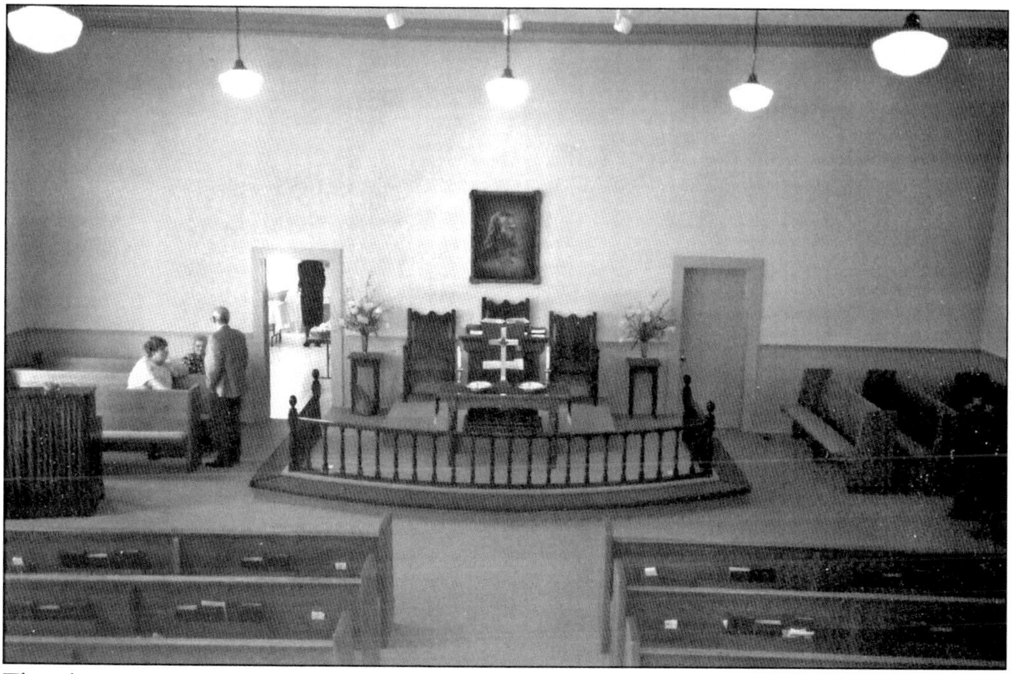

This altar was transferred from the old Bethel Methodist Church to the new church constructed in 2001 on Stemley Bridge Road. (Courtesy of Joe Williams.)

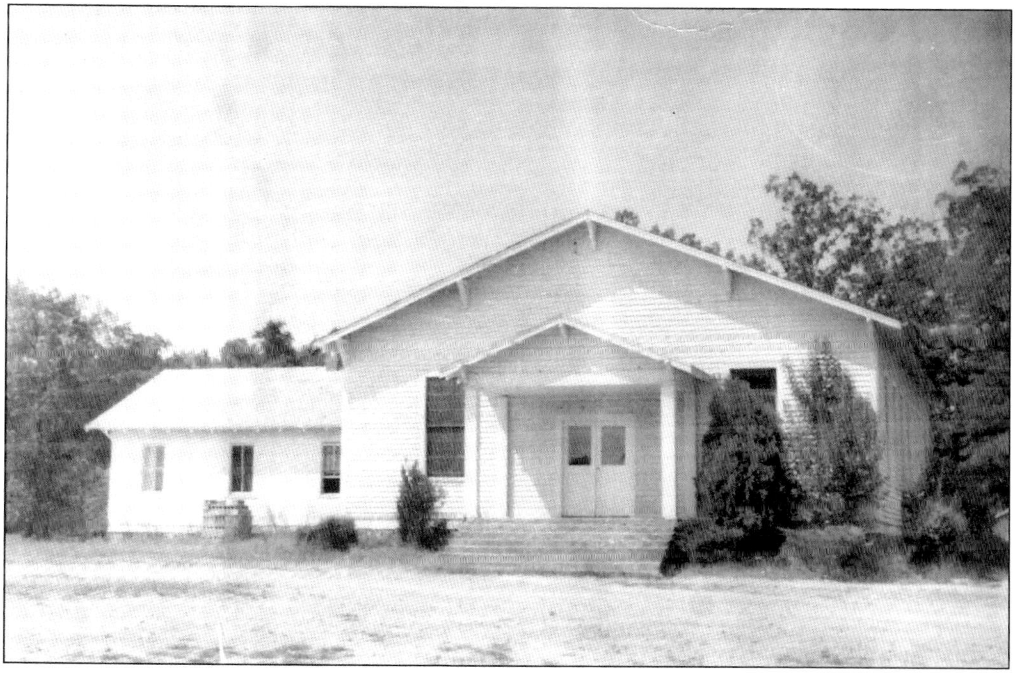

Hepzibah Baptist Church joined the Coosa River Baptist Association in 1937 as Clear Creek Baptist Church. Clear Creek was organized prior to 1837 in a one-room log structure one-and-a-half miles southeast of the present site of Hepzibah. Destroyed by a cyclone in 1852, the church was moved from Clear Creek to its present location. Its name was changed to Hephzibah and later to Hepzibah. (Courtesy of Sid Gambrell.)

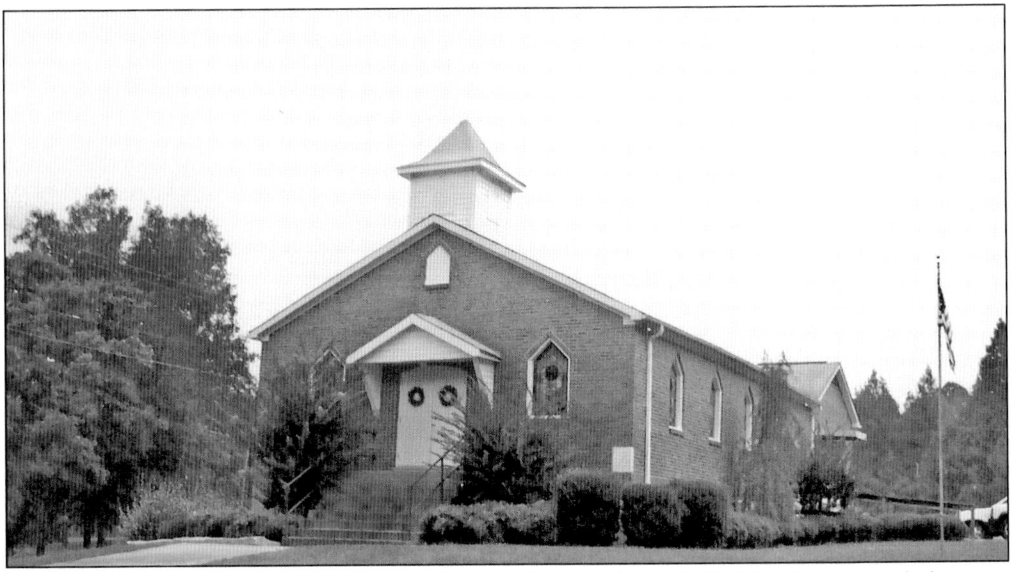

Records of Concord United Methodist Church date back to 1855. The first recorded pastor was Reverend Dickerson followed by John Deupree, whose descendants' names flow through Concord membership rolls for years. In the 1880s, a large lumber mill was located at Renfroe; the town flourished and was incorporated until 1892. In the churchyard are two historical stones from that era: a square stone, part of the post office, and an upright stone, the base for a gristmill. (Courtesy of Patsy Fulmer.)

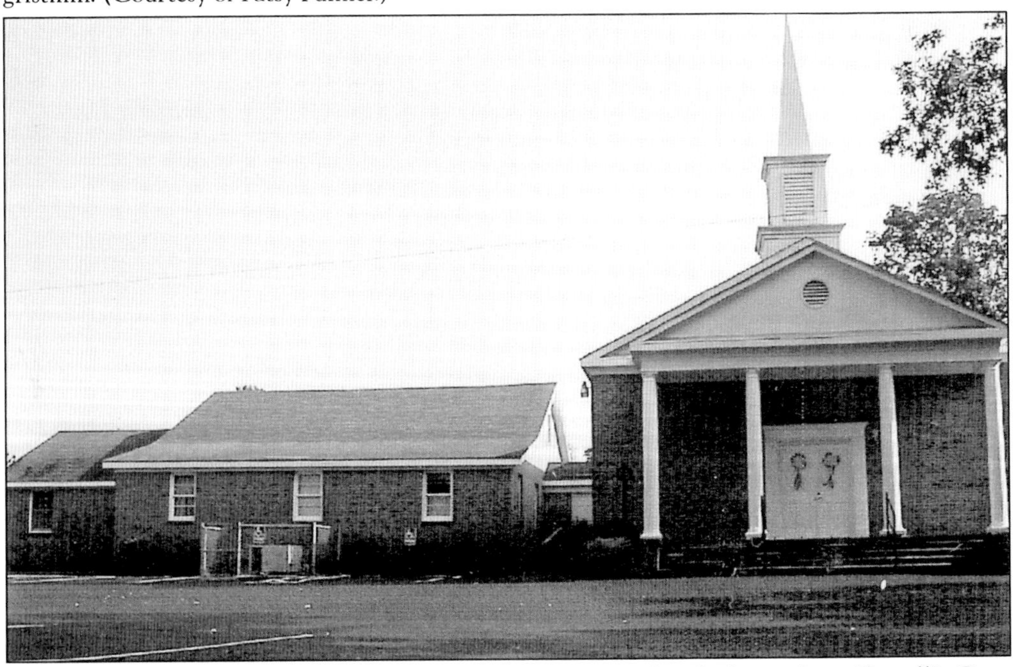

This photograph from 2003 is of Pleasant Grove Baptist Church, located on Howell's Cove Road. The church, second oldest in the Coosa River Baptist Association, was constituted in 1856 in a small log cabin. Among the charter members were J. J. Abbott, M. Turner, and T. C. Wood. Its first pastor was J. H. Franklin; the current pastor is Clyde Pettus, Th.D. (Courtesy of Paul Medlock.)

The marketing and distribution system of a man who made moonshine whiskey in the Stemley area is unique. In the cemetery at Shiloh Methodist Church, one gravesite was covered by a marble slab. Anyone wanting to make a purchase went to the cemetery, moved the slab aside, selected a full jar, left a quarter and an empty canning jar for the next batch, and replaced the slab. (Courtesy of the Wells family.)

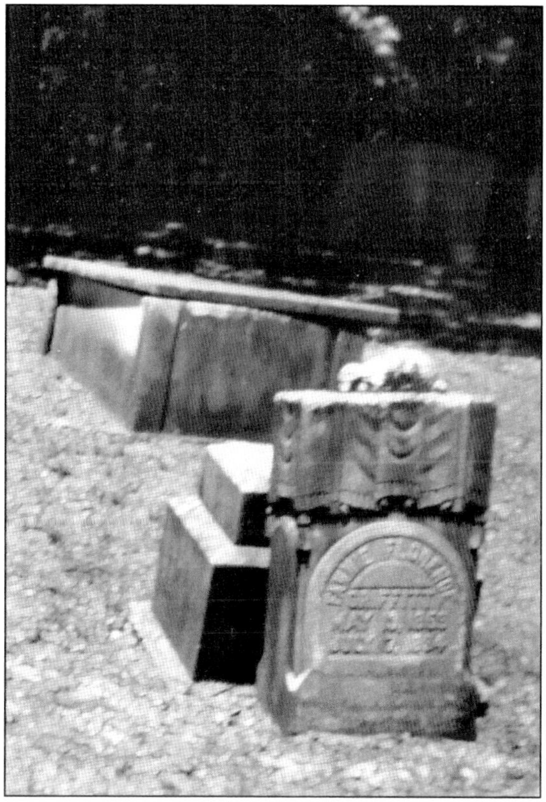

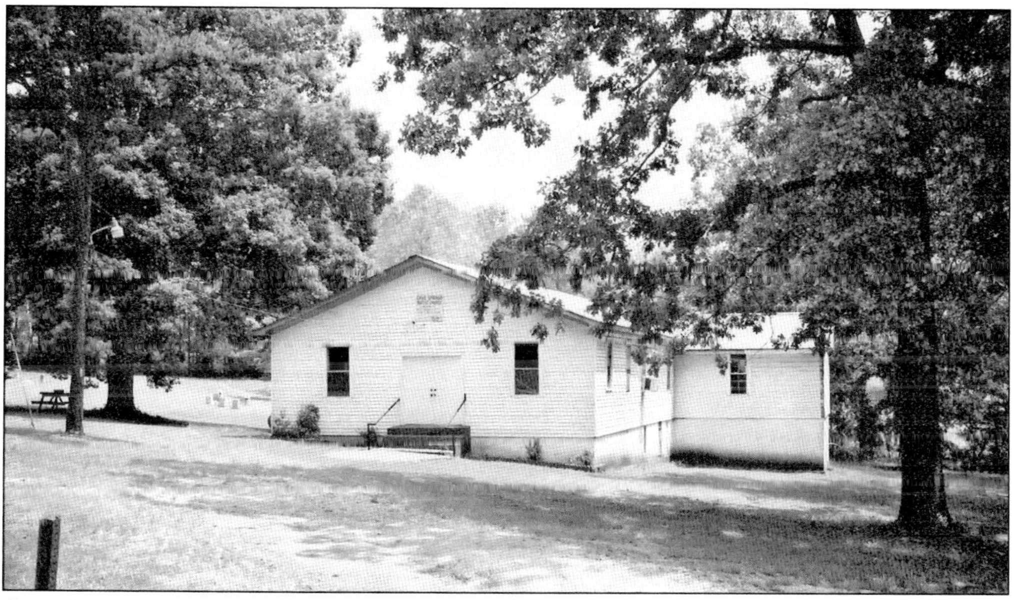

Cave Springs Baptist Church, located at the foot of Ragland Mountain on Highway 77, was previously located off Tipton Road near the cave springs in Dry Valley. Constructed sometime before 1892 by Pastor Sam Madden on land donated by a Mr. Norris, it was used both as a church and a school. Pastor David Hendrix built the present church sometime in the 1960s, using some of the wood from the original building. (Courtesy of Ollis Madden.)

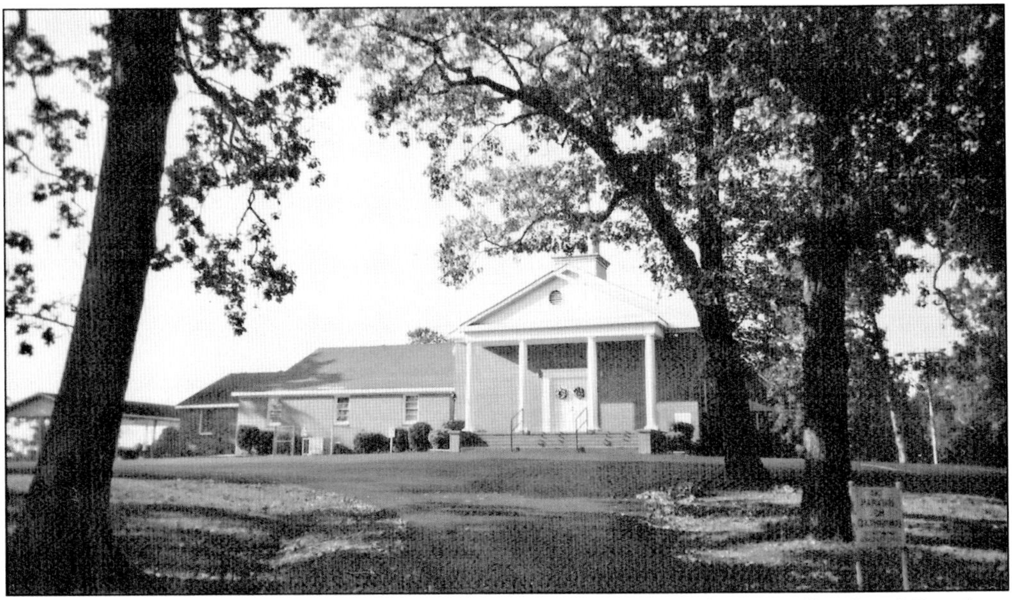

Antioch Missionary Baptist Church, shown here, was organized on Griffitt Bend Road on October 3, 1872. M. G. Cooley was the first pastor. In 1884, the second church building was constructed on land donated by Butt and Jane Buck on the Old Collins Ferry Road. The church is now in its third building, acquired from Antioch Rosewall School. It has been renovated several times since then. The present pastor is Dr. Matthew Leonard. (Courtesy of Robertha Gooden.)

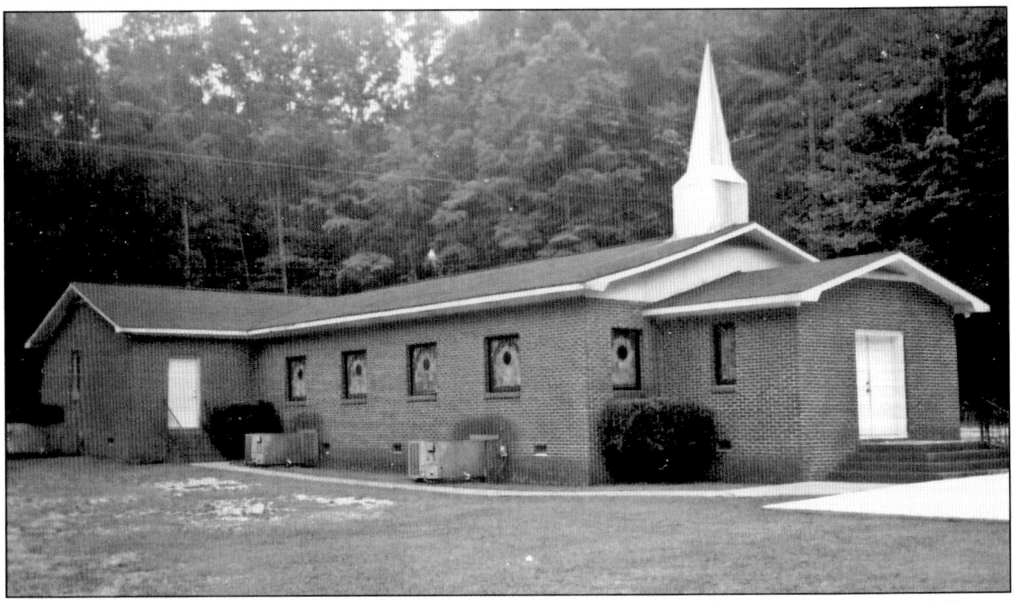

Macedonia Baptist Church, established in 1875, has been housed in at least three different buildings. The first building was on a small dirt road, and they met only once a month. They presently meet full-time, and the road has been widened and paved. In its early years, the congregation walked from the church to Williamson Store, baptized new members in nearby Poorhouse Branch, changed clothes in Williamson Cotton Gin, and walked back to the church for worship service. (Courtesy of Rosa Morris.)

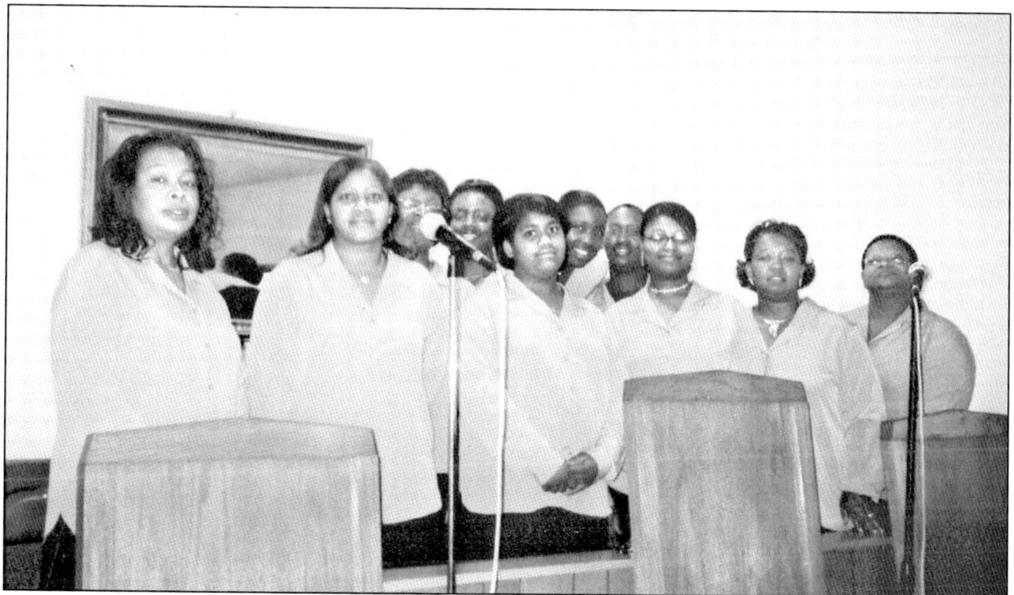

The Macedonia Baptist Church Choir, from left to right, is Vanessa Wilson, Fannie Barnes, Barbara Morris, Cheronia Morris, Jocoby Cochran, Charlotte Briskey, Rosa Briskey, Tiffany Babley, Felishia Garrett, and Dee Elston; not pictured are director Carl Barnes, Tim Cochran, Richard Briskey, Carderious Cochran, Danny Morris, and Brice Stockdale. (Courtesy of Rosa Morris.)

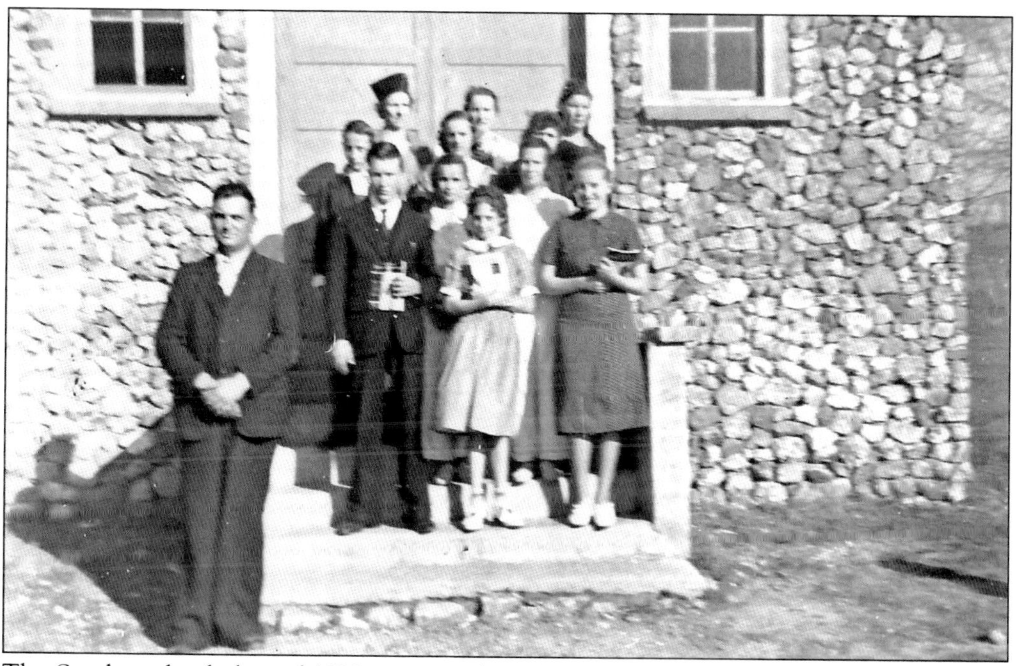

The Sunday school class of 1938 is pictured on the steps of the Little Rock Church. Those identified in the photograph from left to right are (first row) teacher Dwight Martin, Calvin Sanders, Elizabeth Sanders (Evans), and unidentified; (second row) Ola Fulmer and Pattie Fulmer; (third row) Paul Fulmer, Marie Fulmer, and unidentified; (fourth row) Donnie Bynum, Lucille Fulmer, and Gertrude Harris. (Courtesy of the Sanders family.)

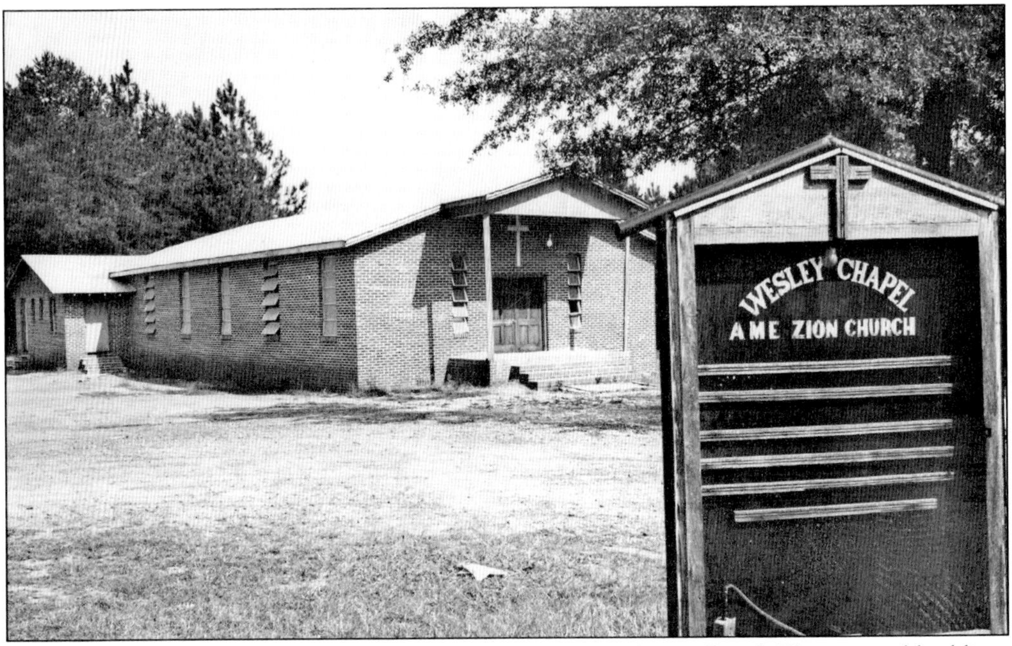

Wesley Chapel AME Zion Church is located at 1426 Cove Access Road. The original building, from *c.* 1900, was located about half a mile east of there. Its present site is on land bought from Julian and Margaret J. Elliott. In 1932 and again in the early 1960s, the church was blown away by a storm and was rebuilt. (Courtesy of Jeraldine Draper Reynolds.)

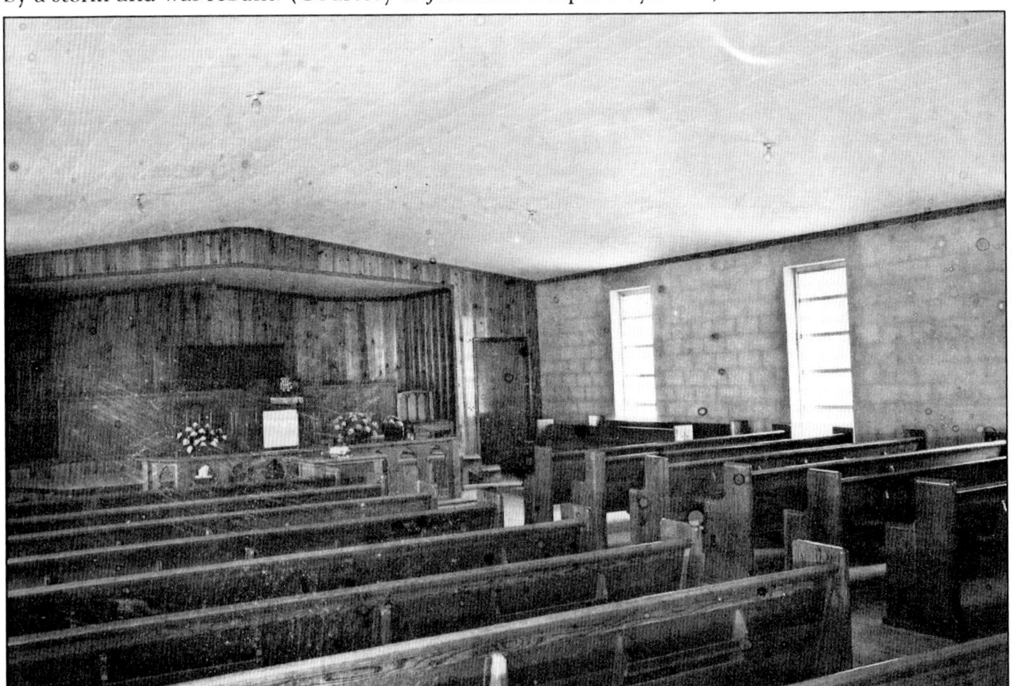

This photograph shows the inside of Wesley Chapel. The present pastor of the church is Melvin Perry, presiding elder is D. A. L. Wilson, and presiding probate bishop is James E. McCoy. (Courtesy of Jeraldine Draper Reynolds.)

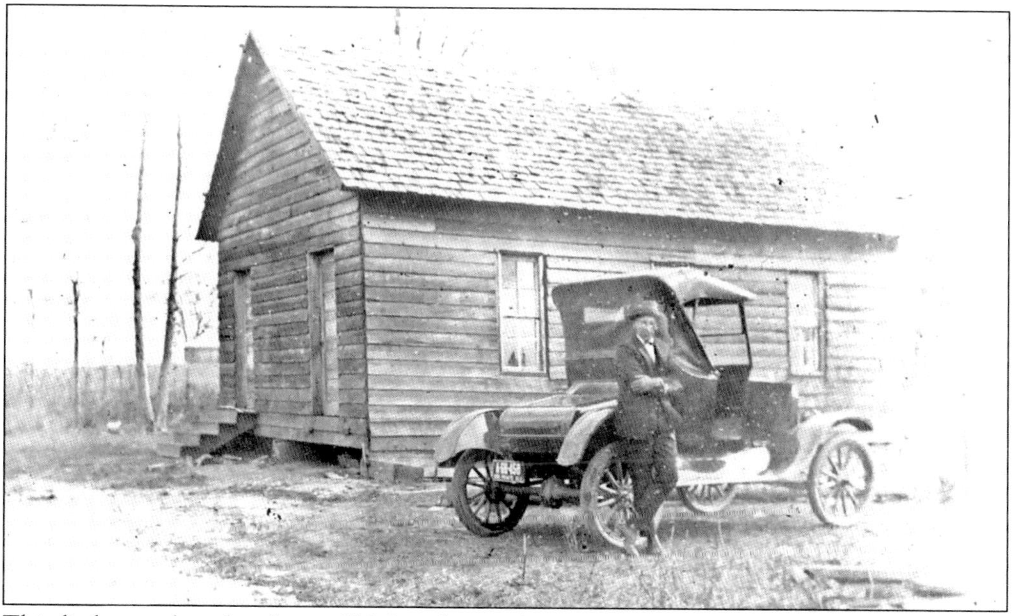

This little wooden church on Old Stemley Bridge Road, built in 1922, was used briefly as a schoolhouse and as a Methodist meetinghouse for many years afterwards. Leslie Kilgroe Johnson, pictured here by his Model T Ford, was the first pastor. Later the Methodists and Baptists held services there on alternating Sundays. It was "rocked" (the exterior walls covered with rocks) in 1935 (see photograph below) and then was called the Little Rock Church. It now stands empty and in need of restoration. (Courtesy of Jo Ann Bishop.)

Audrey Delle Disspain (1910–1998) was the daughter of William Walter and Minnie Etta (Sisson) Forrest. She is shown here in front of the Little Rock Church on Old Stemley Bridge Road. Audrey attended school here in 1923, the only year it held classes. (Courtesy of Dave Disspain.)

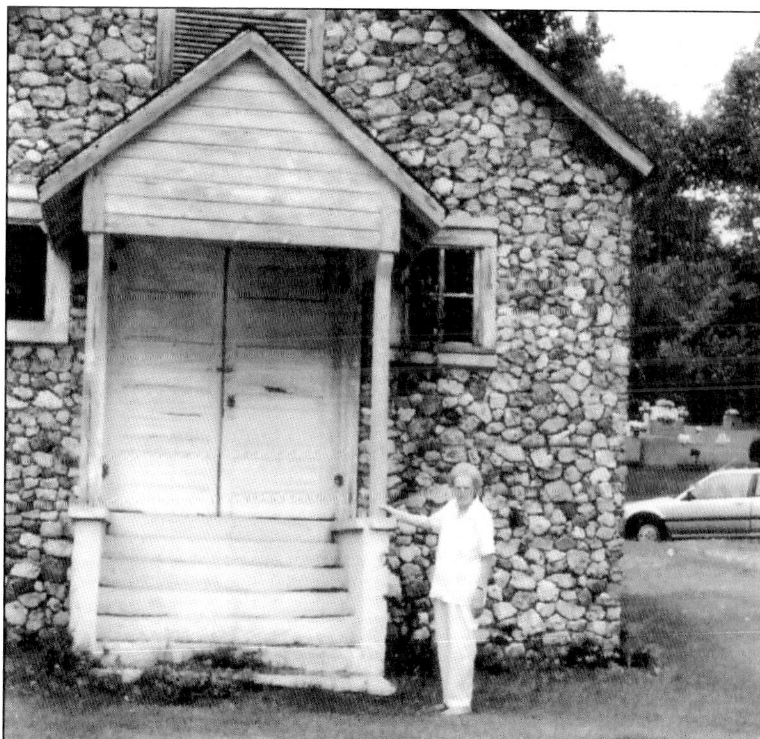

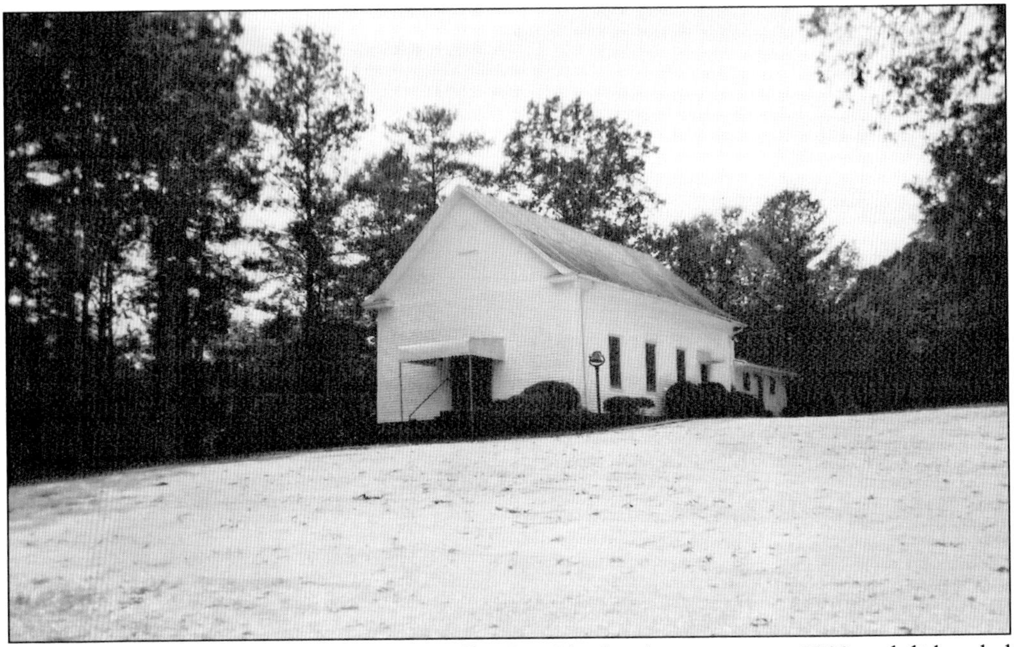

Shiloh United Methodist Church near Griffitt Bend had its beginnings in 1909 and disbanded in 1958. At that time, it was meeting only one Sunday each month. Twenty years later, new interest was generated, and the church was restored. It regained membership in the Sylacauga District of the United Methodist Conference in March 1978 and soon began having weekly services with Reverend Griffitt as pastor. Sunday school classes started the following June. The present pastor is Ricky Rushton. (Courtesy of Mavis Kennedy.)

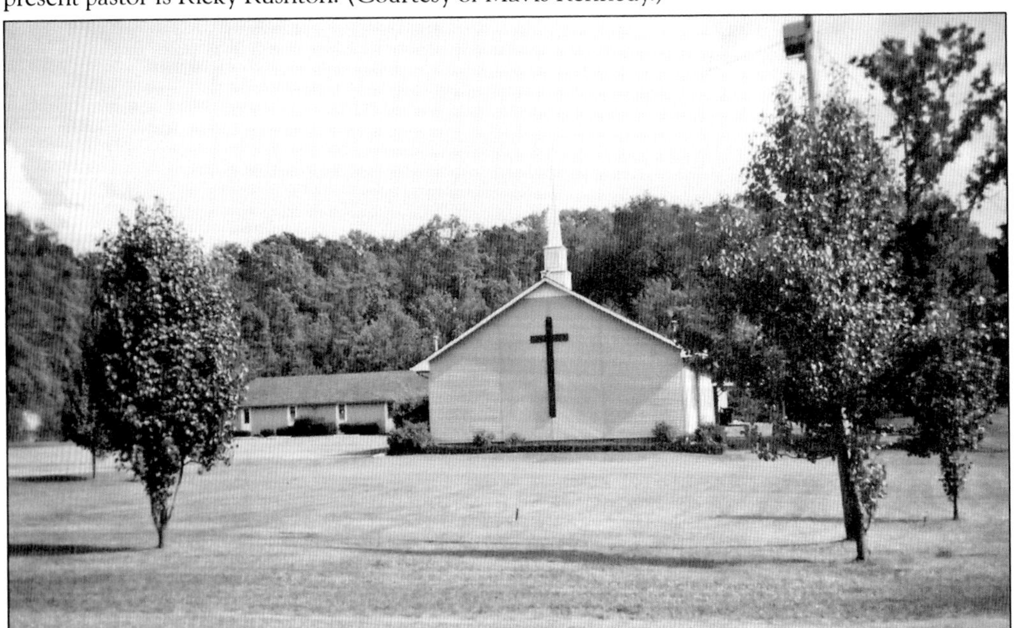

Stemley Baptist Church on Old Stemley Bridge Road began as a mission in 1973. It was constituted in 1978 with 59 charter members. The first pastor was James E. Darden; the present pastor is Joe Adams. (Courtesy of the Dewitt Johnson family.)

Three

SCHOOLS

Before schools were built around Stemley Bridge, skills necessary for one's livelihood, including homemaking skills and the basic school curriculum, were all taught at home. The earliest schools were one-room schoolhouses, which were funded and built by the community usually on donated land. For early inhabitants, an elementary education was a privilege, and the gathering of the crops took priority over schoolwork. By the mid-1900s, a high school education was considered an accomplishment, and college graduates were few. Today a college degree is easily obtainable and is almost a necessity.

There is information for several of the early schools, but no known photographs exist. This includes Boom's Bend, across Stemley Bridge Road in St. Clair County towards May's Bend. Boom's Bend was taught by Dwight Adair and Dan Funderburg, then by Ross Wyatt, and it closed about 1921. Other schools were Cropwell, which was taught by Billy Cummings; Eureka; the school at Williamson's store; Village Academy; Renfroe; Talladega Academy; and a school between Howell's Cove and Choccolocco across from Neville Thornton's that opened in 1879.

One early school was Antioch Rosewall School, which served the black community from the late 1800s until the early 1960s. Some black students went to the Hannah Mallory School in Alpine.

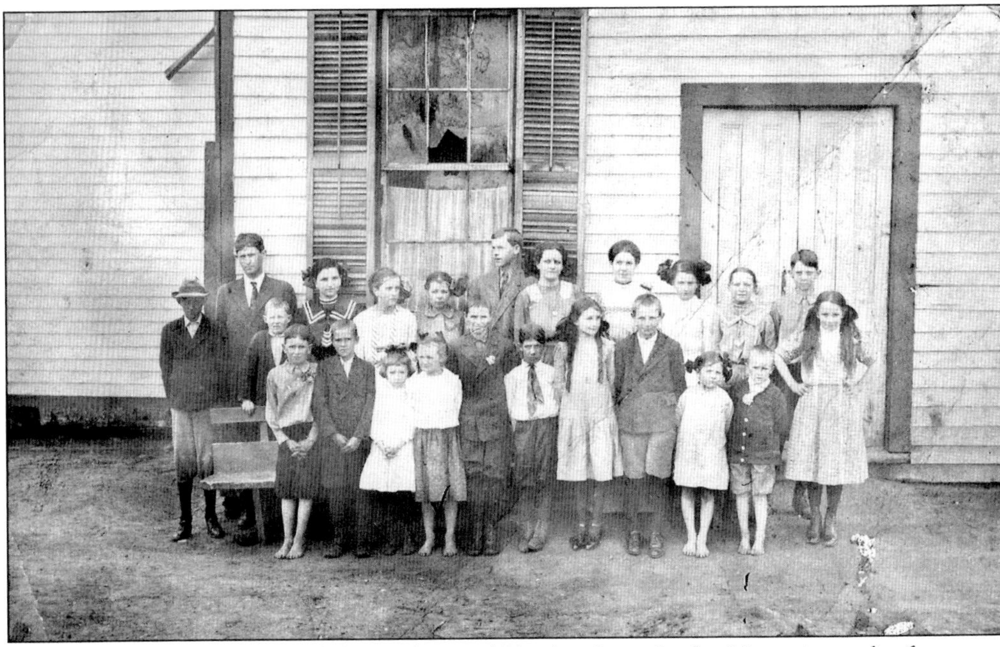

In this *c.* 1908 photograph of the students of Ida Academy, Leslie Hutto is on the front row, second from the right, and Venice Hutto is third from the right; the others are unidentified. (Courtesy of Mary Virginia Macon.)

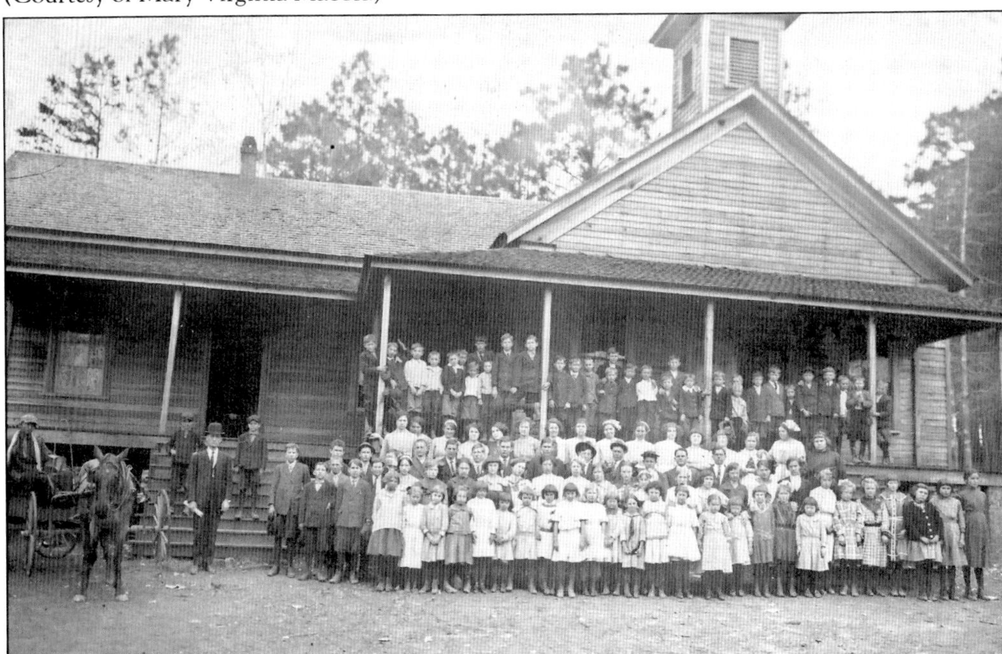

Pineview School on Plant Road opened in 1924 and burned in 1928. It had at least 10 grades. Mrs. Pete Burk taught grades one through four, and Mrs. Frieze taught grades five and six. There was a teacher for every two to four grades. Ivanette Martin was one of the students, and she now lives on the old school site. (Courtesy of Sid Gambrell.)

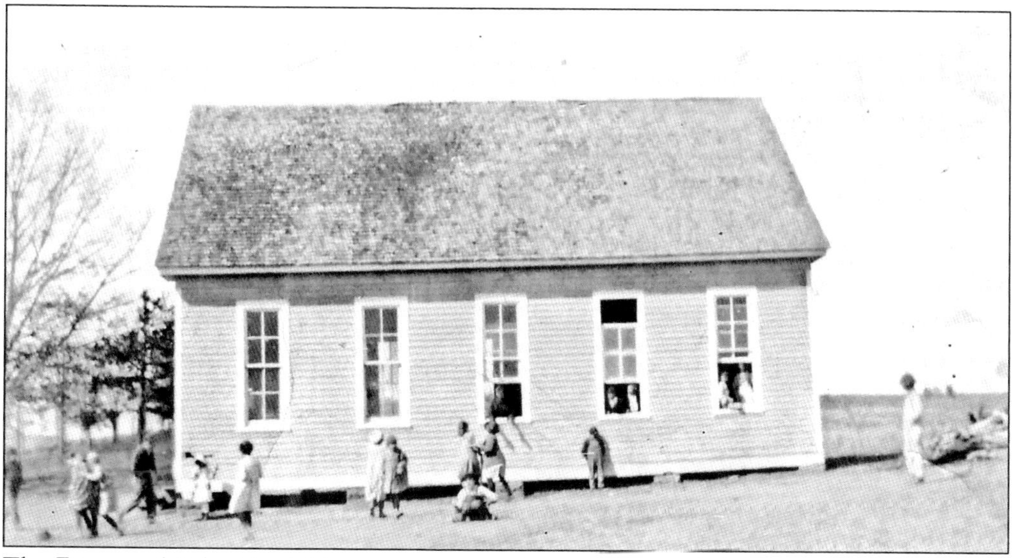

The Fricze and Schmidt children were among those who attended Conchardee School until 1912 when Talladega County High School opened in Lincoln. Alma Schmidt later taught at Conchardee along with Mae Belle Acker and later Mary Jane Hackney. Inez Schmidt taught Sunday school there on Sunday evenings. It was later a rental home and still later was used to store hay. It eventually burned down. (Courtesy of Laura Schmidt.)

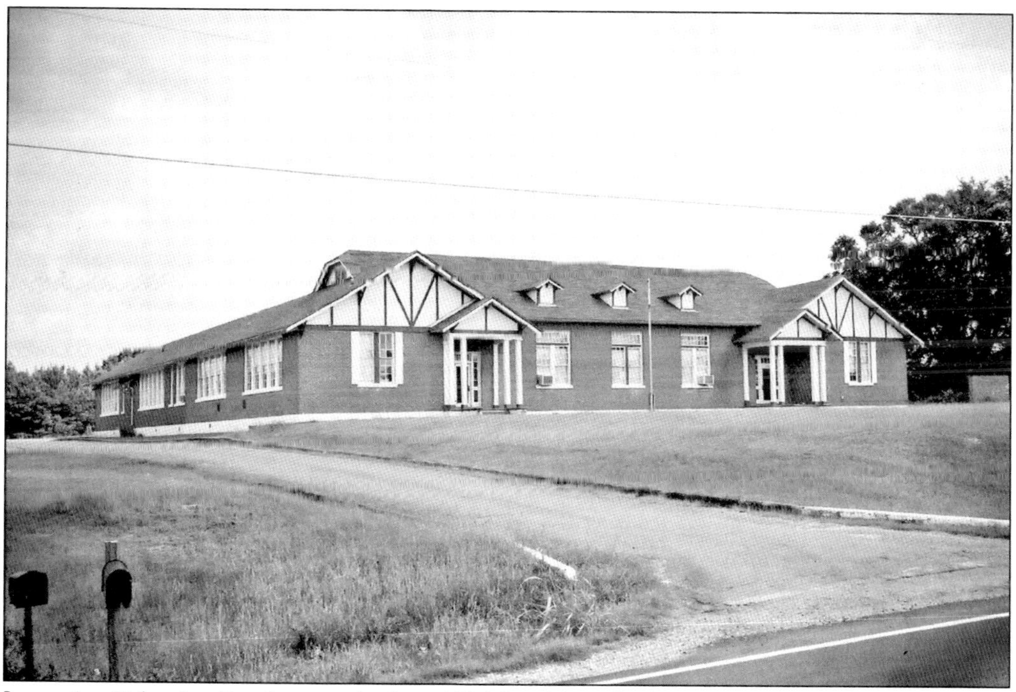

Jonesview School at Renfroe was built in 1926. In 1954, it had 9 grades, 214 students, 7 teachers, and 4 school buses. It closed c. 1990. (Courtesy of Mary Jo and Charles C. Hodge.)

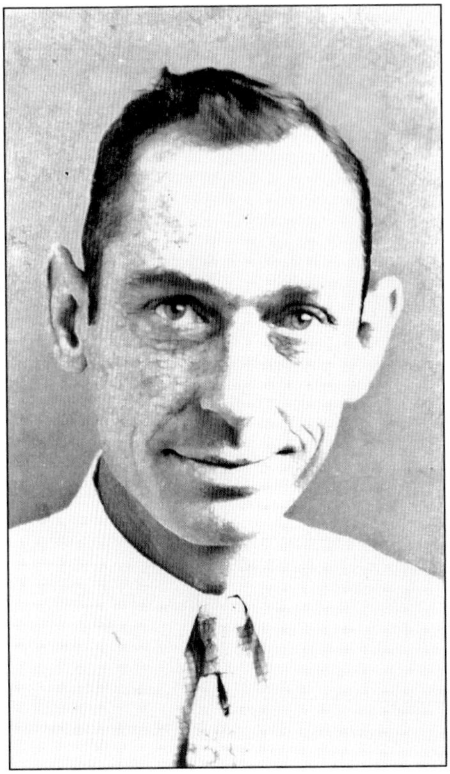

J. E. McCarn, shown here, was principal of Idalia Elementary School in 1930 and 1931. He taught the seventh and eighth grades and was well liked and respected. He drowned at Lake Chinnabee in Talladega National Park. (Courtesy of Thelma Daffron.)

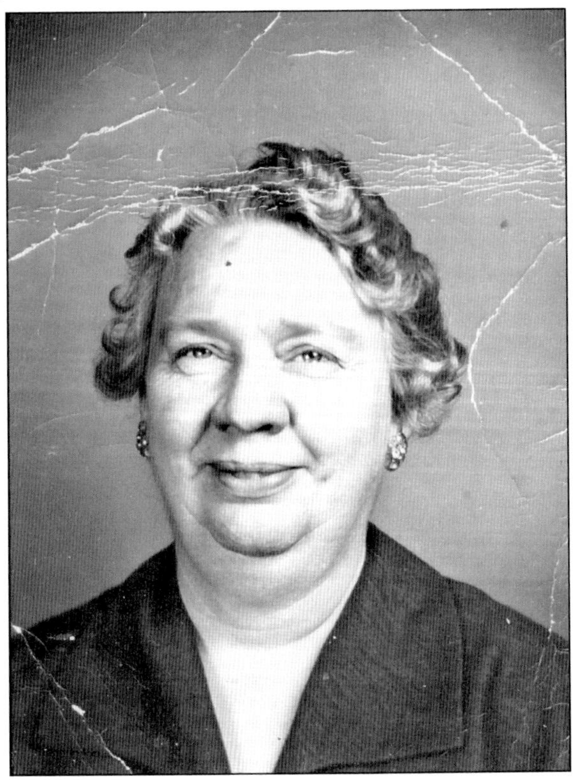

Conola Shaddix graduated from Talladega County High School in 1922 and immediately began teaching at the new Stemley School, later to become the Little Rock Church. In 1924, Stemley School and Ida Academy were consolidated and Idalia Elementary School was formed. Shaddix was one of its first teachers. She later taught at Choccolocco, which was consolidated with Munford, and then at Eastaboga before returning to Idalia, where she taught 24 more years before retiring. (Courtesy of John Shaddix.)

Addie Shaddix taught second grade at Idalia Elementary School for many years. She was the sister of Conola Shaddix, who taught first grade at Idalia. Between them, the two sisters hold the longest service record in the Talladega County School System of 49 years each. She retired in 1971. (Courtesy of Dorothy Bates.)

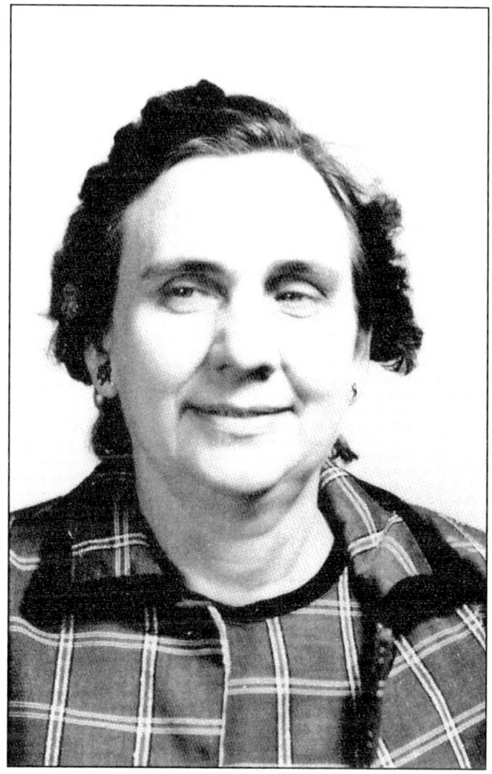

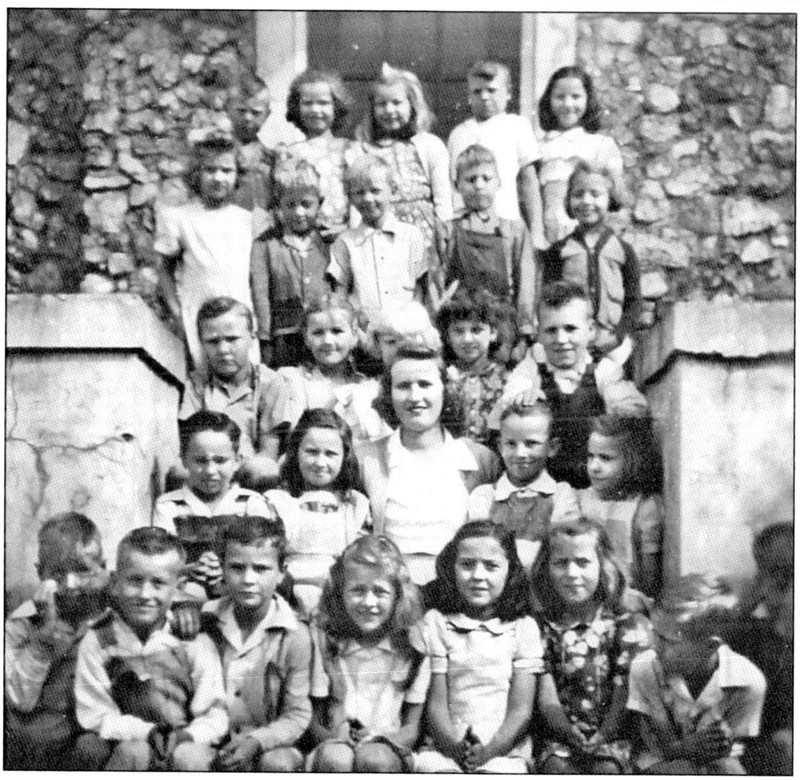

The first- and second-grade classes of 1943 pose on the steps of the auditorium building of Idalia Elementary School. Students include, in no particular order, Clarence Hutto, Betty Paul Hutto, Mildred Johnson, Mary Jo ?, George Fulmer, Frankie Spencer, Paul Proctor, ? Proctor, Shelby Jean Nix, Bill Henderson, Peggy Sue Fulmer, and Johnnie Mae Johnson. (Courtesy of JoAnn Gauldin.)

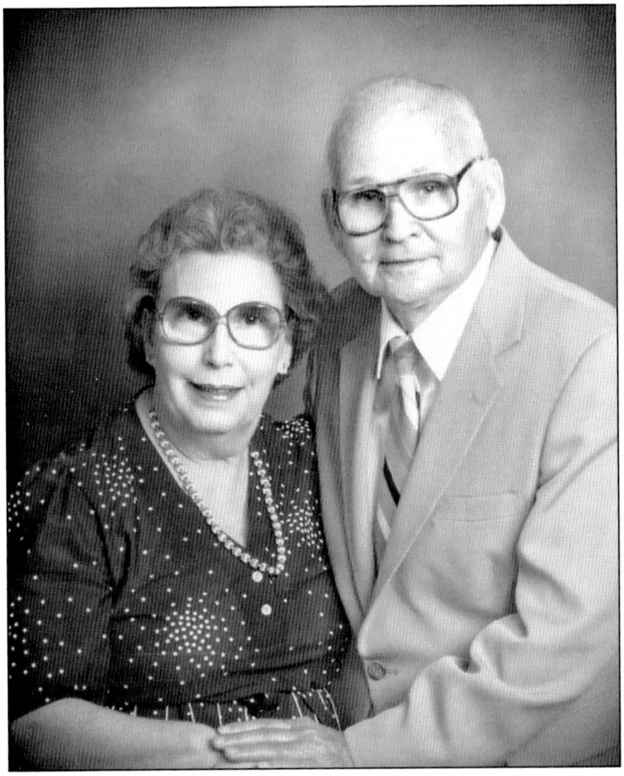

C. D. Thomas (1915–1989) was principal of Idalia Elementary School from 1948 to 1973 and taught the sixth grade for most of those years. His wife, Reba, also taught at Idalia. She taught the fourth grade and half of the fifth grade until the school was integrated in the 1970s. At that time, the school acquired a teacher for each grade, one through six, and Reba taught the fifth. Lois Houston, who previously taught at the Talladega County Training School, was the first black teacher at Idalia. (Courtesy of Reba Thomas.)

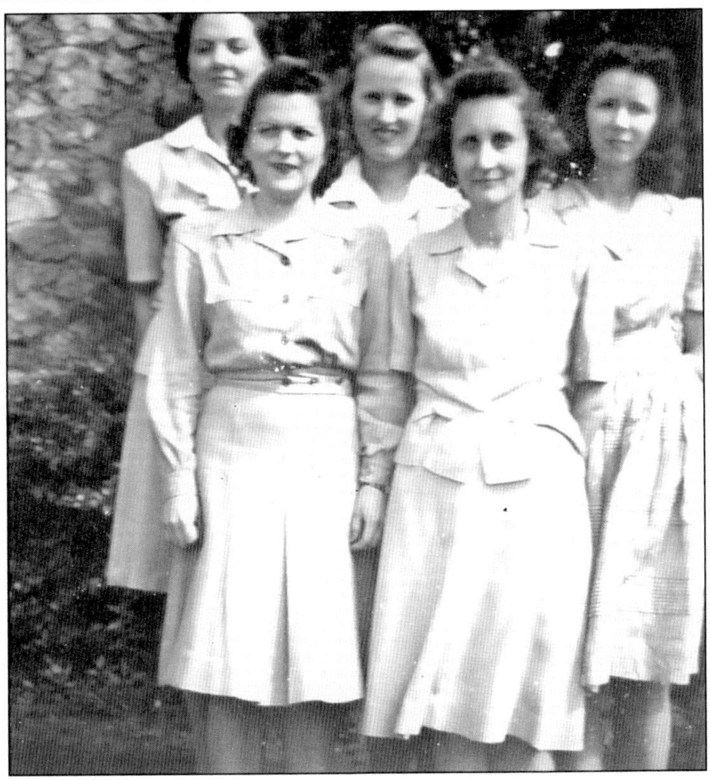

During World War II, most teachers were women. In this photograph, the teachers of Idalia Elementary School from left to right are (first row) principal Doris Bazemore and Ms. Southerland; (second row) Grace Payne, Thelma Daffron, and Ms. Harrington. (Courtesy of Thelma Daffron.)

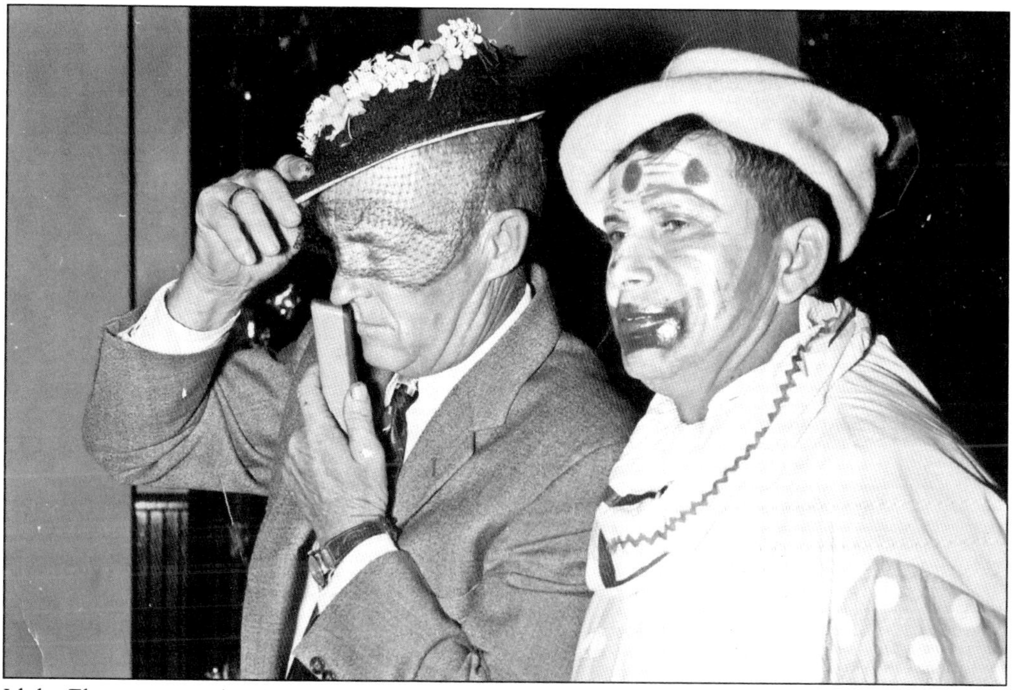

Idalia Elementary School traditionally held a Halloween Carnival every year until around 1980. Auctioning hats in this 1956 carnival photograph are Leslie Hutto, auctioneer, and Chester Parker, clown. (Courtesy of Jo Ann Bishop.)

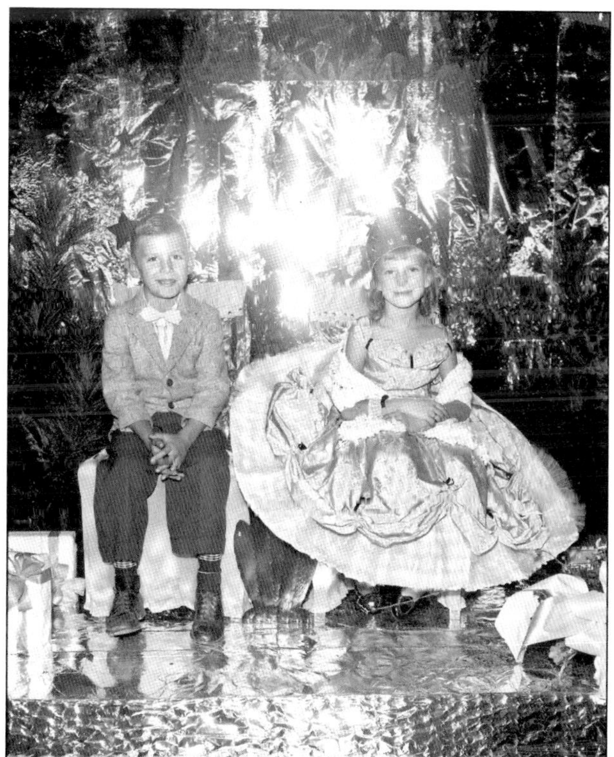

Gary Moore and Dianne Parker were crowned Halloween king and queen at the 1956 Idalia Elementary School Halloween Carnival. (Courtesy of Jo Ann Bishop.)

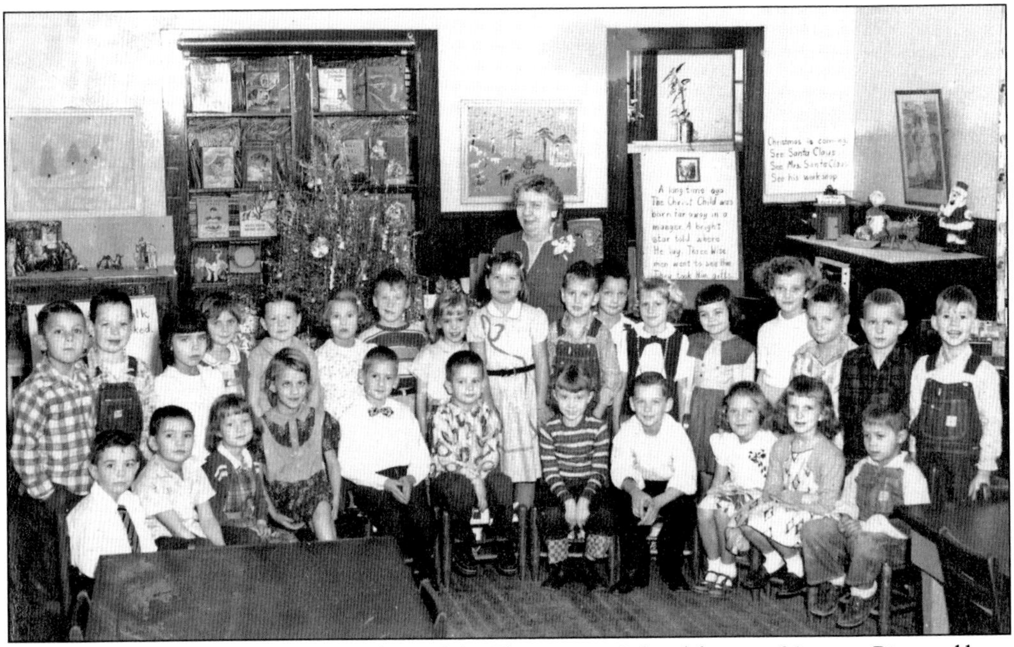

Conola Shaddix taught the first grade at Idalia Elementary School for over 30 years. Pictured here with her is the class of 1957. From left to right are (first row) Bernard "PeeWee" Hollingsworth, Wesley Mitchell, three unidentified, James Sides, unidentified, Lester Goray, Linda Watts, Dianne Parker, and unidentified; (second row) Johnny Wayne Sims, Wesley Gurley, four unidentified, Micky Miller, Virginia Martin, unidentified, Donald Matson, unidentified, Rita Howard, Brenda Bannister, three unidentified, and Edward Jones. (Courtesy of Jo Ann Bishop.)

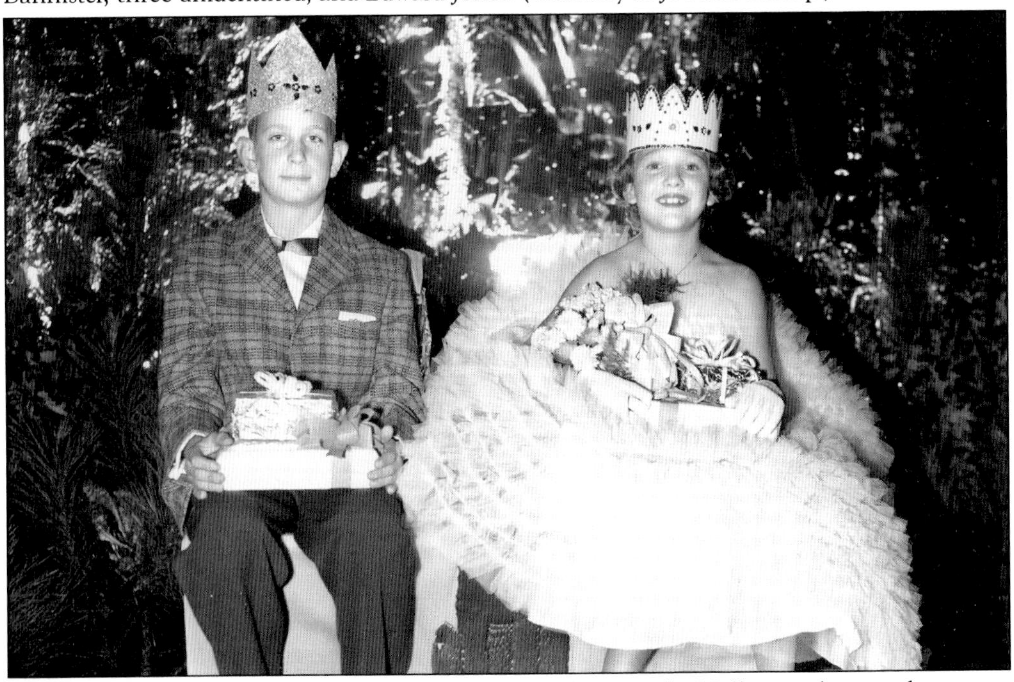

Joe Williams, fifth grade, and Elaine Jeter, fourth grade, were the Halloween king and queen at Idalia Elementary School in 1957. (Courtesy of Joe Williams.)

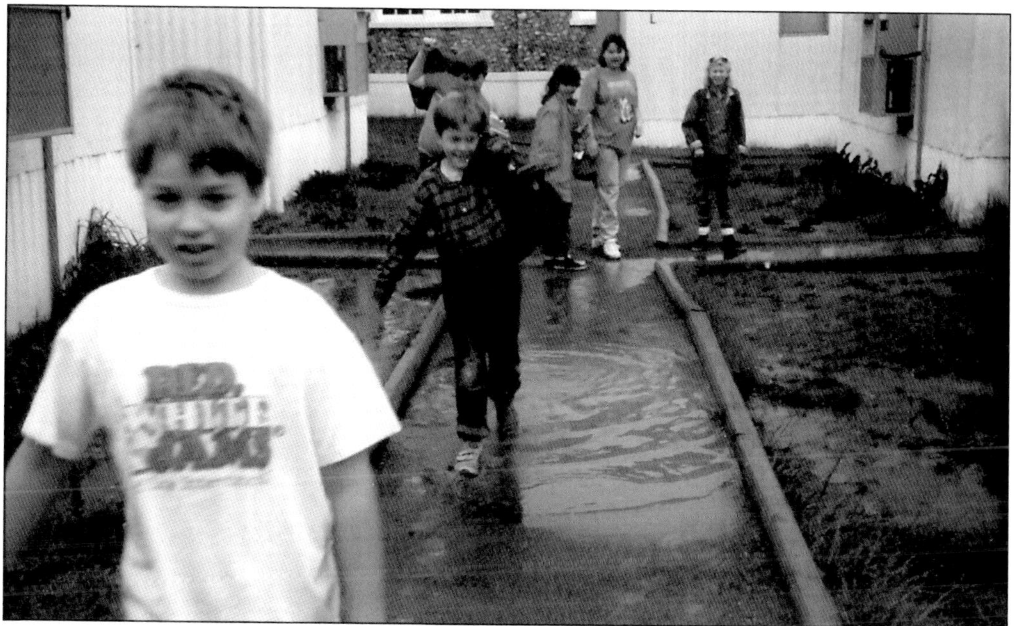

During the transition from Idalia Elementary School to Stemley Road Elementary School Idalia, classes were set up in temporary, individual, mobile units. Walking to class in the rain in April 1988 are students (front to back) Jay Mizzell, Scott Pilkington, William Vincent, Bethanne Barber, Mikki Mizzell, and Michelle Horton. (Courtesy of Beverly Gene Caldwell Pope.)

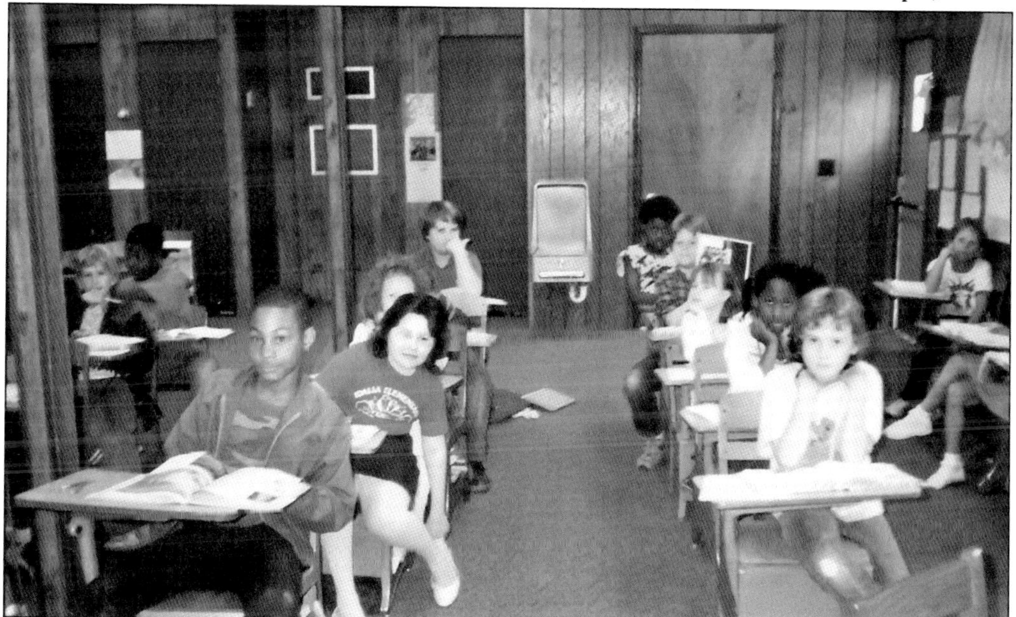

This photograph was taken of the fourth-grade class of Idalia Elementary School in 1988 when the classes were being held in temporary mobile buildings after the schoolhouse burned in 1986. From front to back are (first row, far left) Chris Belcher and Kendrick Tuck, (second row) Gray Smith, Adelia Hurst, Beth Lackey, Cory White, and William Vincent; (third row) Judy Harris, Liz Brown, Amanda Hillburn, Scott Pilkington, and Tenille Jackson; (fourth row) Bill Fetner. (Courtesy of Beverly Gene Caldwell Pope.)

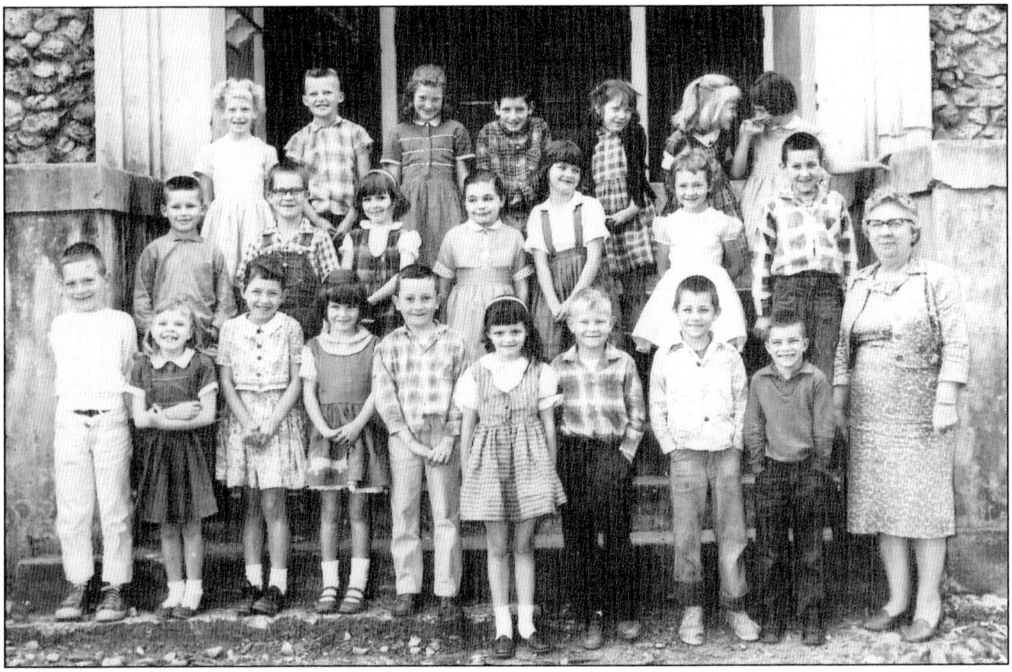

This photograph shows the Idalia Elementary School first-grade class of 1960–1961 with teacher Conola Shaddix. (Courtesy of Belle Hutto.)

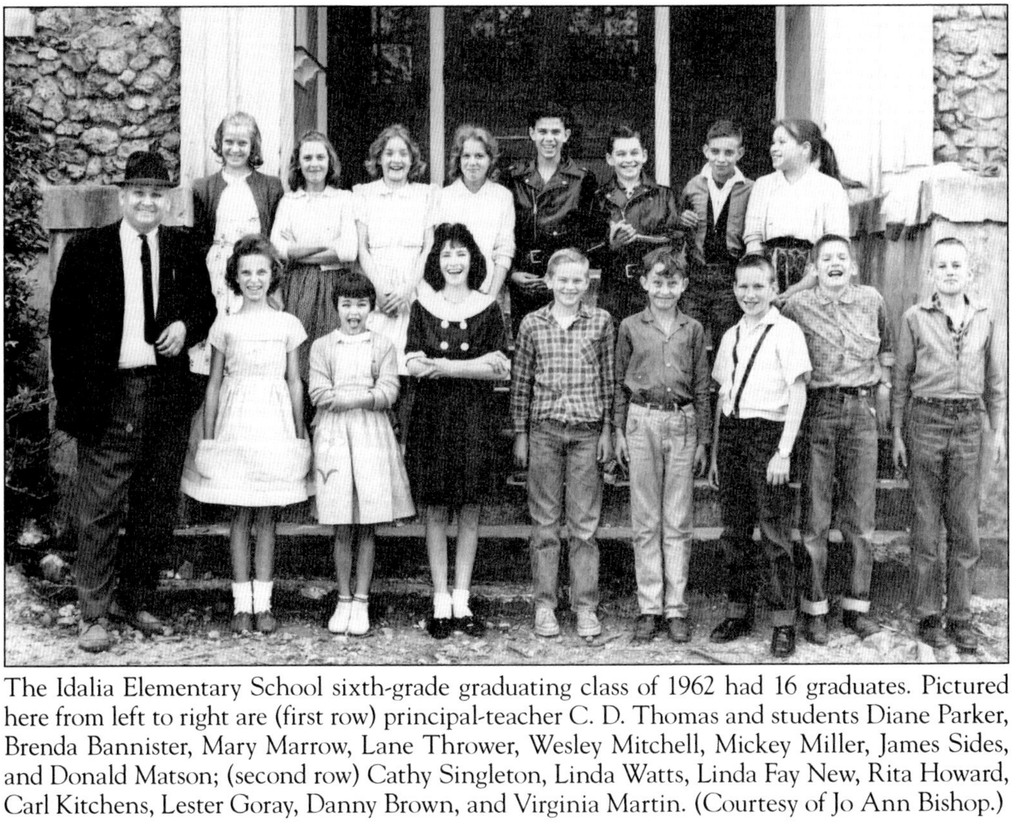

The Idalia Elementary School sixth-grade graduating class of 1962 had 16 graduates. Pictured here from left to right are (first row) principal-teacher C. D. Thomas and students Diane Parker, Brenda Bannister, Mary Marrow, Lane Thrower, Wesley Mitchell, Mickey Miller, James Sides, and Donald Matson; (second row) Cathy Singleton, Linda Watts, Linda Fay New, Rita Howard, Carl Kitchens, Lester Goray, Danny Brown, and Virginia Martin. (Courtesy of Jo Ann Bishop.)

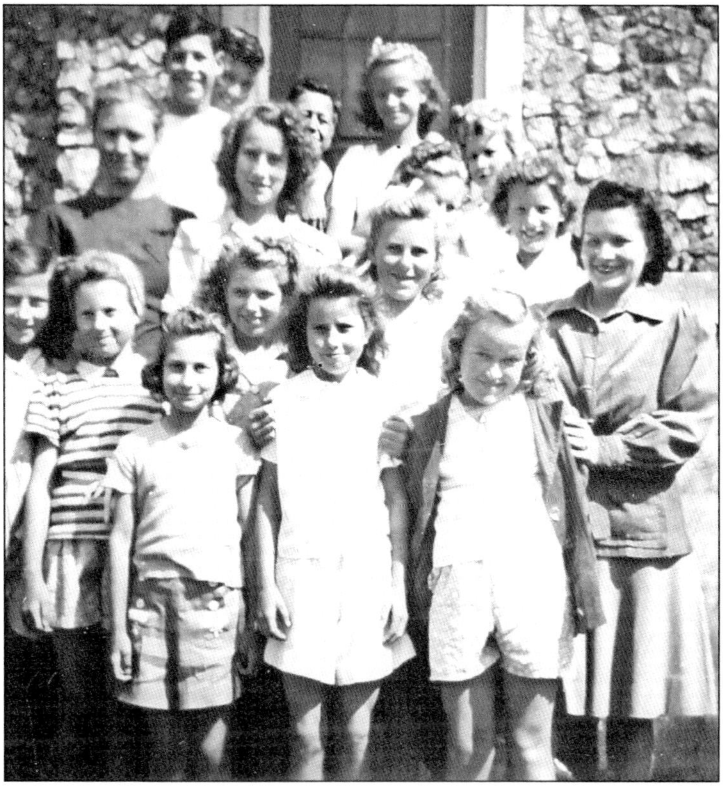

Shown in this 1942 photograph of Idalia Elementary School from left to right are (first row) Dot Johnson, Evelyn Hall, Sara Nell Hutto, and teacher Doris Bazemore. The rest are unidentified except for Clara Jean Fulmer, second from the left, and Lula Mae Williams, fourth from the left, in the second row. (Courtesy of Thelma Daffron.)

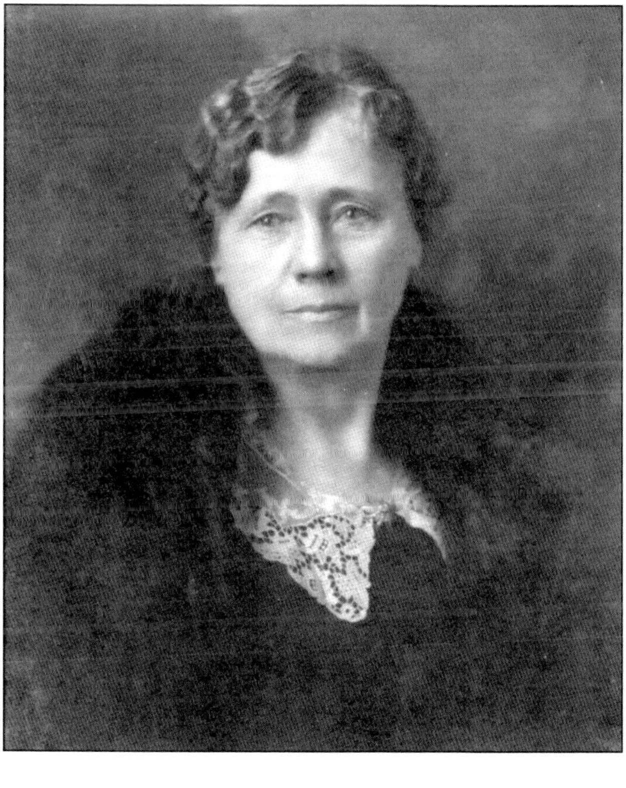

Ida Wallis Elliott (1867–1961) was the daughter of Charner and Isabell Van Wallis. Ida married Thomas Elliott, and they had three children. Ida organized the people of Howell's Cove and had a school built. In her honor, the school was named Ida Academy. In 1924, Ida Academy consolidated with Stemley School and became Idalia Elementary School. (Courtesy of Beverly Gene Caldwell Pope.)

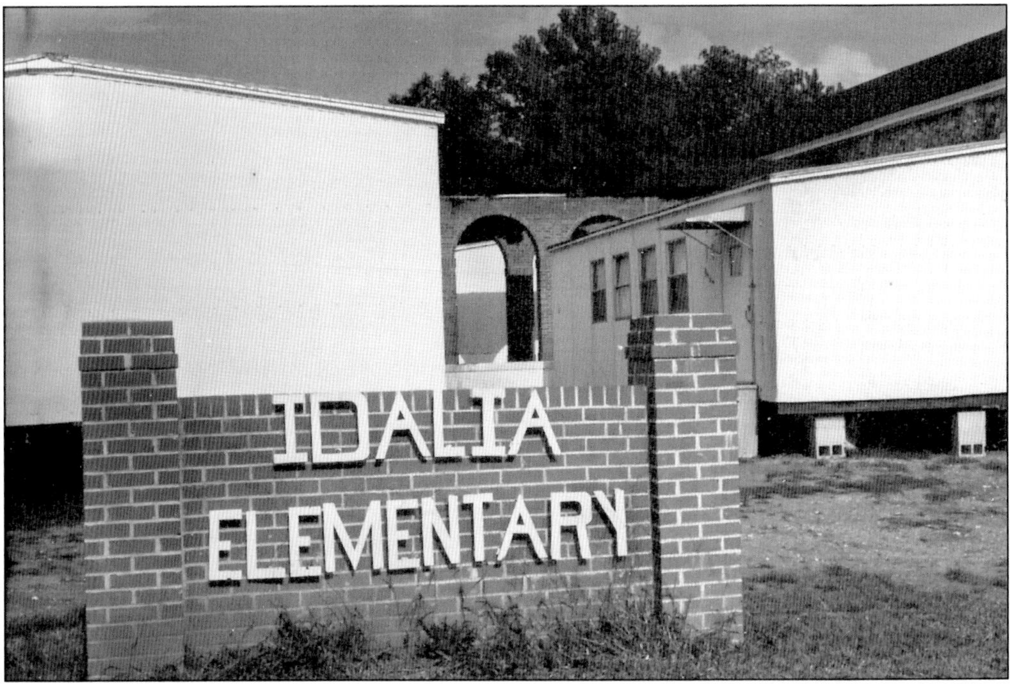

For four years after Idalia Elementary School burned in 1986, classes were held in temporary mobile units. Shown here are some of the mobile units that were converted into classrooms, an office building, a library, and restrooms. (Courtesy of Beverly Gene Caldwell Pope.)

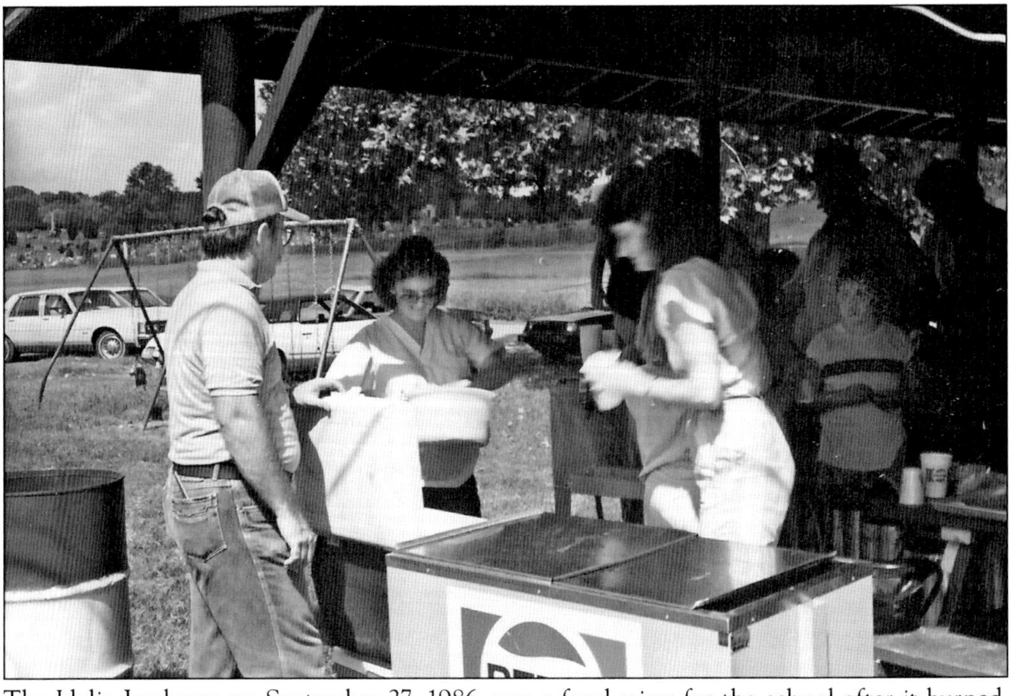

The Idalia Jamboree on September 27, 1986, was a fund-raiser for the school after it burned. Pictured from left to right in the foreground are Pete Gaither, a former student; Carlene Owens, a bus driver; and Rita Coppedge, a teacher at Idalia. (Courtesy of Beverly Gene Caldwell Pope.)

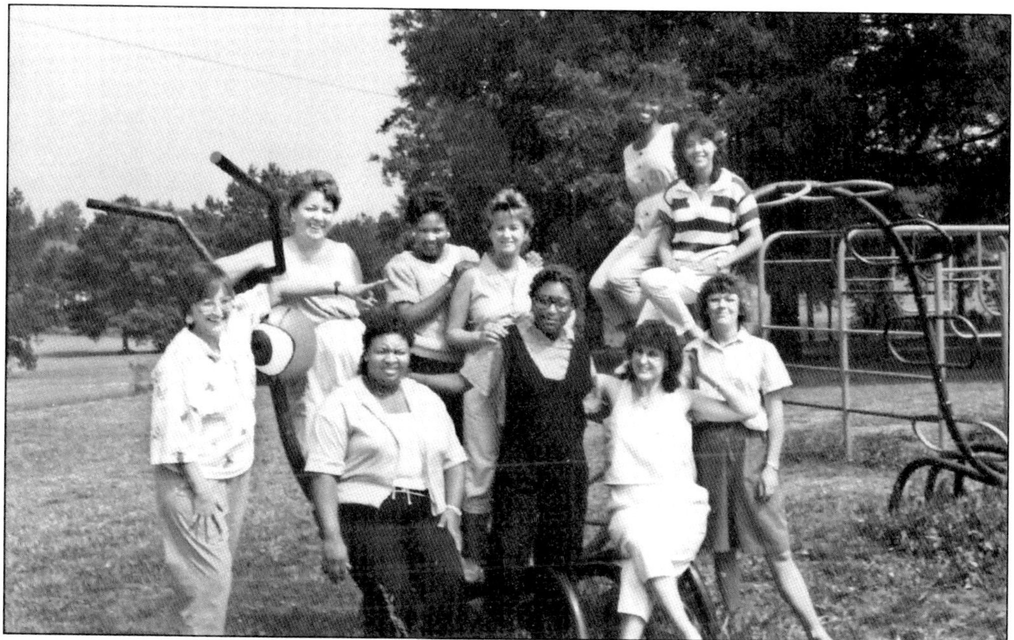

The faculty of Idalia Elementary School gathered for this photograph on May 29, 1987. From left to right are (first row) Mary Ann Hubbard, Emily Studdard (mother of Ruben Studdard, winner of the 2003 *American Idol* contest, who attended kindergarten at Idalia), Doris Hawkins, Rita Pilkington, and Linda Frank; (second row) Jo Reaves, Ms. Varner, Vicki Hester, Sylvia Tucker, and Trina Pettus. (Courtesy of Beverly Gene Caldwell Pope.)

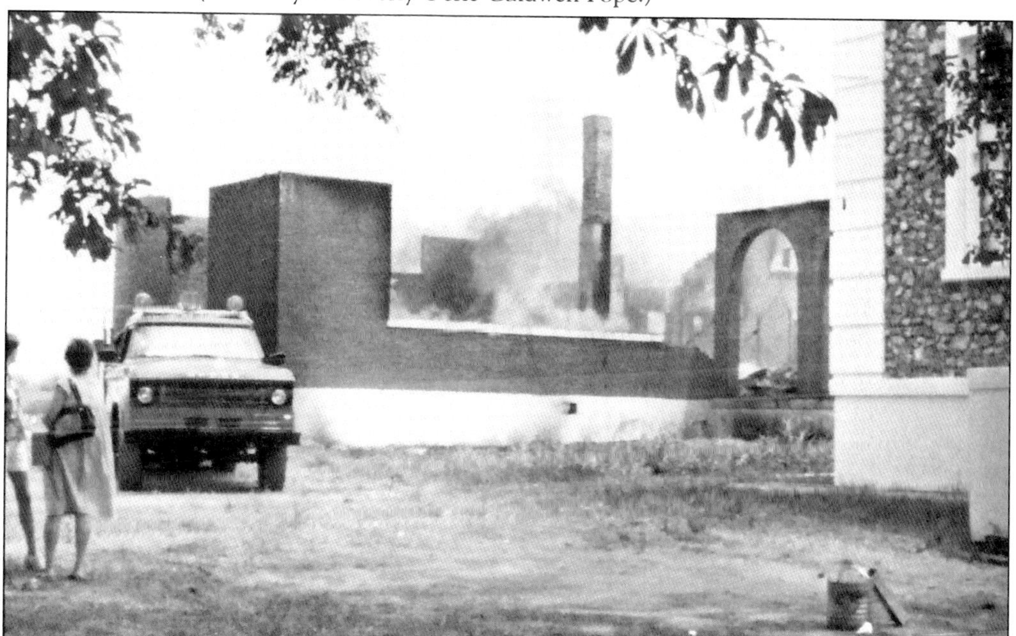

Idalia Elementary School burned on June 27, 1986, probably because of faulty wiring in the attic. This picture was taken in front of the auditorium looking toward the second-grade room. Only the auditorium and two of the classrooms were salvaged. (Courtesy of Beverly Gene Caldwell Pope.)

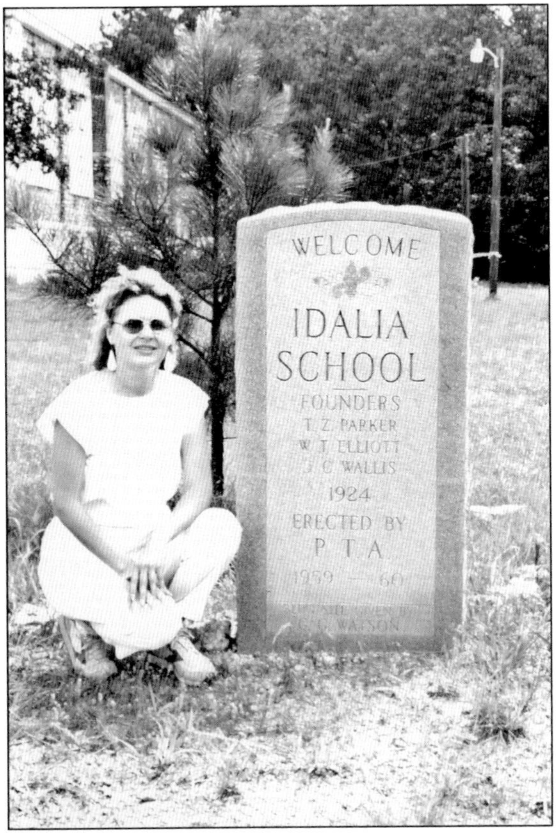

The day after Idalia Elementary School burned, June 28, 1986, Beverly Gene Caldwell Pope posed by this monument in front of the auditorium. Beverly Pope is the great-niece of Ida Wallis Elliott. Beverly taught fourth grade at Idalia from 1982 to 1990. (Courtesy of Beverly Gene Caldwell Pope.)

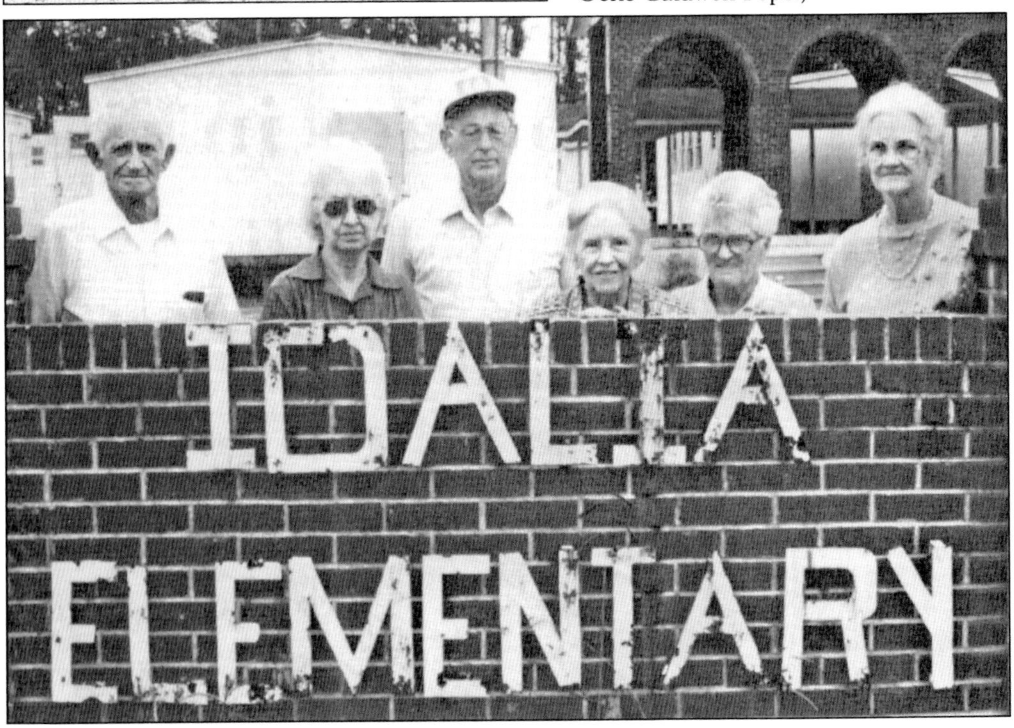

After Idalia Elementary School burned, the Talladega County Board of Education planned to name the new school Stemley Road Elementary, but members of the community came out to voice their dissenting opinion that the name not be changed from Idalia Elementary School. After the protests, the sign in front of the new school read Stemley Road Elementary School Idalia. The lunchroom in the new school was named in honor of Ida Elliott. Pictured here behind the old Idalia sign from left to right are Paul Hutto, Ora Goray Gaither, Tom Parker, Ettielyn Huston Simpson, Nannie Gaither, and Sadie Irwin Newsome. (Courtesy of Beverly Gene Caldwell Pope.)

Hattie Cunningham is shown at Talladega County Training School sometime in the 1940s. Hattie worked for the school administrators who lived in a building on campus. (Courtesy of Lois Embry.)

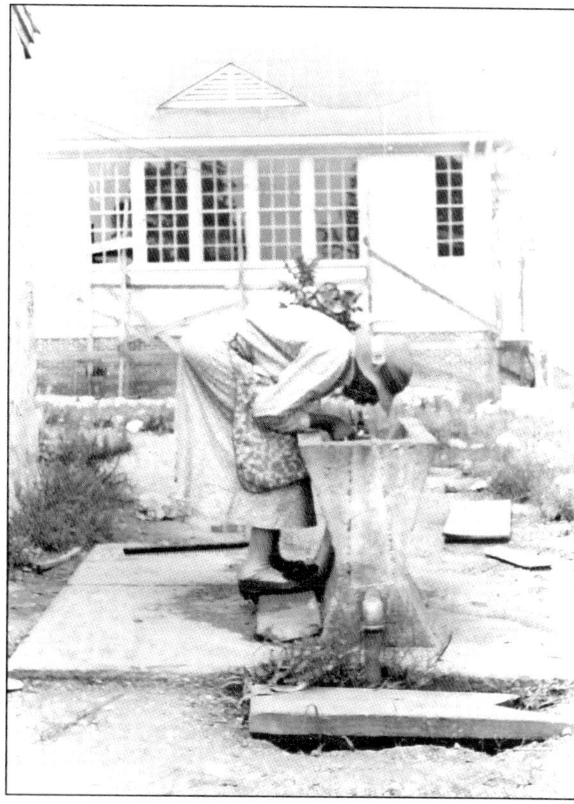

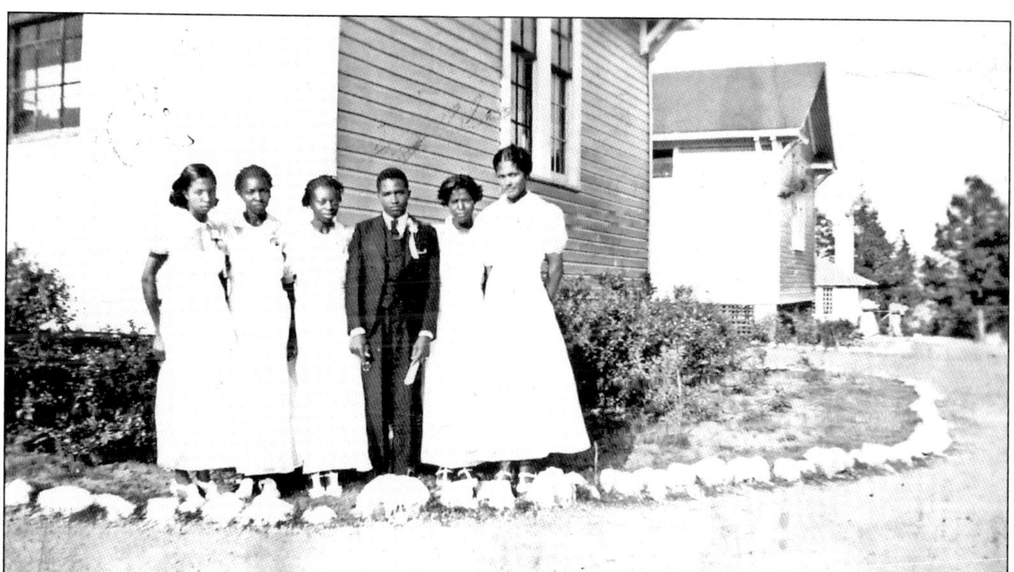

Standing in front of Talladega County Training School is the class of 1937. They are, from left to right, Ollie Lawson, Louise Sawyer, Josie Cross, Willie Lawson, Mary Julia Tuck, and Maie C. Phillips. (Courtesy of Barbara Dunn.)

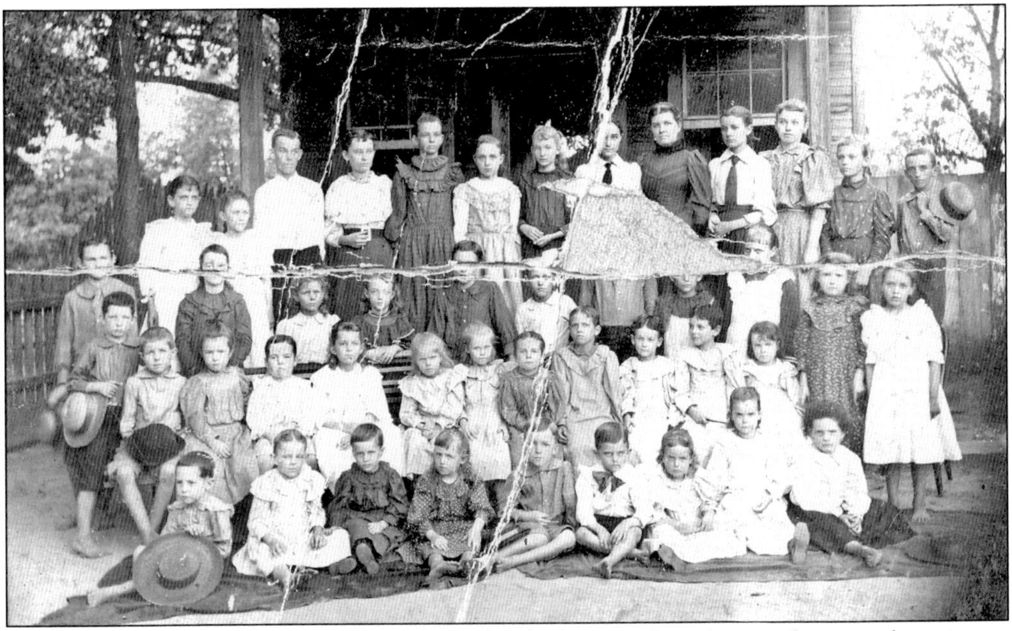

Do you recognize anyone in this long-ago school photograph or know when or where it was taken? Note every student is wearing long sleeves and a number of them are barefooted. Also note the hats. (Courtesy of Rosemary Robinson.)

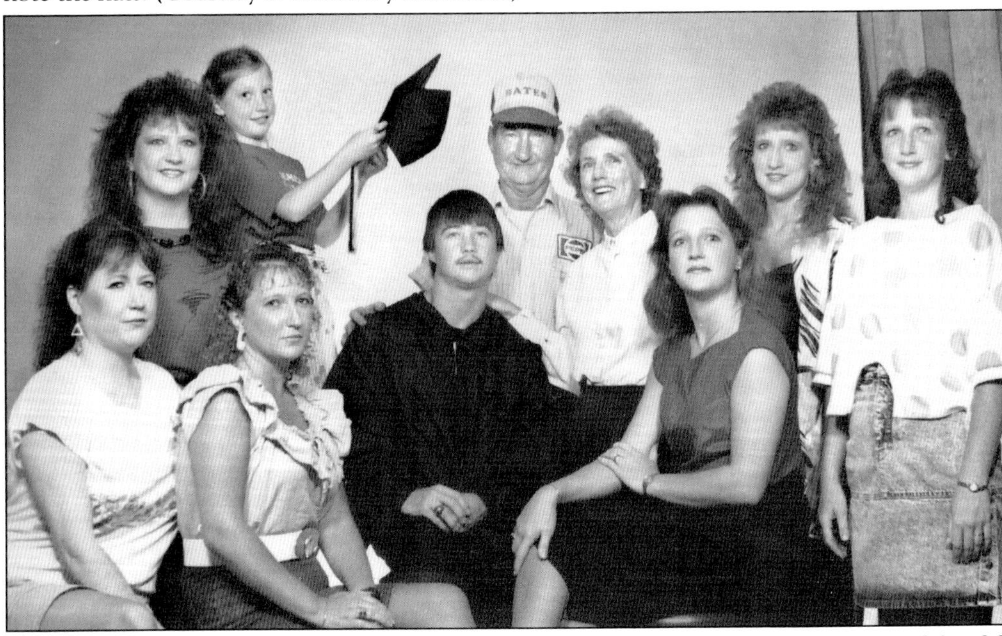

The *Daily Home* featured this photograph of the Bates family on the front page on May 26, 1988. The family had a remarkable perfect attendance record throughout school. All eight children of Horace and Dorothy Bates went to Idalia Elementary School, Drew Middle School, and Talladega County High School in Lincoln without missing a day of school. Horace and Dorothy Bates are pictured in the center next to their only son, Glenn. On their left, from left to right are daughters Amy, Rita, Beth (with cap), and Kathy, and on their right are Glenda, Cindy, and Tracey. (Courtesy of Dorothy Bates.)

Four

PEOPLE

Early settlers of the greater Stemley Bridge area were farmers and planters, millers and merchants. A partial list of their names includes Harmon, Lundie, Ragland, Beavers, Davis, Franklin, Collins, Maclin, Gover, Cunningham, Scales, Rutledge, Elrod, Ridout, Howell, Willenburg, Watkins, Estill, Smoot, Gray, Burchfield, Hobbs, Seay, Hammonds, Hallmark, Chapman, Curry, Elston, Henderson, Overman, Deel, Tarrant, Greene, Terry, Flynn, Lawson, Thornton, Newsome, Schmidt, Lanniester, Allen, Duncan, Morris, Stockdale, Sims, Smith, Bates, Thomas, Parks, Hodge, Henley, Armbrester, Hubbard, Gambrell, Lowry, Floyd, Hann, Rowell, Sanders, Johnson, Fulmer, Truss, Finley, and Castleberry.

Since 1964, when Logan Martin Dam began operation, much of the lake shoreline has been sold, and many homes are being built, bringing in people who enjoy the lake and lakeside activities such as fishing and boating.

Around Stemley Bridge, there lies a feeling of togetherness and equality among its people who have made this community diverse and alive with an incredible human spirit. These photographs give vivid evidence of the people who made this community their home and life, and it is obvious that the Stemley area carries a heritage dear to many hearts.

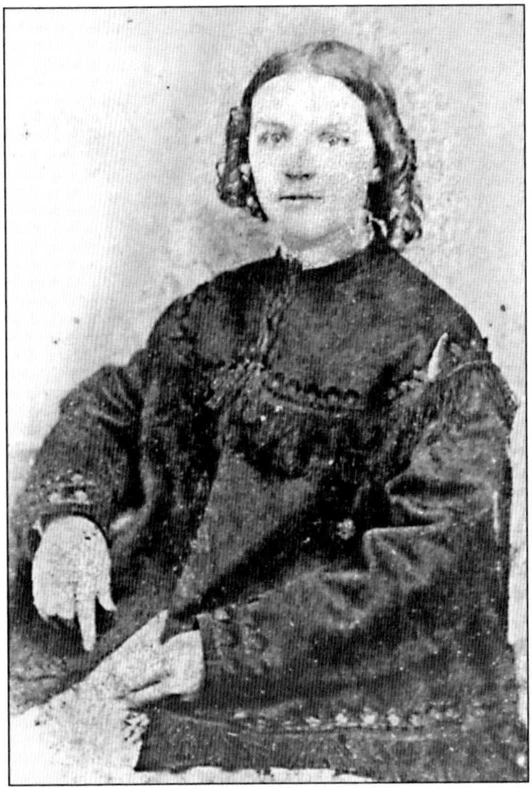

Edith Eloise Johnson (1850–1917) was the wife of Civil War veteran James Thomas Johnson. The buckskin jacket she is wearing was given to her by an American Indian friend of the family. (Courtesy of Jeanette Zachero.)

George Adam Fulmer (1851–1941) and his second wife, Ella (Davis) Fulmer, are standing in front of the family home. Ella helped George raise the six children of his first wife, Lavinia Morgan, who died at the age of 34. Lavinia was the daughter of Philander Morgan, brother of U.S. Sen. John Tyler Morgan. (Courtesy of Jeanette Zachero.)

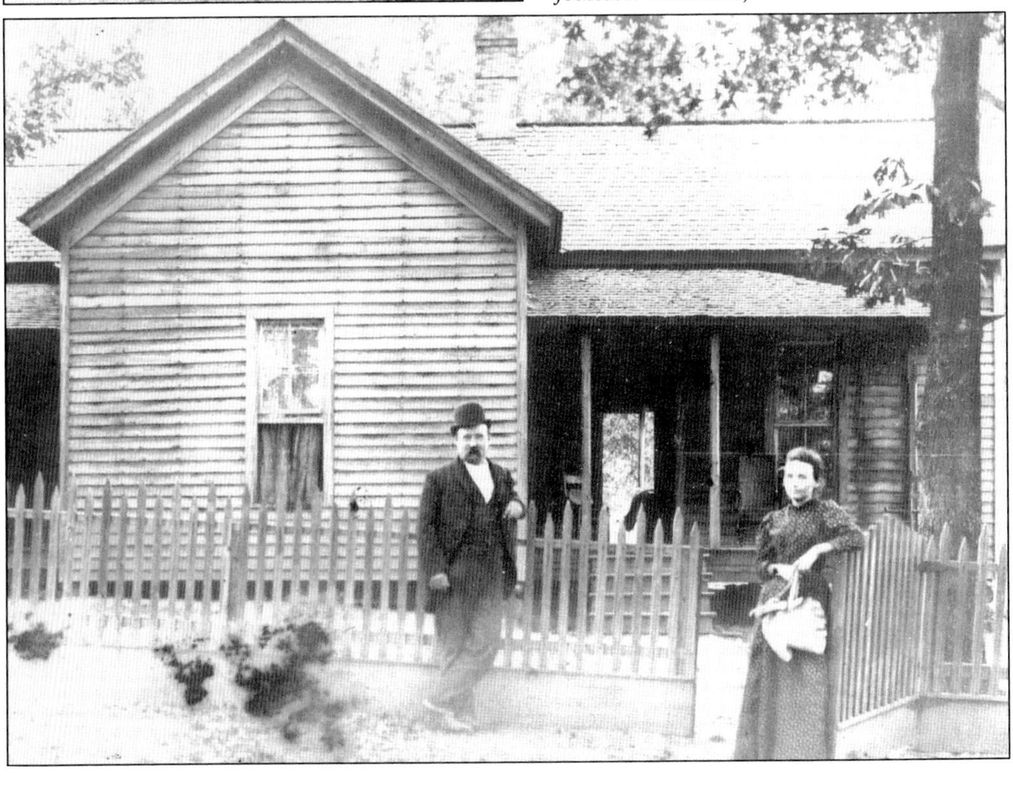

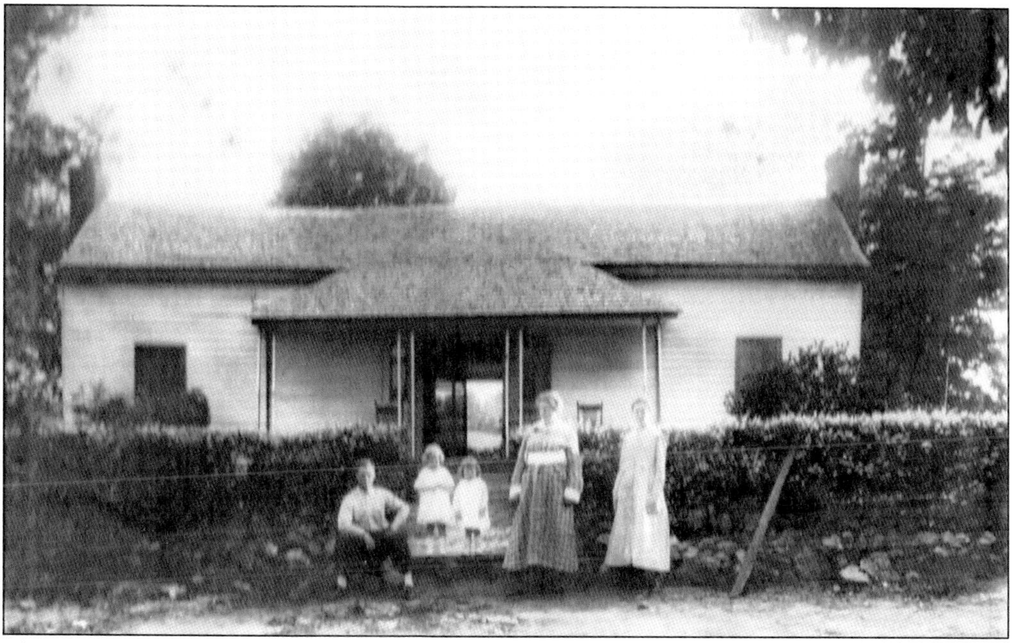

This c. 1919 photograph shows J. W. Avery and his family in front of their home. Pictured from left to right are J. W.; children, Margaret Avery (Williams) and Nandean Avery (Parker); his wife, Myrtle (Coker) Avery; and Myrtle's sister, Mattie Laura Coker. (Courtesy of Alta and MariAnne Williams.)

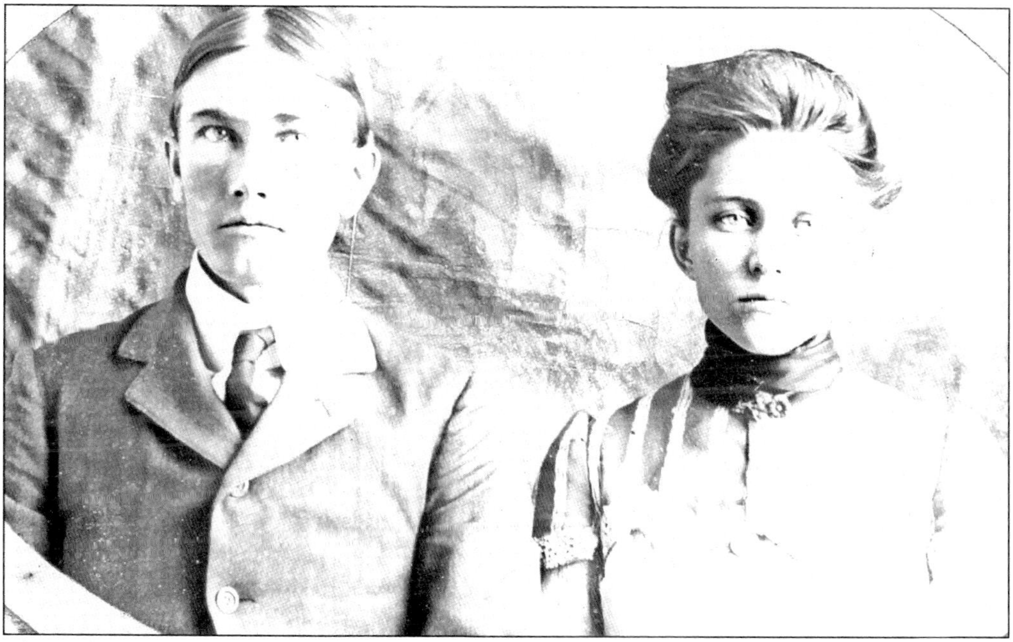

This is the wedding picture of Timmons Hendrix Floyd and Maggie Grimes, c. 1900. They bought their home and farm from Fall Robinson of Cropwell. Timmons built, owned, and operated the Little Rock Store and Camp Pleasure. Maggie kept the record books for Timmons's businesses and crops. Twice a day, Timmons read and recorded the meter gauge that monitored water levels of the Coosa River at Stemley Bridge. (Courtesy of Rosemary Robinson.)

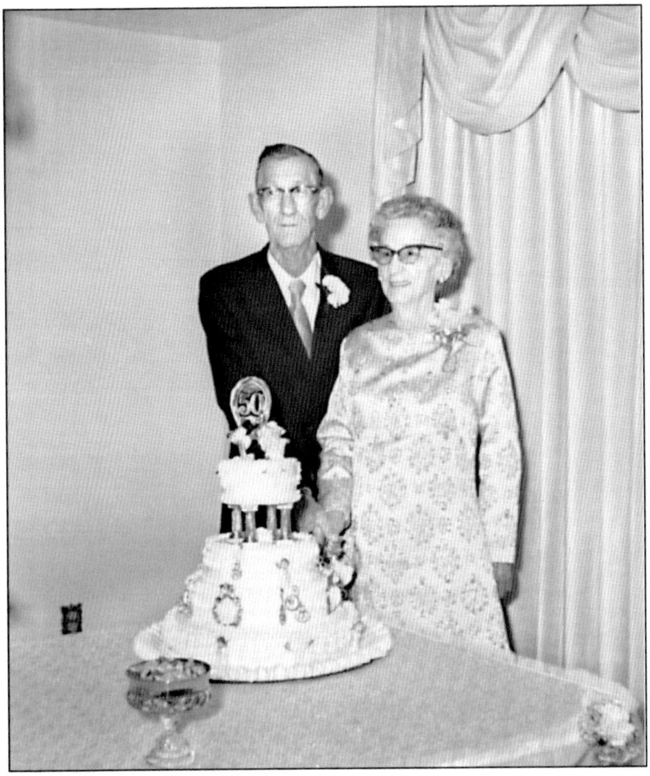

Henry Austin Hubbard (1899–1994) and Jennie Brince Glenn Hubbard (1895–1978) were married December 26, 1922. In this photograph, Henry and Jennie are at their 50th wedding anniversary celebration. They earned their living by farming. (Courtesy of Sara Goucher.)

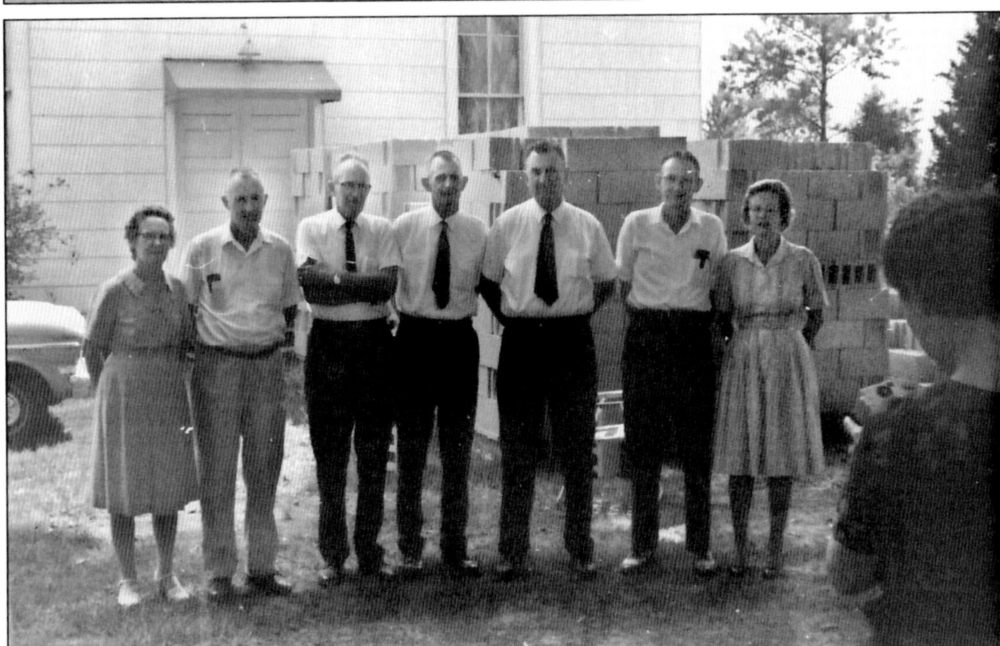

The Hutto family posed for this photograph outside the old Bethel Church in the 1960s. From left to right are Venice Hutto; Leslie Hutto, who served as Talladega County commissioner; Eugene Hutto, who served on the Talladega County Board of Education; Paul Hutto; Cloyd Hutto; Hugh Hutto; and Lora Hutto Shearing. (Courtesy of Frances Barber.)

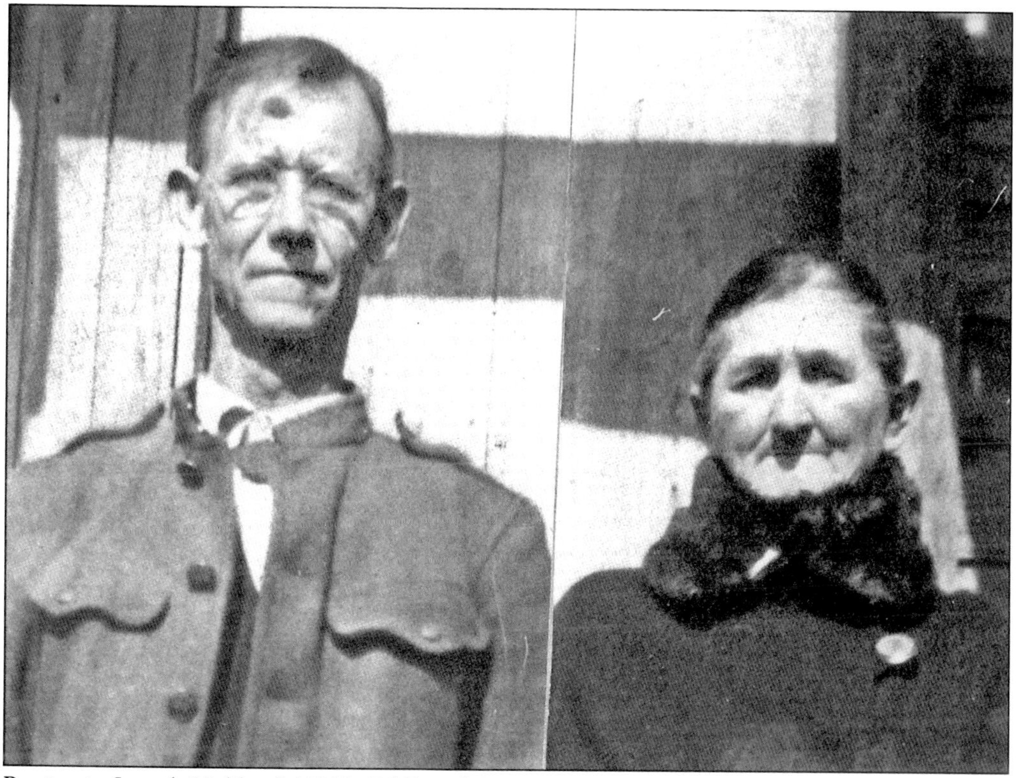

Benjamin Joseph Hubbard (1867–1956) and Sara Frances (Parks) Hubbard (1869–1941) posed for this photograph in the early 1900s. Benjamin worked as a farmer on Plantersville Road. He and Sara were the parents of eight children: daughters Phenie, Mildred, Fannie, and Lucille, and sons Jack, Dude, Ophus, and Austin. (Courtesy of Sara Goucher.)

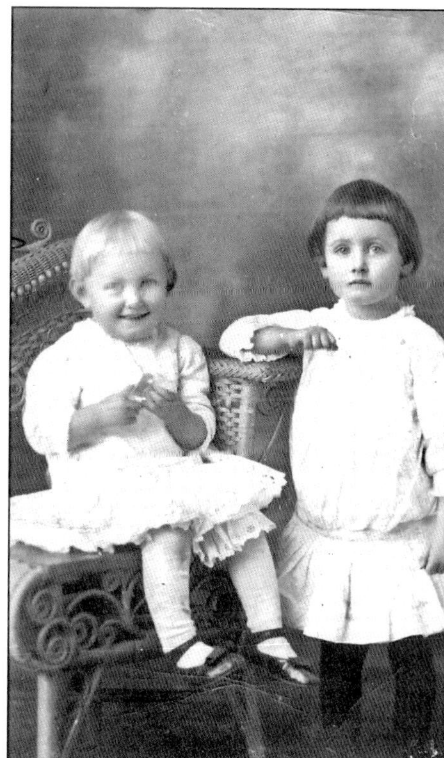

This is a photograph of Estelle Goray, left, and her sister Ora. The two sisters attended school at Ida Academy, a one-room school, until Ida Academy and Stemley School were combined to form Idalia Elementary School, c. 1923. They attended Idalia through the eighth grade before going to Talladega County High School at Lincoln. (Courtesy of Ora Gaither.)

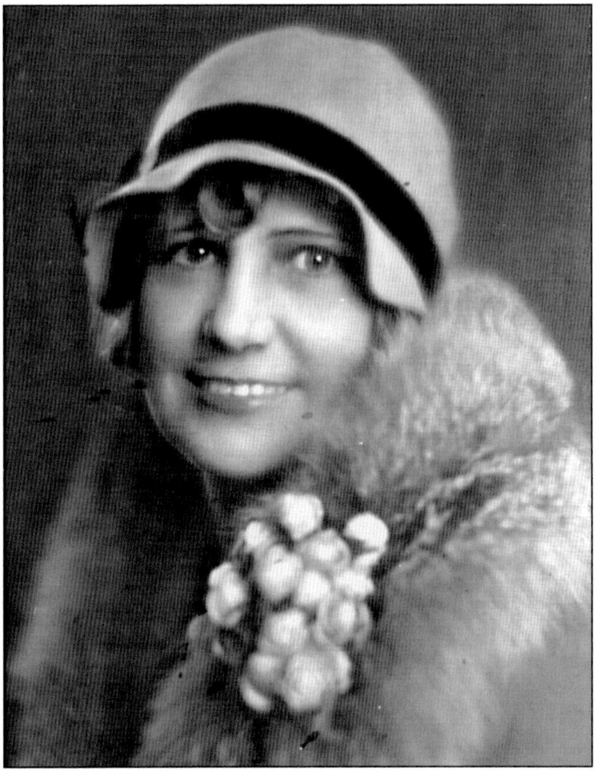

Shown here is Davy Florence (Griffitt) Myles. Davy lived in Memphis for a while but moved back to Griffitt Bend after the Depression. She was always "on call" to go to the home of any black woman giving birth without medical aid. With no formal training, Davy always seemed to know how to help, and in appreciation for her care, she was often given the honor of naming the baby she helped deliver. (Courtesy of Joe and Sue Wells.)

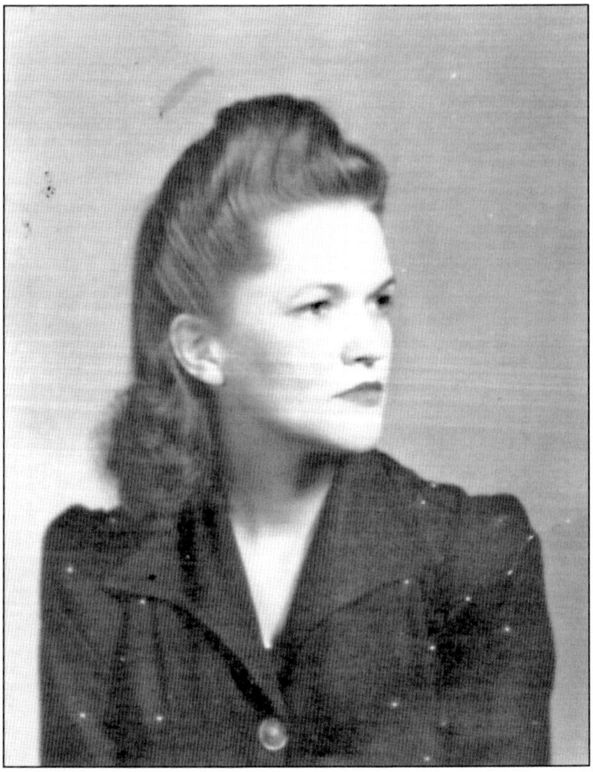

Ruby Key has lived in the Stemley area since 1942. In 1949, her home was a typical farmhouse with no telephone and no running water. However, there was electricity: she remembers the small electric bulbs. To get a telephone, they had to pay for the line by having $2 per month added to their bill until it was paid. She was on an eight-party line. In the early 1950s, the Keys were one of the first families in the neighborhood to own a television. (Courtesy of Ruby Key.)

As was common in the 1860s, Will Griffitt had several slaves to help with the crops. Will's slave families (tenants) lived in their own houses. When they were freed, they continued to live on the property and care for it. Lula and Elder Abercrombie raised five girls and one boy in the same house in which their family had lived as slaves. Their oldest child, Rosalie, cared for Will Griffitt's granddaughter, Floriene (Whitson) Parsons, and her child, Sue. This photograph of Rosalie and Sue was taken in 1939. (Courtesy of Joe and Sue Wells.)

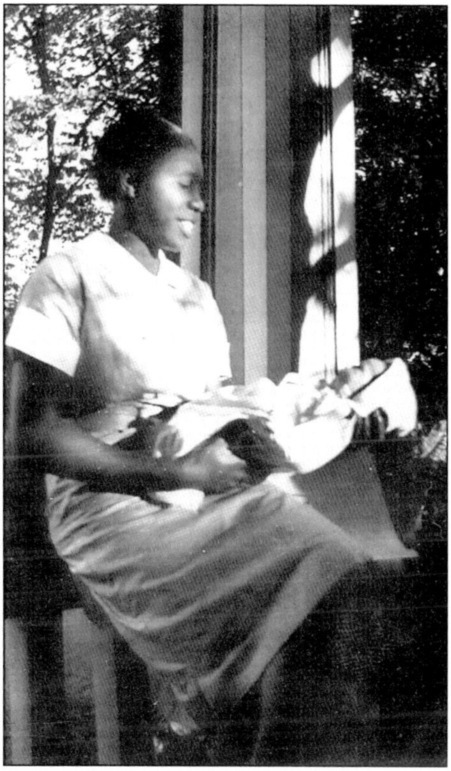

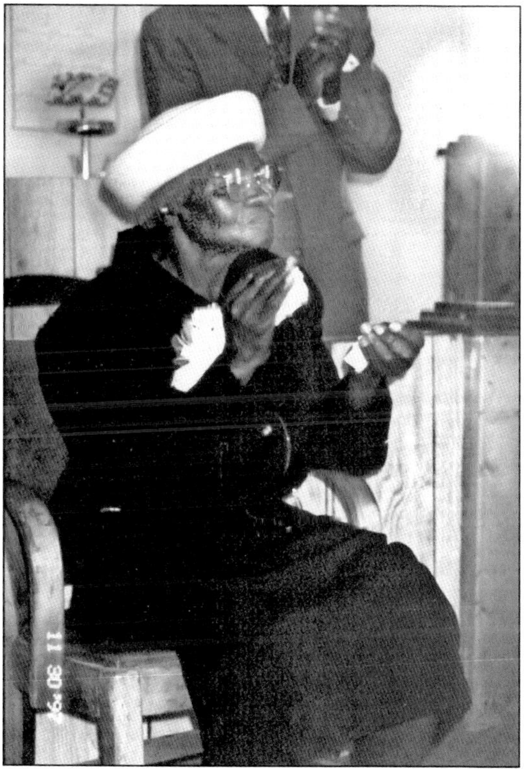

This photograph was taken of Nealie Kidd during a church service. Nealie was married to George Kidd, who purchased their Logan Martin lakefront property from Timmons Floyd. Nealie and George named their only child George Floyd Kidd after Timmons Floyd. In 2005, Nealie is 87 years old and still owns the lakefront property. (Courtesy of Johnnie Mae Cochran.)

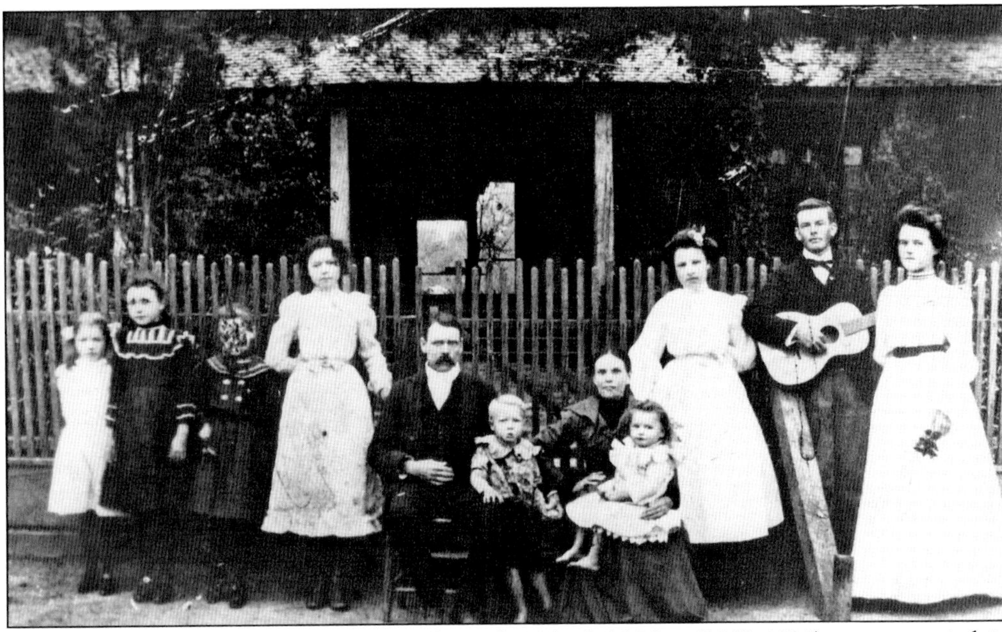

William "Bill" Bynum (1860–1932) and Sarah Whitfield Hitt (1862–1934) were married in 1879. Their children were Josie, Willie, Georgia, Villa, Webb, Cliff, Frank, Vera, Zula, Tom, and Minnie. They lived at the Laney place near Cropwell, and the children went to school in Cropwell. At the time of their deaths, Bill and Sarah were living in the home of their daughter, Josie Bynum Fulmer, at Stemley. (Courtesy of Jeanette Zachero.)

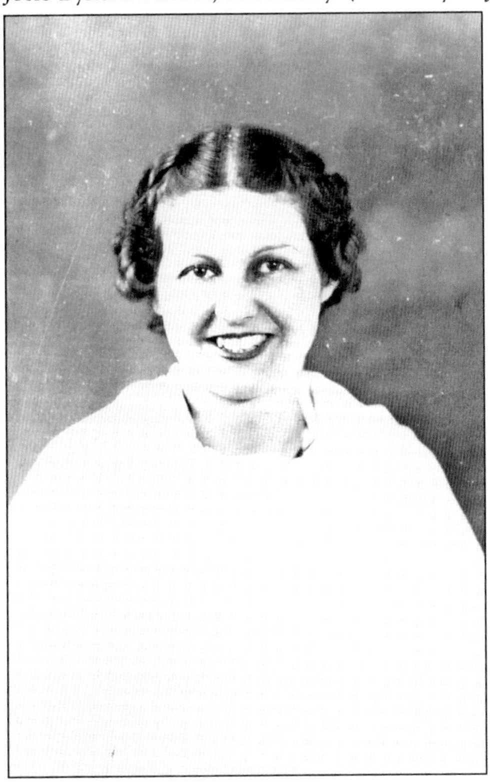

Margaret Avery was a wife, mother, and nurse; she was married to Robert A. Williams. Margaret died in March 1999. (Courtesy of Alta and MariAnne Williams.)

Annie (Lackey) Spencer was the widow of John Nielson Spencer, who died when their youngest son, Thomas, was just a toddler. Annie is shown here c. 1940 with her children. Pictured from left to right are (first row) Geraldine Medlock and Annie; (second row) Ray, Thomas, Graves, Burk, and Clinton. The Spencers were farmers. Most of them lived in the Stemley Bridge Road area. (Courtesy of Mary Frances Spencer.)

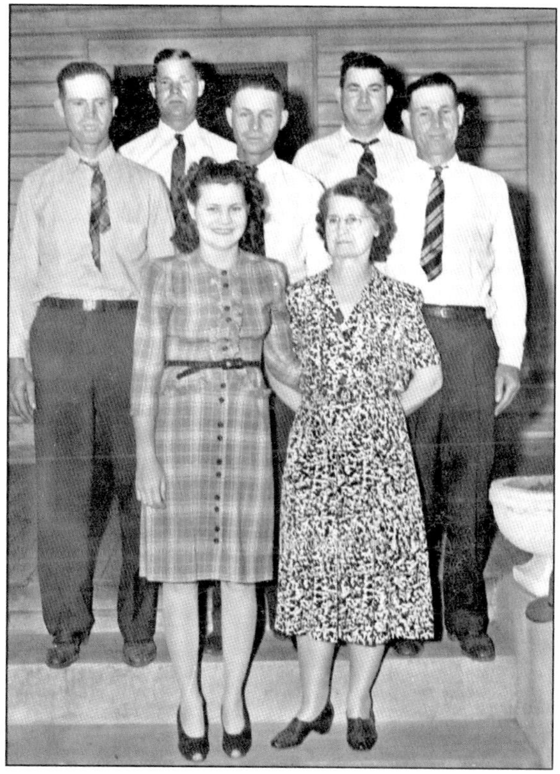

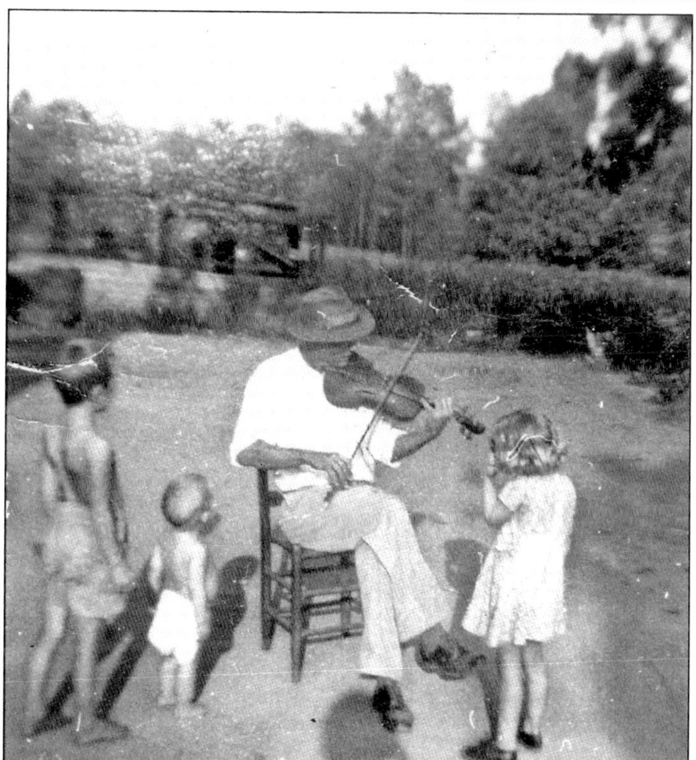

Pictured here from left to right are Bill, Charles, Winston, and Thelma Henderson around 1942. Winston played the fiddle for community dances, and many times he played just for the family. (Courtesy of Charles Henderson.)

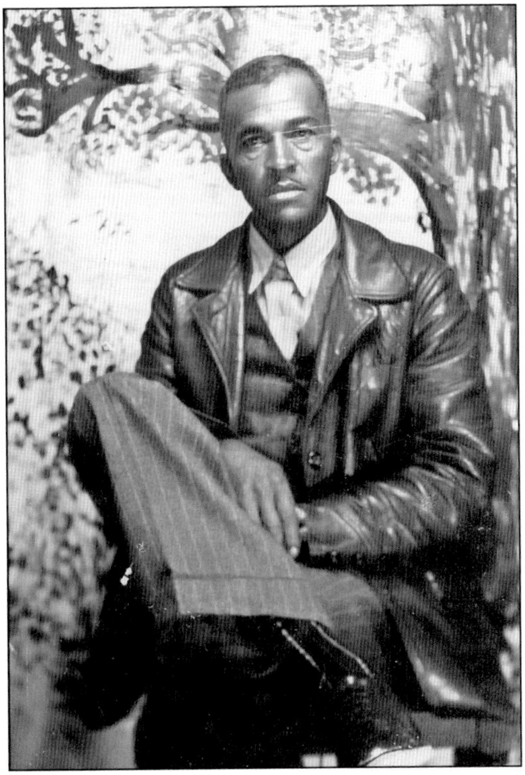

Burt Lawson and his wife, Claudia, along with Ida Elliott and her son Julian, donated the land on which Talladega County Central High School is currently located. Otis Lawson moved his store across the street in order for the TCC gymnasium to be built close to the school. The football field and the original principal's home were purchased from Burt and Claudia Lawson. Burt died November 23, 1973. (Courtesy of Barbara Dunn.)

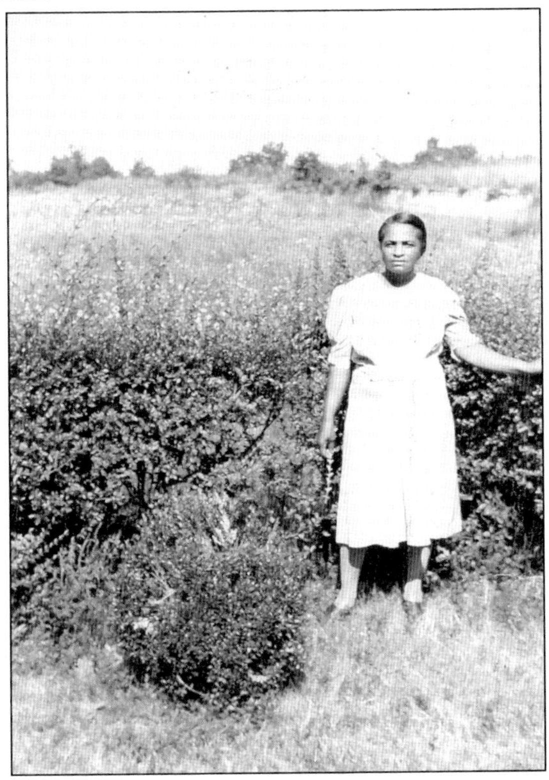

Claudia Lawson was the wife of Burt Lawson, who donated the land for Talladega County Training School. Among the many people who assisted with the formation of the school were Eliza Tuck, Agnes and Charlie Phillips, and Lune and Sadie Draper. (Courtesy of Barbara Dunn.)

Grover and Ethel Heath posed for this photograph on their wedding day, April 6, 1929. Ethel remembers that Grover bought her wedding dress for $25. (Courtesy of Grover and Ethel Heath.)

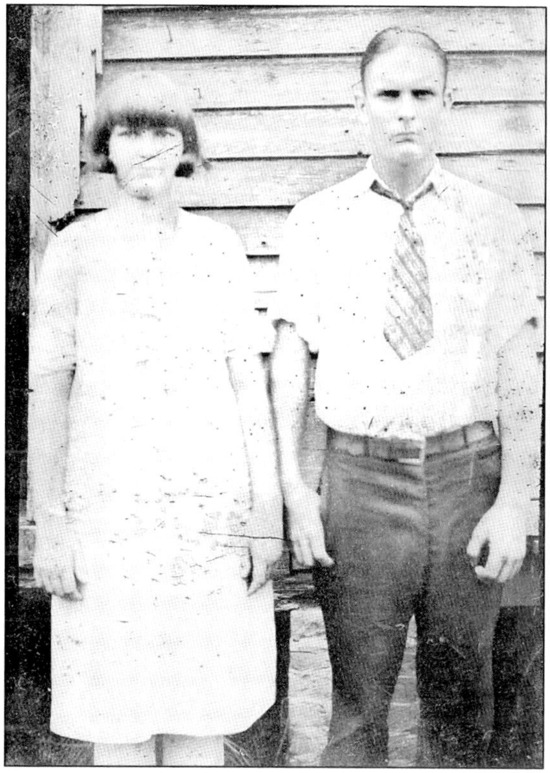

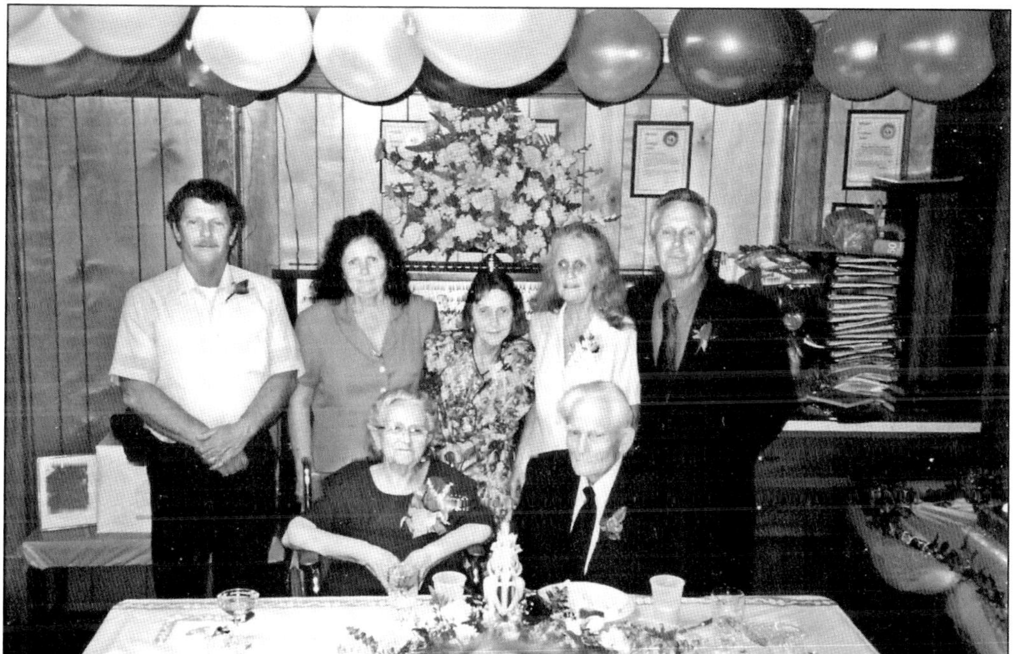

Grover and Ethel Heath (seated) posed with their children at a celebration in the late 1990s. Standing from left to right are Lamar Heath, Shirley Heath (Smith), Joyce Heath (McDonald), Virginia Heath (Davison), and Robert Joe Heath. (Courtesy of Grover and Ethel Heath.)

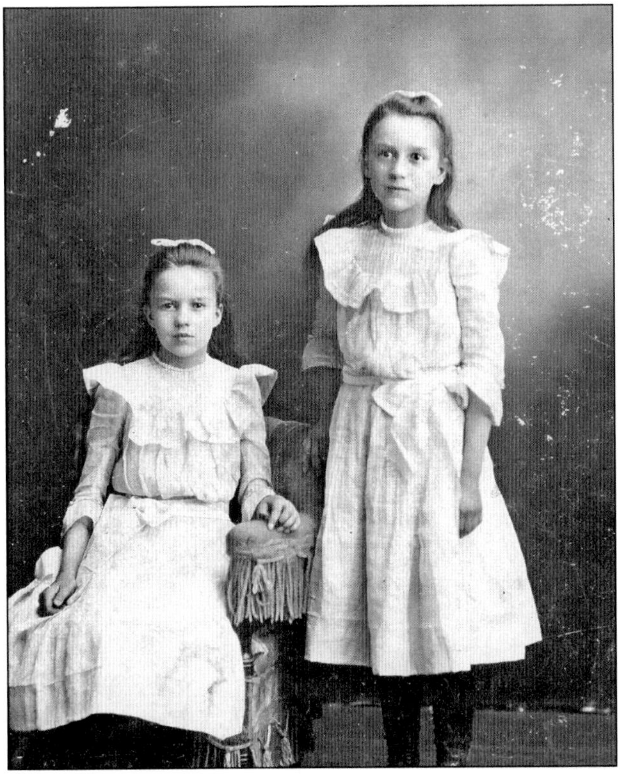

This is a photograph of twins Deloris (left) and Delola Thomas. Deloris married Morgan Howell, and they were the parents of Charlotte Eloise. Delola married Richard Howell, Morgan's brother. (Courtesy of M. H. McCary.)

The Leslie Johnson family poses in front of the family Model T Ford. Standing from left to right are the children of Leslie's wife, Maudie Jane (Fulmer) Johnson: Dewitt; Weaver; Mark; Lillie Mae; and Jewel; Leslie's wife, Caty; Leslie; and two unidentified ladies. This photograph was taken in the early 1930s. (Courtesy of Derrell Hann.)

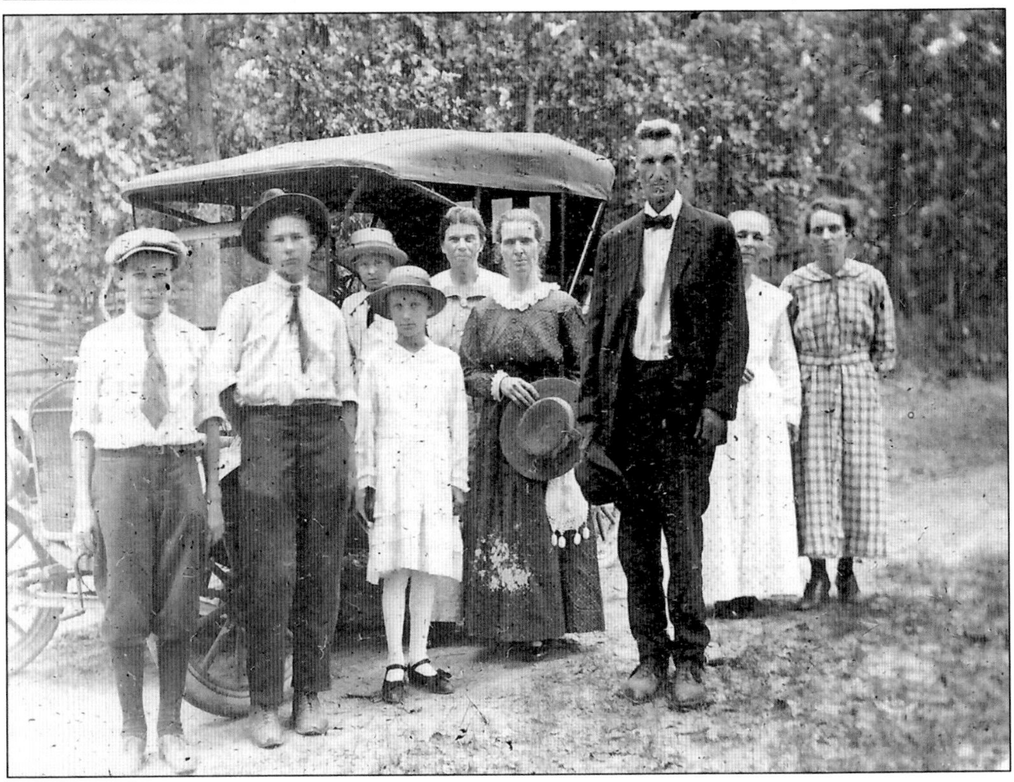

Jimmy Grimes lived in the Stemley area with his daughter, Maggie, and son-in-law, Timmons Floyd. Jimmy provided financial assistance for Timmons and Maggie to build and operate the Little Rock Store and Camp Pleasure. (Courtesy of Rosemary Robinson.)

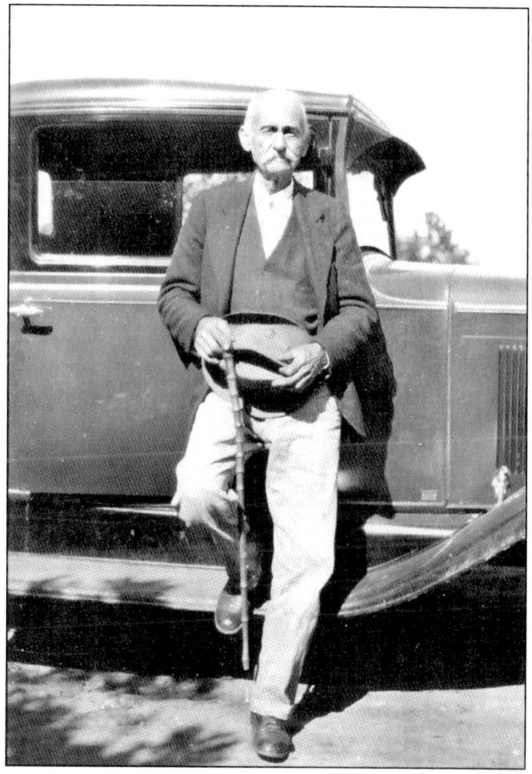

This photograph of the family of Johnnie C. and Nannie Lee Barnes was taken in 1954. From left to right are (first row) Donnie Lee, Daniel H., Annie Realta Kearley, and Larelle "Belle" Hutto; (second row) Nannie Lee, Johnnie C., John Harold, and Alton. (Courtesy of Dan and Mary Barnes.)

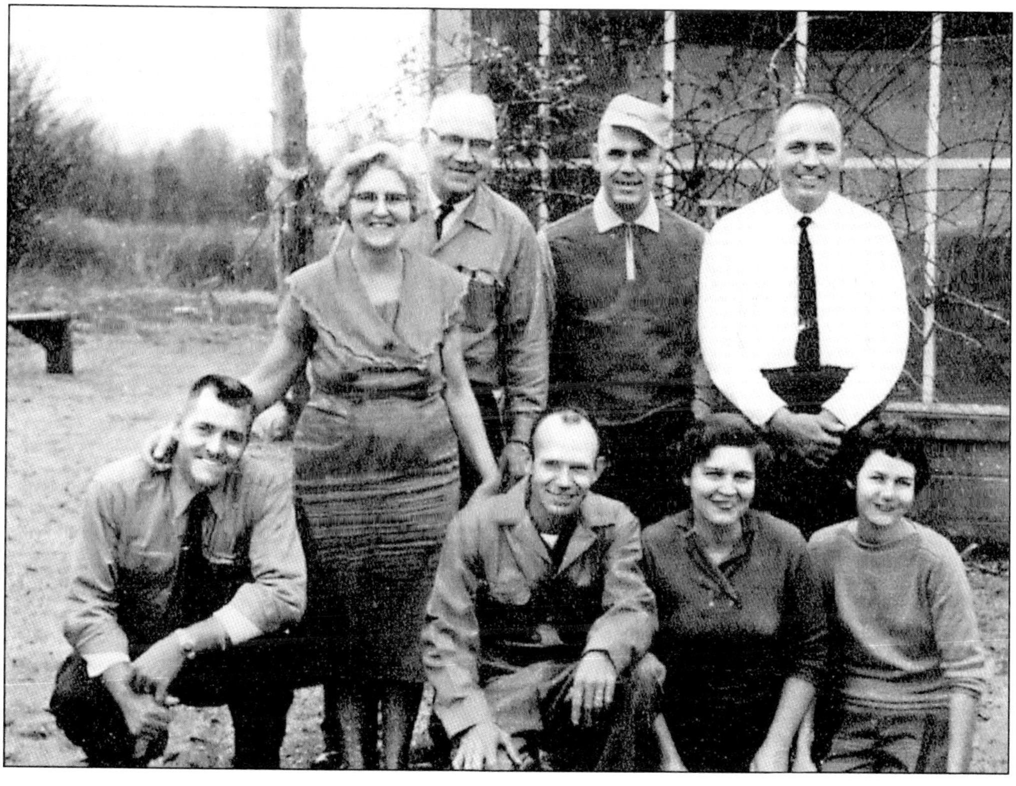

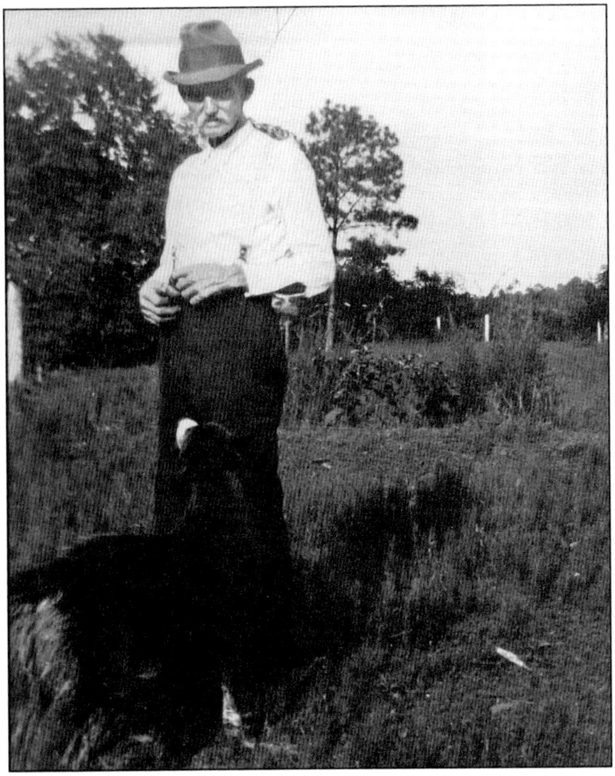

William Griffitt captained a riverboat in the mid-1800s that moved people and goods up and down the Coosa River. When the government opened the land that is now Griffitt Bend for settlement, Will purchased a section and moved his family here. Gradually other settlers came. He carried their household goods to his boat landing and arranged for a horse and wagon to complete the move inland. After his three daughters were born, he no longer made the long boat trips. He is shown here with his dog, Pal. (Courtesy of the Wells family.)

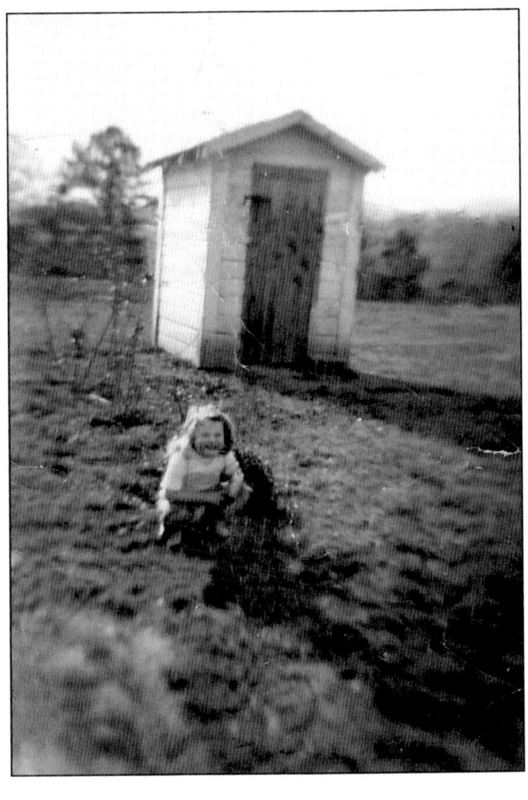

Faye Fulmer is in front of an outhouse c. 1949 before their family had indoor plumbing. Outhouses were seen in the Stemley area as late as the mid-1950s. (Courtesy of Peggy Hall.)

This photograph of Alta Williams (left), MariAnne Williams (center), and Gerri Duckworth was taken at the home of Maude Williams around 1945. (Courtesy of Alta and MariAnne Williams.)

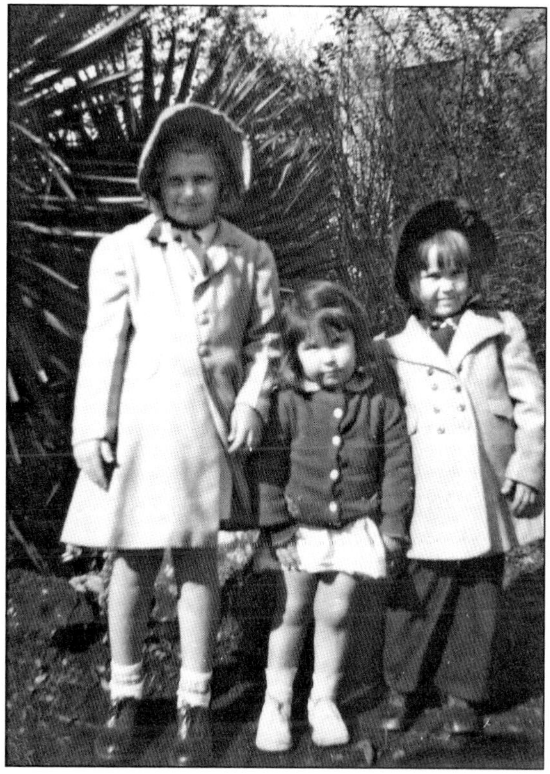

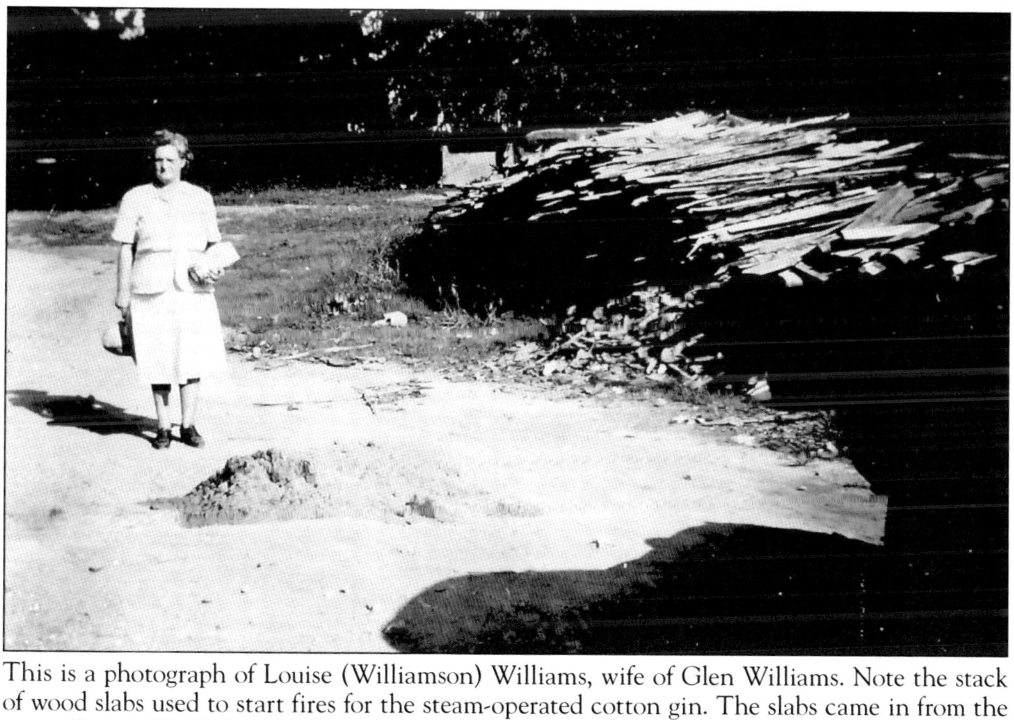

This is a photograph of Louise (Williamson) Williams, wife of Glen Williams. Note the stack of wood slabs used to start fires for the steam-operated cotton gin. The slabs came in from the sawmill owned by Robert Williams. The cotton gin whistles would blow every morning at 4 a.m. to let farmers know it was time to start ginning. (Courtesy of Joe Williams.)

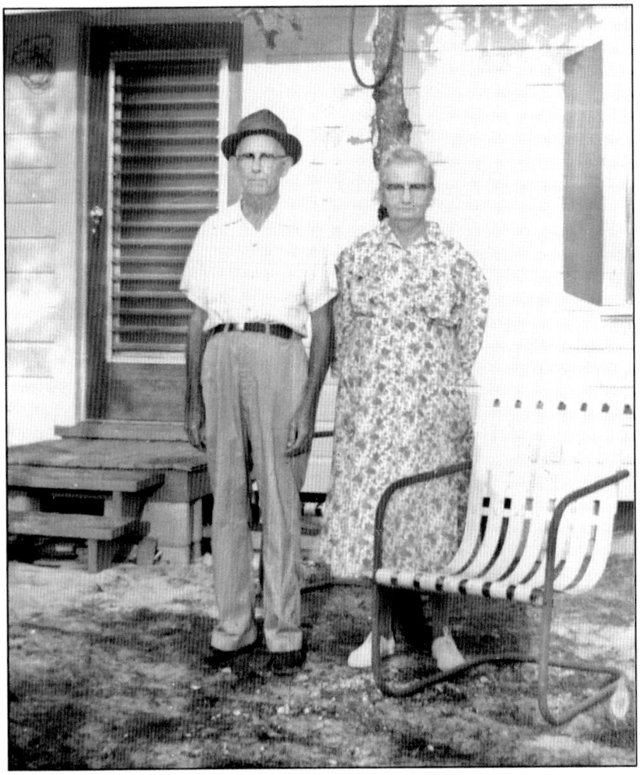

Tom and Myrtie (Endfinger) Sanders, shown here *c.* 1958, lived on Stemley Bridge Road from 1934 to 1964. They had seven children. Tom was a farmer and held various textile jobs during the Depression. (Courtesy of Calvin Sanders.)

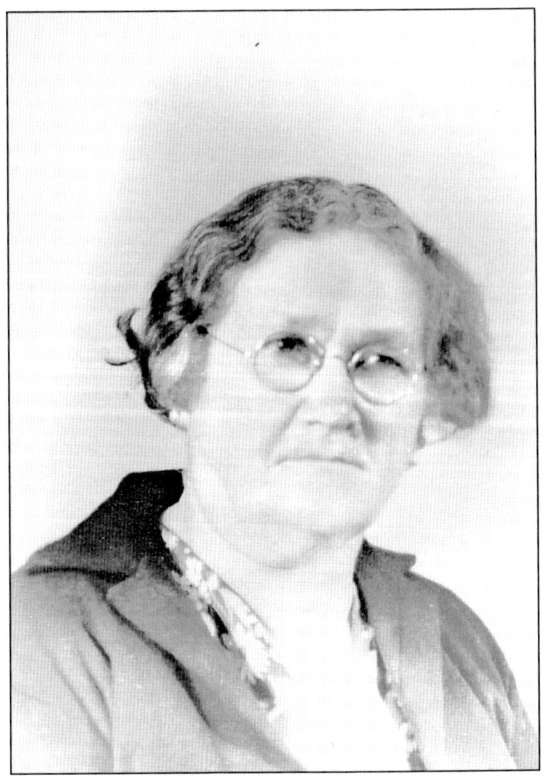

Maude (Hiett) Williams was the mother of Glen and Robert Williams. Everyone called her "Miss Maude." (Courtesy of Joe Williams.)

Claude Chilton Fulmer (1888–1962) and Josie Lee (Bynum) Fulmer (1895–1981) are standing in the front yard of their home. Claude lived his whole life on the family farm except for a few months before his marriage when he worked in Gadsden. He and Josie had been married for 50 years at the time of Claude's death in 1962.

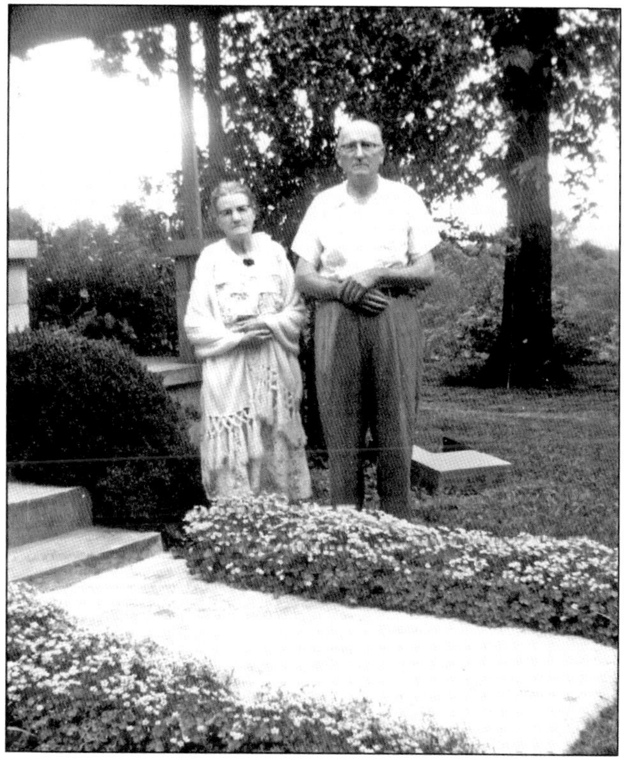

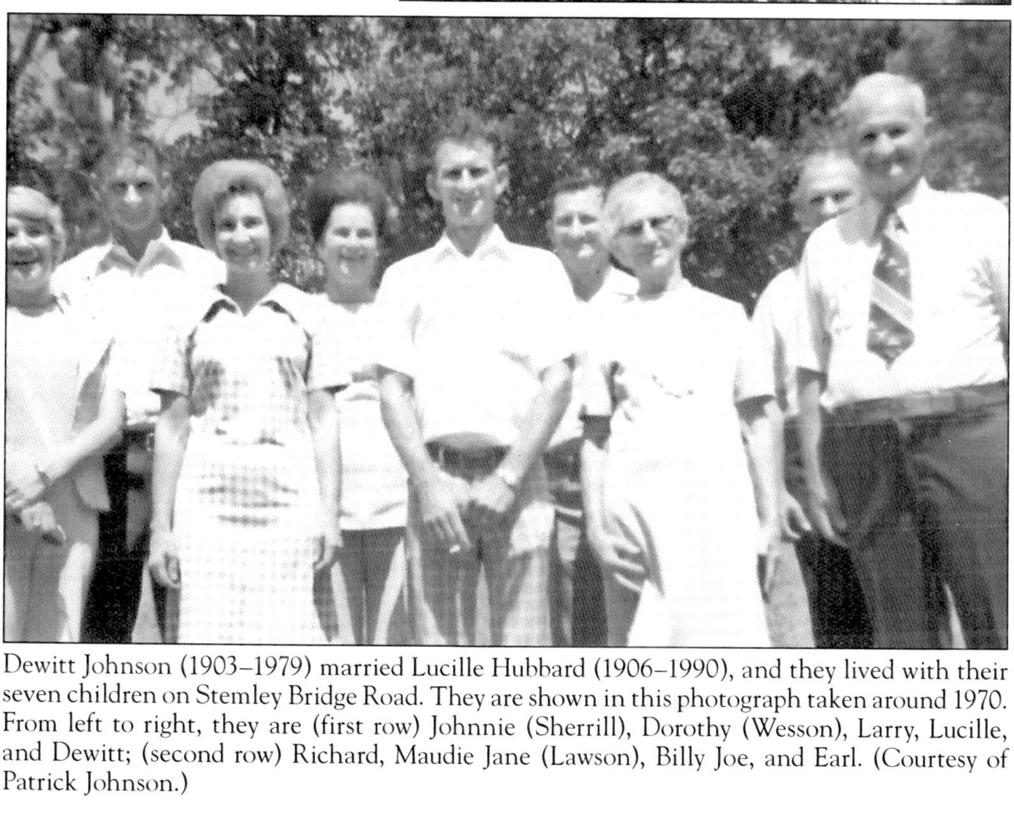

Dewitt Johnson (1903–1979) married Lucille Hubbard (1906–1990), and they lived with their seven children on Stemley Bridge Road. They are shown in this photograph taken around 1970. From left to right, they are (first row) Johnnie (Sherrill), Dorothy (Wesson), Larry, Lucille, and Dewitt; (second row) Richard, Maudie Jane (Lawson), Billy Joe, and Earl. (Courtesy of Patrick Johnson.)

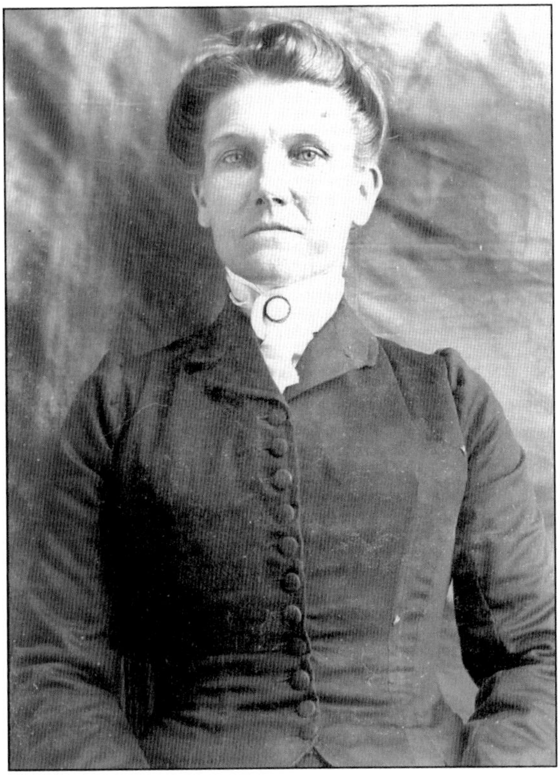

Sarah Cordelia Floyd, shown here in the 1860s, was the mother of Timmons Hendrix Floyd and the grandmother of Benjamin Hendrix Martin, Dwight Martin, and Sarah Martin (Shirling). Sarah moved to the Stemley Bridge area from Timmonsville, South Carolina, with her children. She had three daughters, Myrtle, Minnie, and Ninna, and one son, Timmons. She made her home in the area now known as Horseshoe Circle just off Old Stemley Bridge Road. (Courtesy of Rosemary Robinson.)

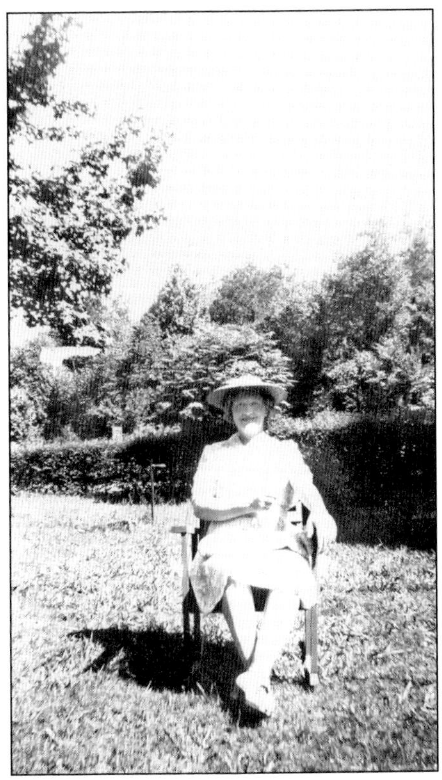

Laura (Hall) Williamson was the wife of Johnny Williamson, who ran a country store at the "Double Bridges" on Stemley Bridge Road. She occasionally helped in the store. (Courtesy of Joe Williams.)

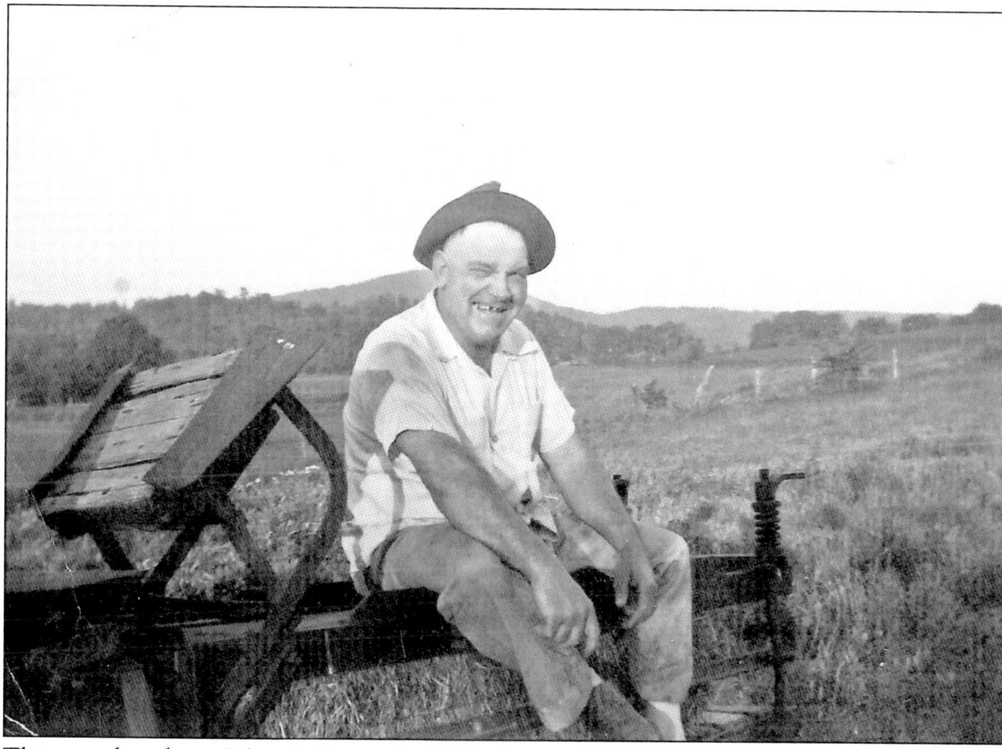

This snapshot shows Johnnie Barnes in 1945 taking time out from his many chores on the farm. His usual chores were milking from 3 a.m. until 6 a.m., delivering milk from early morning until around 3 p.m, and milking again from 5 p.m. until 7 p.m. Somehow he found time to keep the pastures ready for grafting and for hay. (Courtesy of Dan and Mary Barnes.)

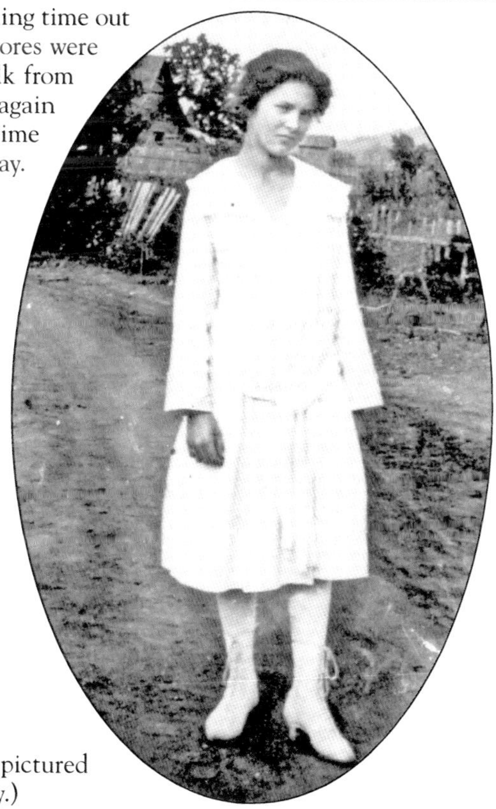

Nannie Lee Barnes, wife of Johnnie Barnes, is pictured here in the 1930s. (Courtesy of the Barnes family.)

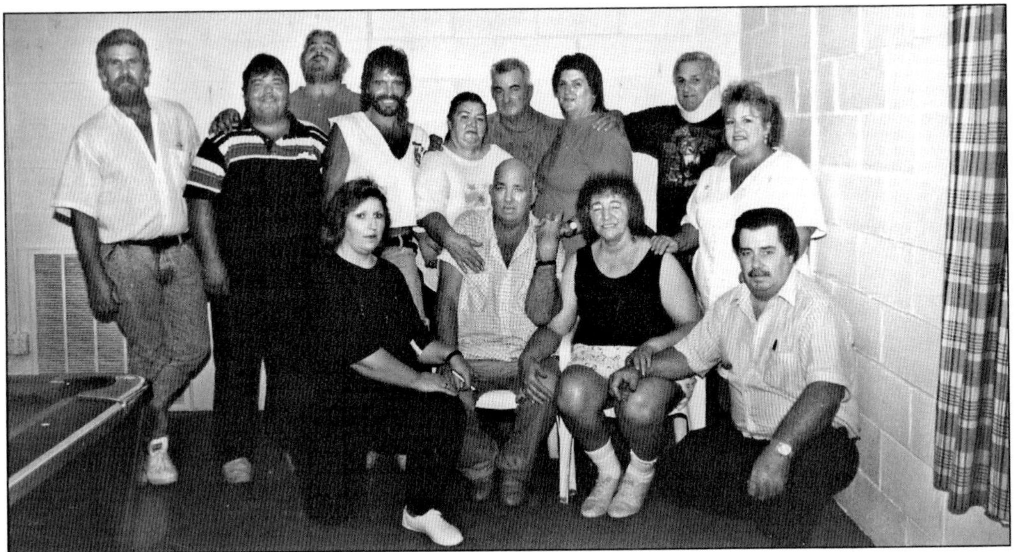

This 1995 photograph shows 8 of Hendrix and Marie Martin's 15 children and a few grandchildren. From left to right are (first row) Janice Kay Martin (15th child), Douglas MacArthur Martin (7th child), his wife, Myra Martin, and Lamar Edwards (1st grandchild raised); (second row) Michael Ray Martin (11th child), Benjamin Barksdale (grandchild), Harvey Burk Martin (14th child), Edward Barksdale (grandchild), Annie Joyce Martin Barksdale (2nd child), Melvin Nixon Martin (8th child), Mary Kathryn Martin Abbott (12th child), Timmons Hendrix Martin (1st child), and Rosemary Edwards Robinson (2nd grandchild raised). (Courtesy of Virginia Martin Gurley.)

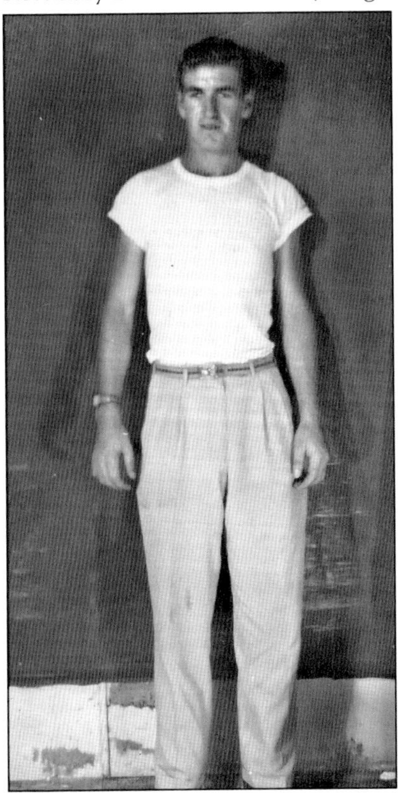

Benny Clarence Martin (1936–1973) was the third child of Hendrix and Marie Martin. Of Hendrix and Marie's 15 children, two died at birth, Jerry Colvin (1938) and Margarie (1941). (Courtesy of Norman Martin.)

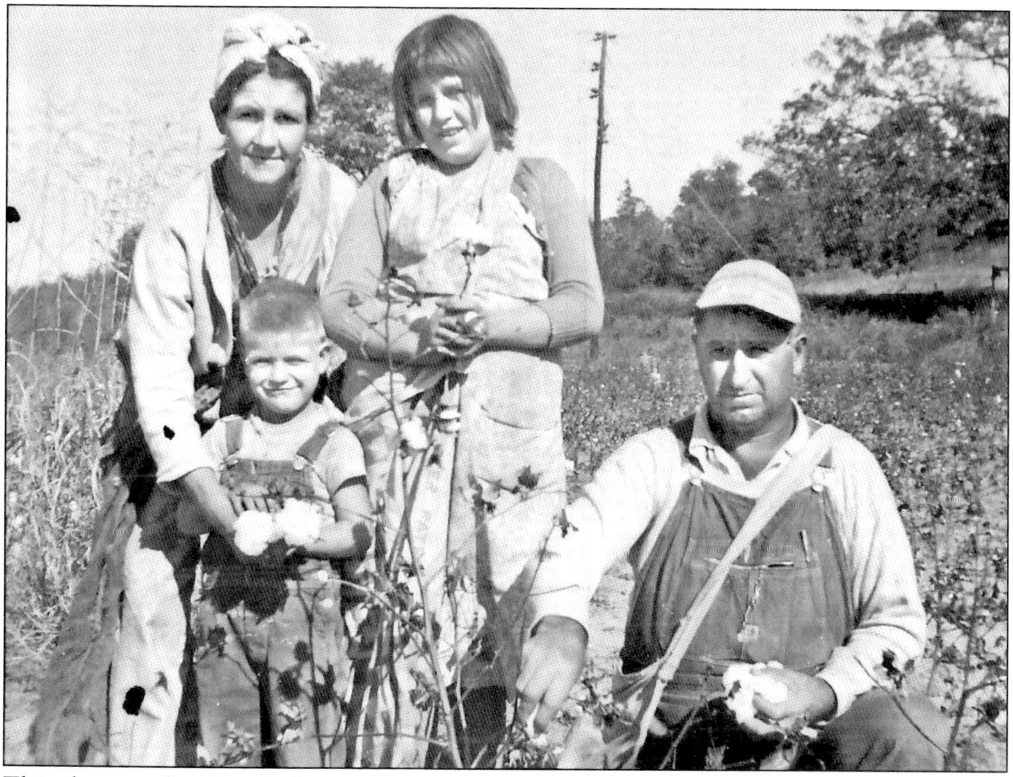

This photograph, taken in the early 1950s, shows Hendrix and Marie Martin with two of their children picking cotton in the fields belonging to Timmons Floyd. The little boy is Norman Wayne Martin (ninth child) and the girl standing center is Hazel Marie Martin (fifth child). (Courtesy of Norman Martin.)

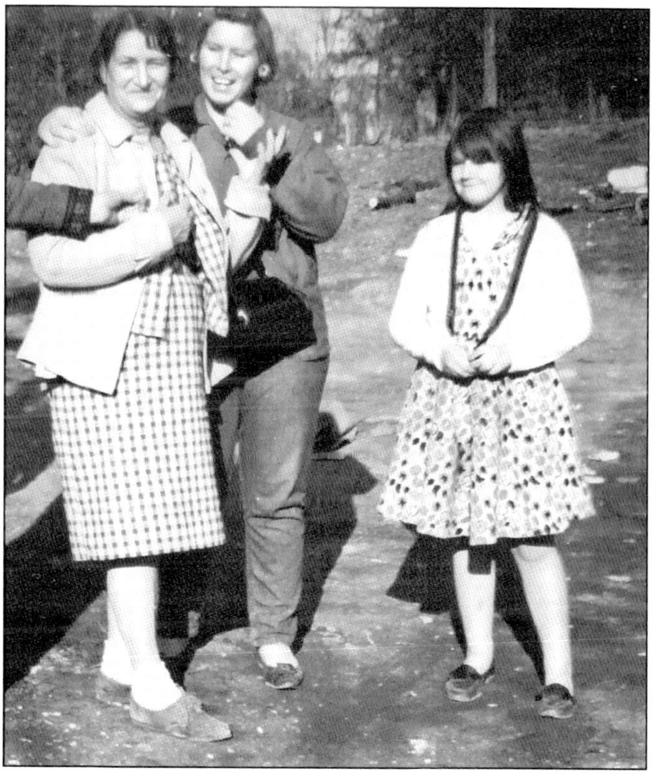

This picture was taken in the 1960s at Hendrix and Marie Martin's home on Stemley Bridge Road. From left to right are Hendrix's sister, Sarah Martin Shirling, Helen Virginia Martin (10th child), and Sarah Cordelia Martin (13th child.) (Courtesy of Norman Martin.)

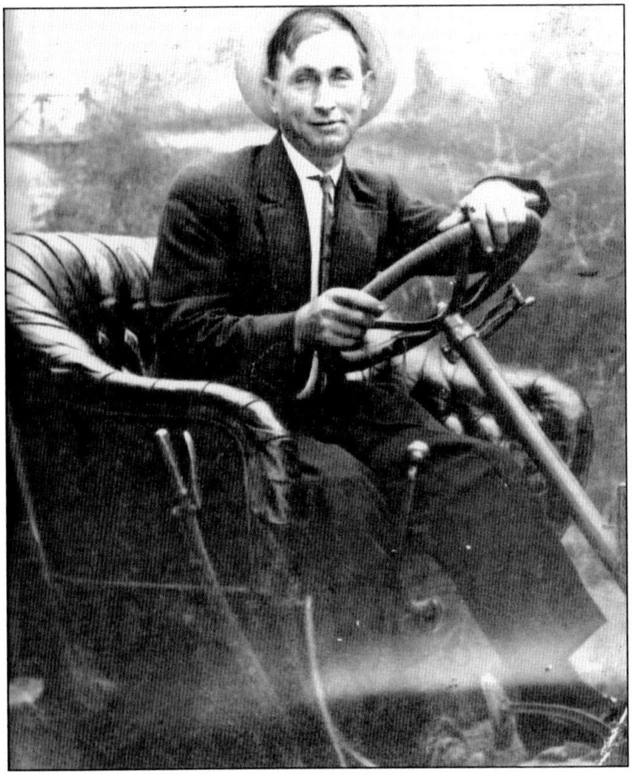

Henry Arthur Gambrell (1887–1958) is shown here in his motorcar. He and his wife, Mamie Jessie (Bonds), raised their children in the Renfroe area. (Courtesy of Sid Gambrell.)

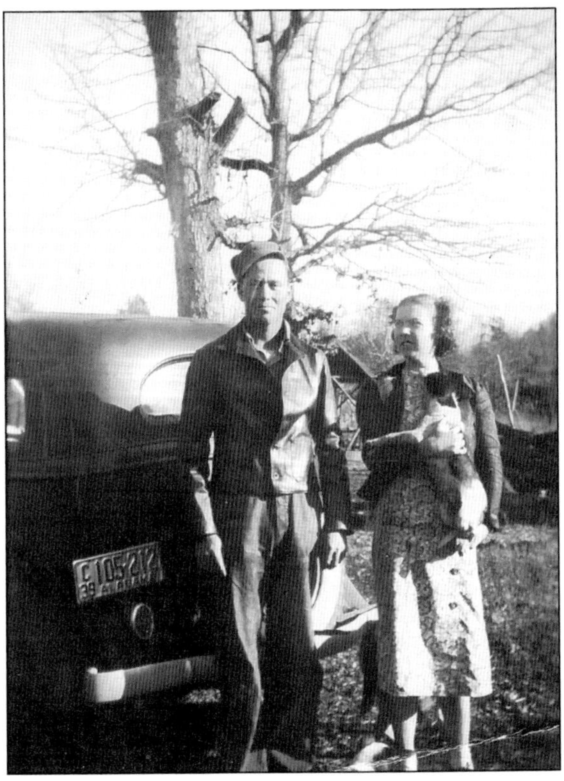

Donald Theo Rigby and Mary Virginia Daffron met when Theo was working with a state painting crew that came to Stemley to paint Stemley Bridge. After the bridge was painted, Theo stayed to work at Camp Pleasure. Their daughter, Judy Lynn, was born when they lived in Stemley. Theo did a lot of hunting and fishing along the Coosa River. (Courtesy of Thelma Daffron.)

Robert Truss married Delia Cunningham, and they had four boys and three girls. The family lived near Talladega County Training School where Robert took part in many of the activities. This photograph was made in 1947. (Courtesy of Lois Embry.)

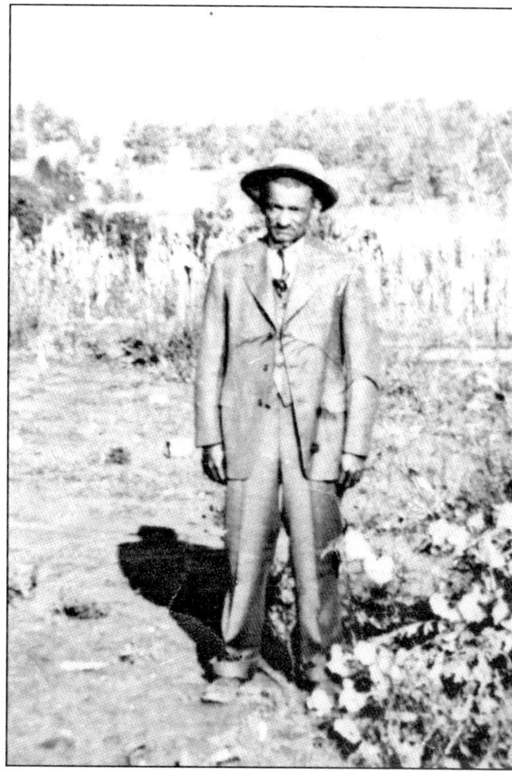

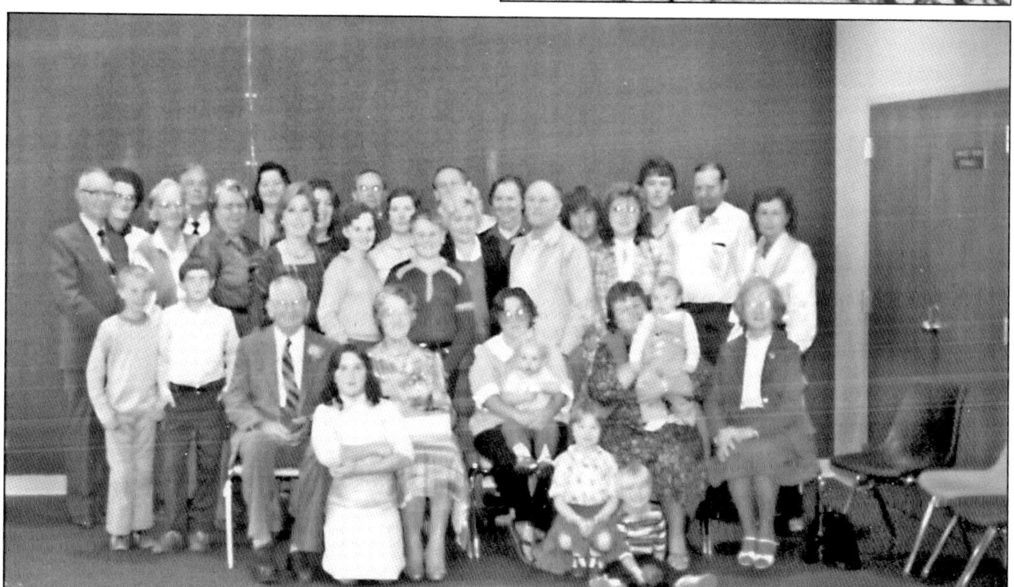

James Walker Johnson (1911–1997) and Beatrice (Fulmer) Johnson (1916–2002), seated far left and shown here with their family, celebrated their 50th wedding anniversary in 1983. After the death of Beatrice's father, Claude Fulmer, her mother, Josie, deeded land to her seven living children. All four of her daughters, Lucille McKee, Beatrice, Thelma Daffron, and Marie Sanders, moved onto their land to be close to their mother in her declining years. (Courtesy of Jeanette Zachero.)

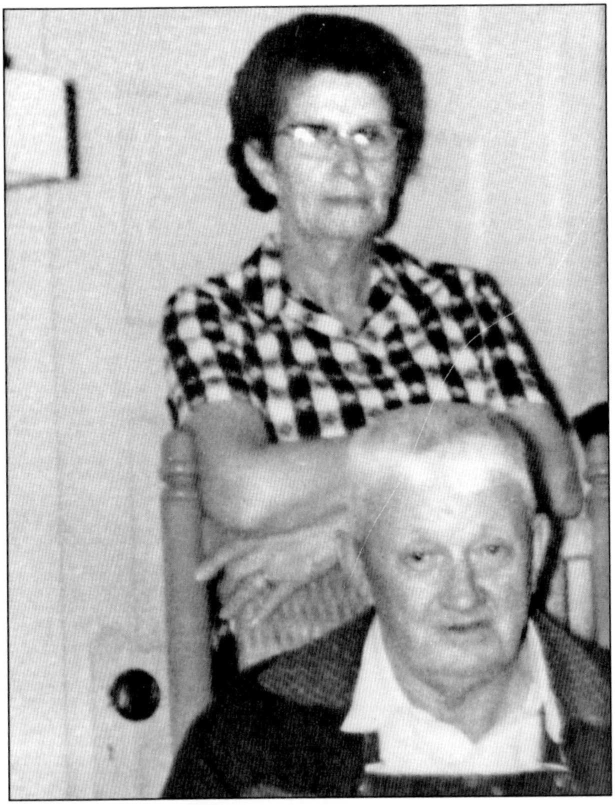

Eugene Fulmer (1902–1961), son of Walter L. and Katie Jane (Johnson) Fulmer, is pictured here with his wife, Mable (Smelley) Fulmer. Eugene was a farmer. The couple lived on Stemley Bridge Road before moving to the Bemiston community in Talladega, where they both worked at the Bemiston Cotton Mill. They had seven children: Lowell, Louise, Christine, Herbert, Clara Jean, Peggy Sue, and Faye. (Courtesy of Peggy Hall.)

Doss Stapler married Lucille Smelley, daughter of John Ed Smelley. They lived on the Coosa River in Griffitt Bend. Doss was a farmer. He is shown here with his plow mule in the 1940s. Even though many farmers were buying tractors, mules were still being used as late as the 1950s. (Courtesy of Peggy Hall.)

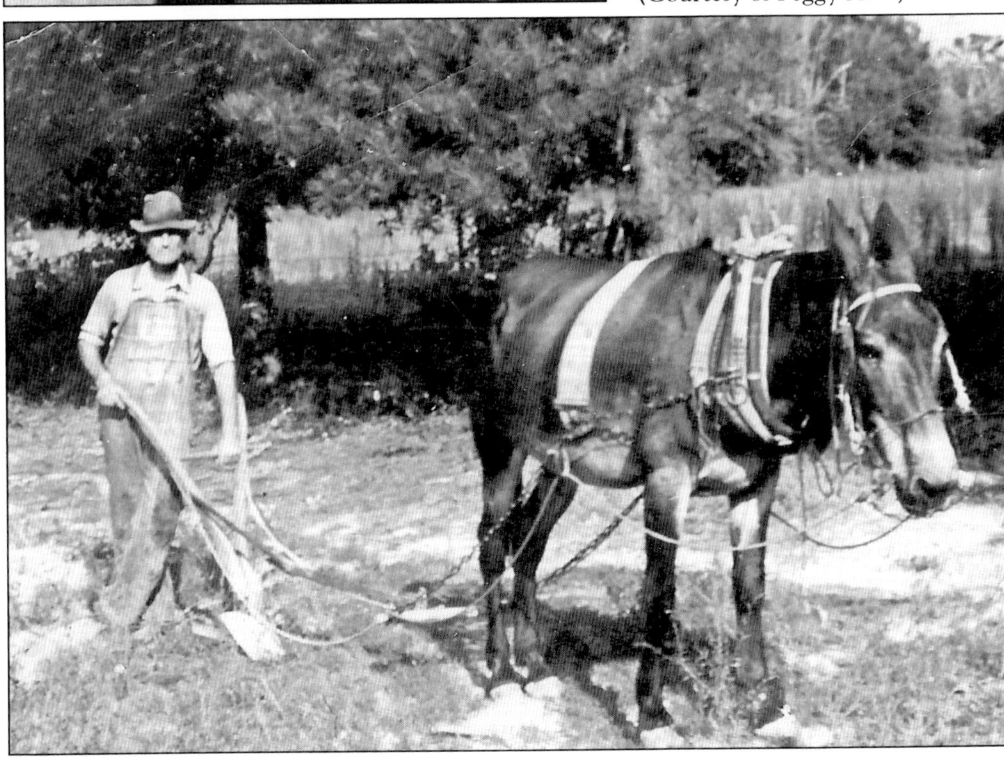

This 1930 photograph shows James Graves Spencer and his wife, Frances Pauline (Franklin), when they were first married. Graves and his brother, Thomas, bought and divided the old Wallace farm. On his portion of the farm, Graves grew row crops and raised cattle. He and his partner, Olan Sims, also owned and operated the old cow sale barn in Talladega. (Courtesy of the Spencer family.)

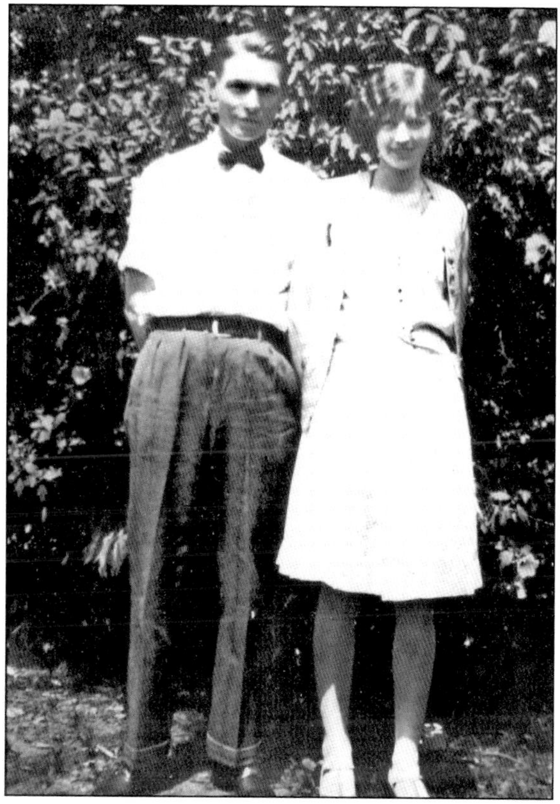

This photograph was taken in 1951 at a Parker family reunion. Seated on the ground from left to right are Vernon Green with sons Robert, James, and Glenn (crouching), Cleonard Parker and son Macheise, and Chester Parker with daughter Dianne; (standing) Leonard Parker, Grady Parker, and Millard Crowe with son Jimmy. (Courtesy of Jo Ann Bishop.)

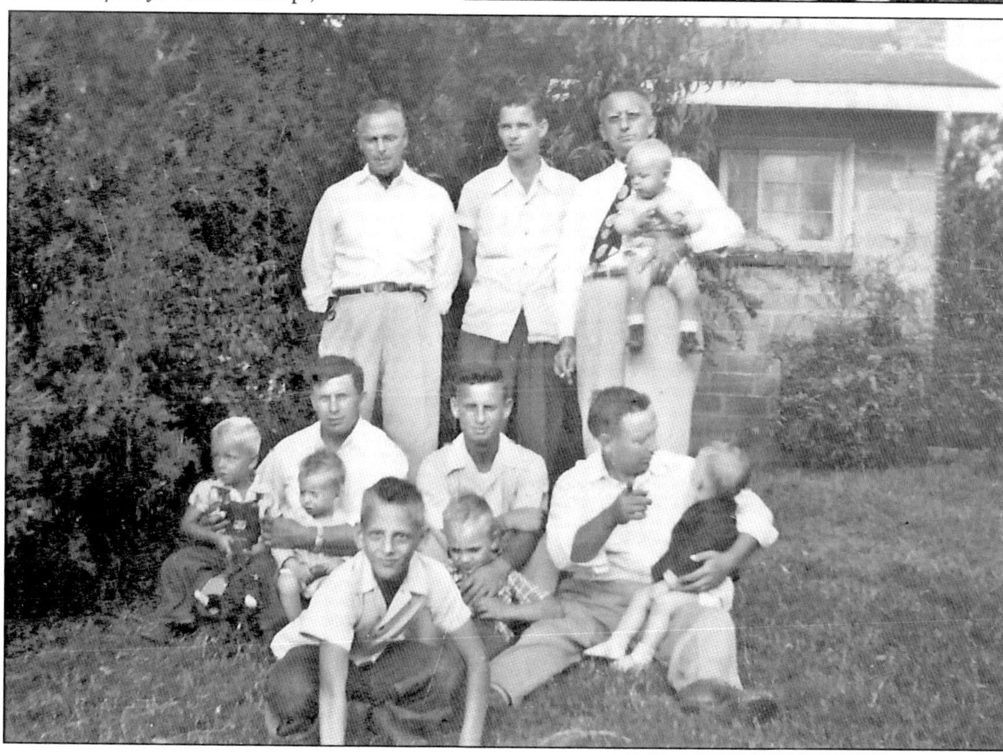

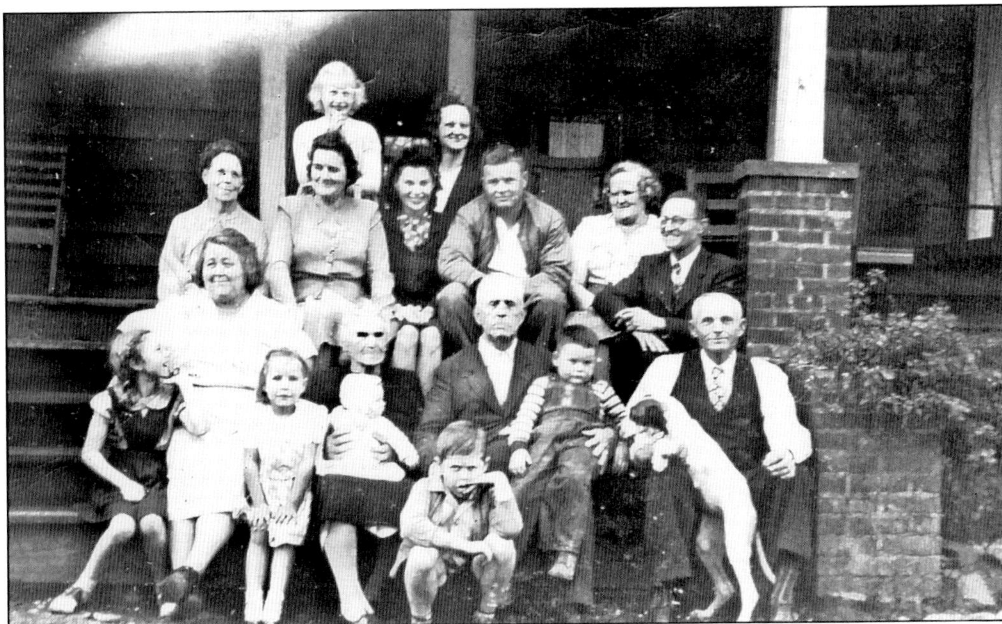

Pictured in this family photograph from left to right are (first row) Celeste Parker, Essie Cline Parker, unidentified, Alice Jane Cline holding Robert Parker Hurst, Tommy Parker Jr., Eugene Cline holding Bill Hurst Jr., and Thomas Zube Parker; (second row) Lena Wallis, Bertha Wallis Lee (who was a missionary), Alice Parker Hurst, William C. Hurst, Myrtle Avery, and Wister Avery; (third row) Pam Parker Hasty and Nandean Avery Parker. (Courtesy of Bill and Alice Hurst.)

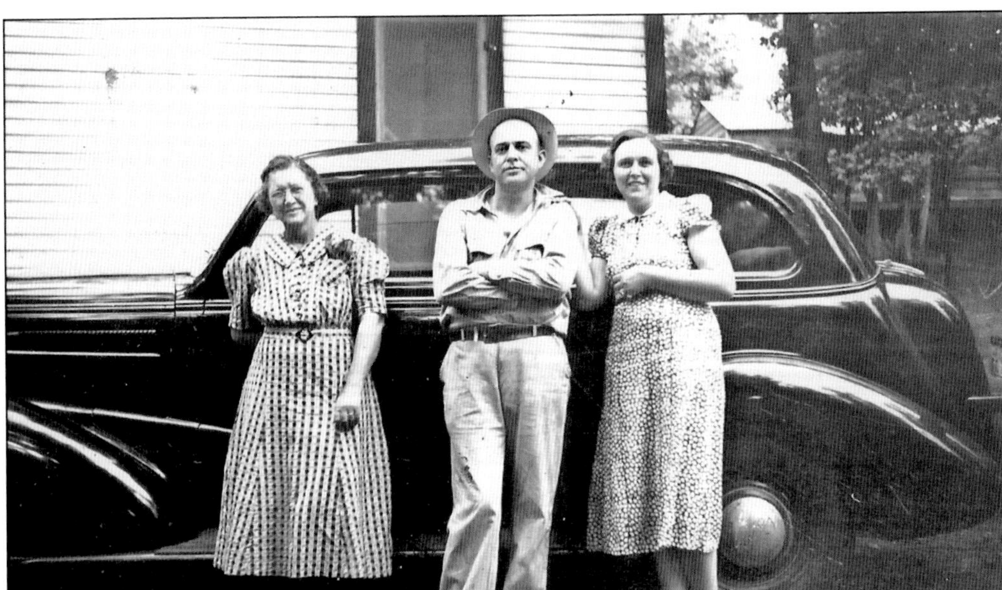

Maggie Floyd, left, and Alfonso Addington and his wife are pictured together c. 1940. Addington was part owner of Camp Pleasure with Timmons and Maggie Floyd. After a disagreement, Timmons Floyd acquired complete ownership of the camp. He sold it to Louis Norred, who sold it to its final owners, Cloyd and Ellory Hutto. (Courtesy of Rosemary Robinson.)

Frances Esther Gaither (1854–1940), left, daughter of Josiah Gunter, is pictured here with her husband, John Jefferson Gaither (1840–1915), and daughter-in-law Emma (Wade), wife of Willie A. Gaither. (Courtesy of Ora Gaither.)

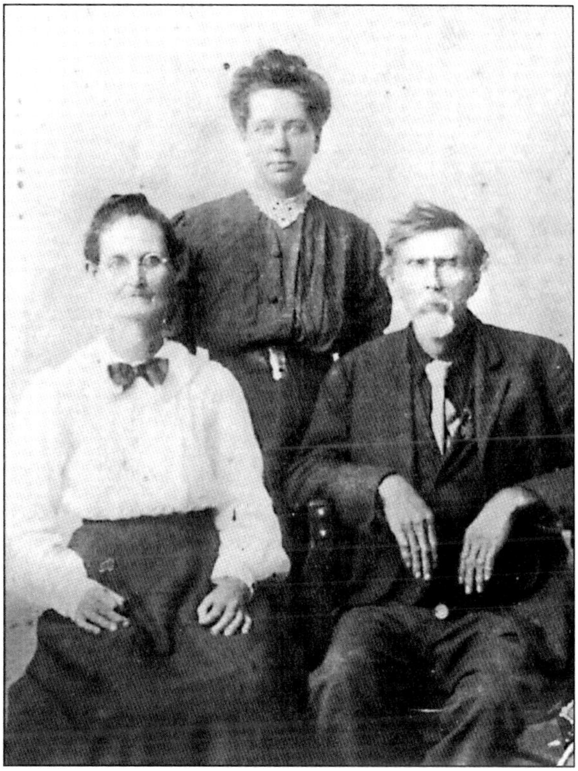

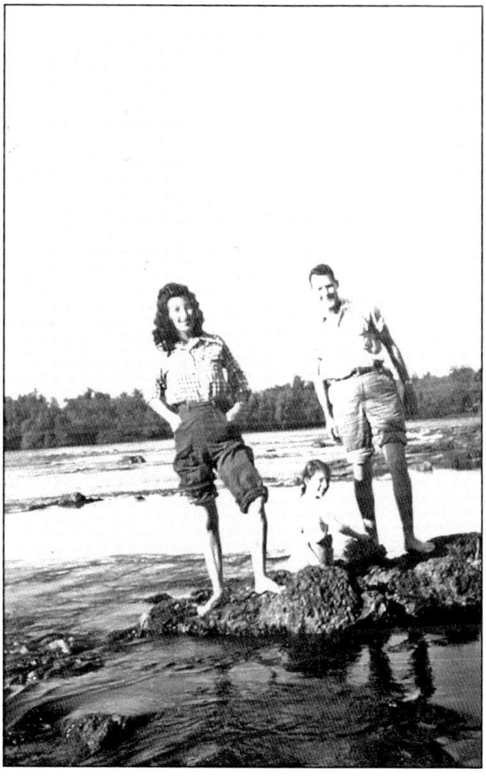

Binnie Parsons, left, her brother, John Parsons, and John's daughter, Sue Parsons (Wells), are having a playtime following a picnic on the big rocks that extended across the river at Griffitt Bend in the 1940s. (Courtesy of Joe and Sue Wells.)

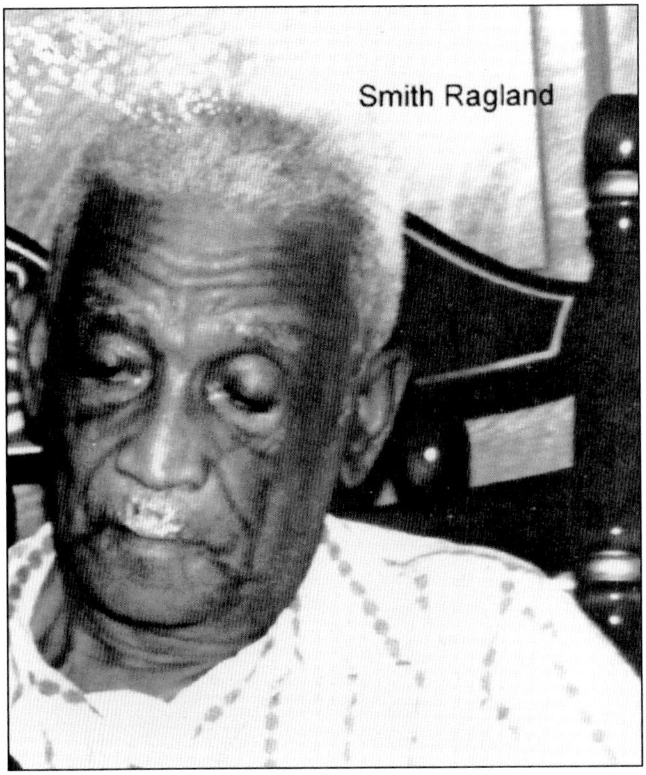

Smith and Luceal Ragland were the parents of four boys and four girls. Smith was a farmer and a good provider. He grew corn, cotton, and vegetables, raised hogs, chickens, and turkeys, and had a milk cow. He smoked pork and beef in a log smokehouse. He never owned a tractor but farmed with two mules, Pete and Jim, and a dog named Buster. He sold wagonloads of charcoal in Talladega for 25¢ a bushel; he cut hair on Sunday mornings for 15¢. Luceal and Smith's offspring included teachers, nurses, barbers, plumbers, two ministers, an electrician, a carpenter, a secretary, a mechanic, a postmaster general of Washington, D.C., a taxi cab company owner, and an account manager for 98.7 Kiss FM. (Courtesy of Rosa Morris.)

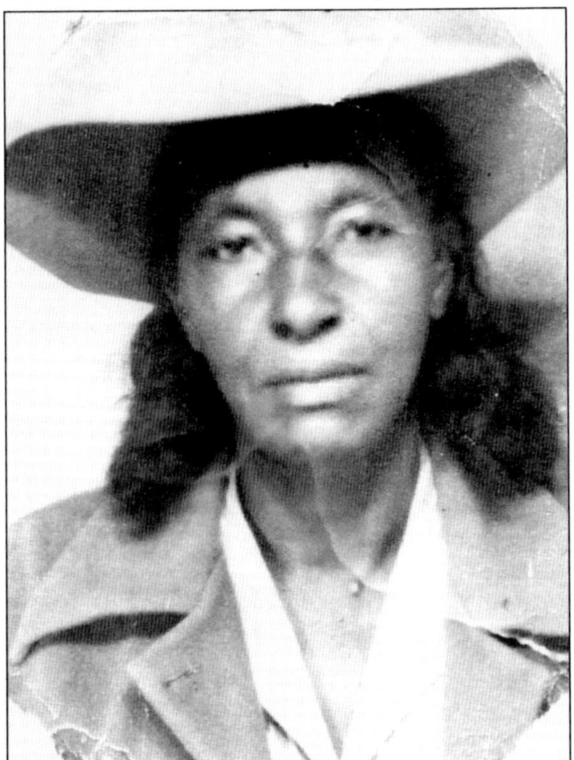

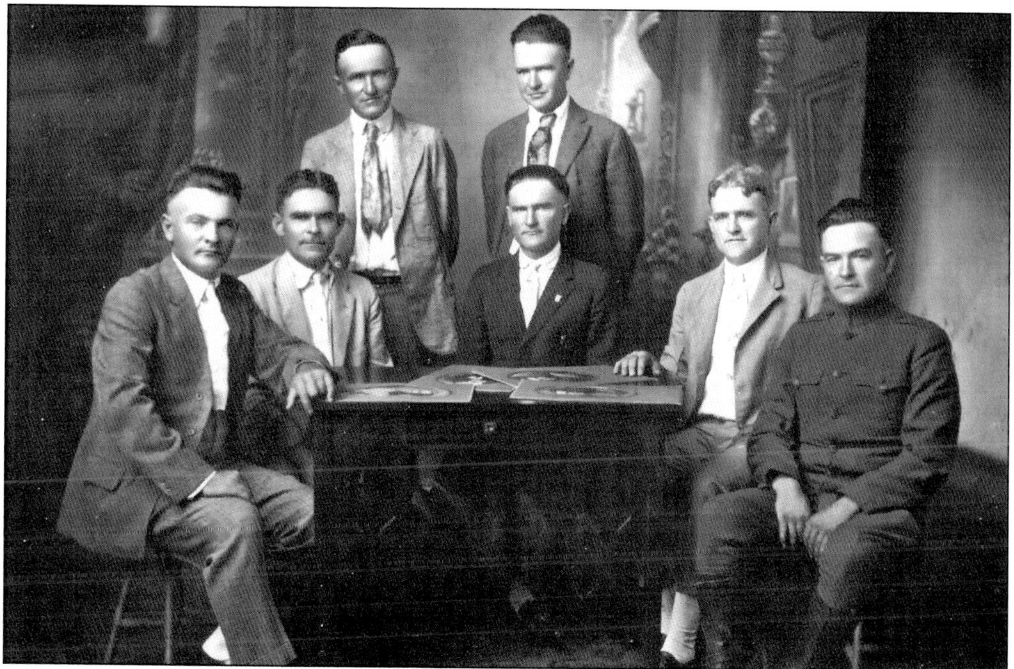

Fannie Beulah Nesbit Tweatt Howell was the mother of 11 children. In this photograph are seven of her sons. From left to right are (seated) Willie, Vurry, Earl (who was sheriff of Talladega County), Dan, and Richard; (standing) Morgan and Carl. Not shown are Mary, Becky, John, and a child who died at birth. John was killed at the age of 21 at Howell's Cotton Gin. After John's death, his mother ordered the gin to be torn down. (Courtesy of M. H. McCary.)

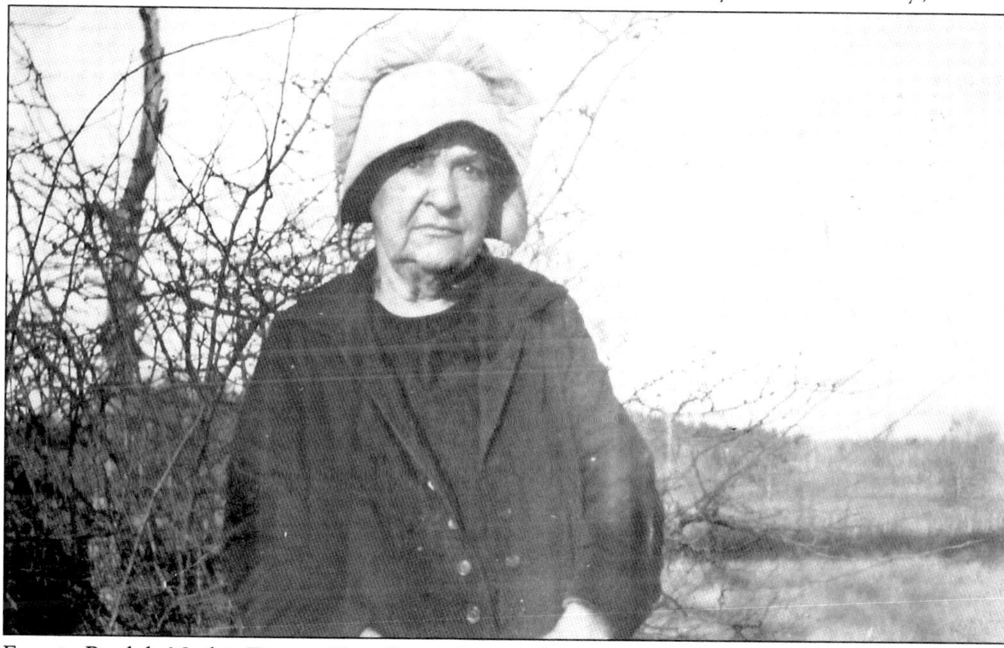

Fannie Beulah Nesbit Tweatt Howell was known by everyone as "Grandmother Fannie." She and her family lived at the Howell's Cove plantation home, one of the oldest homesteads in the county. (Courtesy of M. H. McCary.)

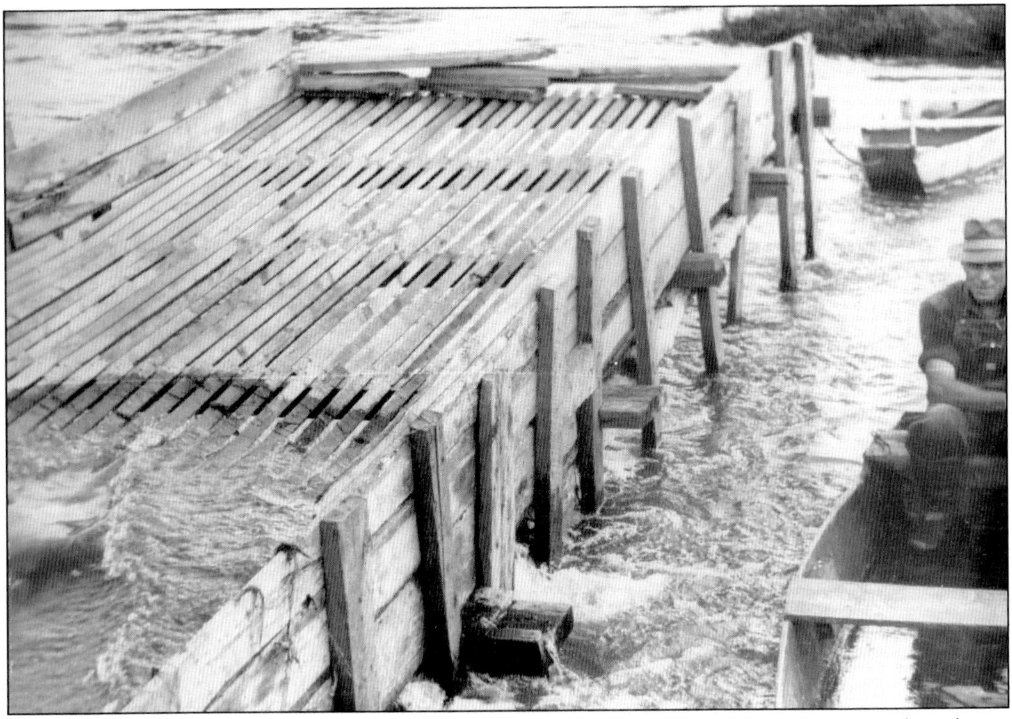

Mack Lee is shown here at the Griffitt fish traps said to have been built by the Creek Indians. Mack was the last operator of the traps, which stayed in service until 1964, when the water was backed up by Logan Martin Dam. (Courtesy of Ed Challender and Harold Jacobs.)

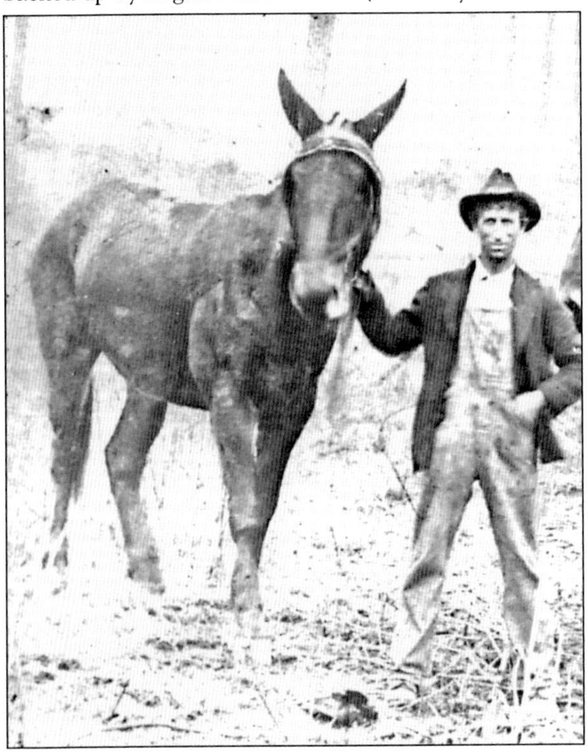

Jay Parker posed with his work mule in the early 1900s. Jay was the husband of Radier Parker. In later years, he was accidentally run over by a logging truck and killed. (Courtesy of Dianna Parker.)

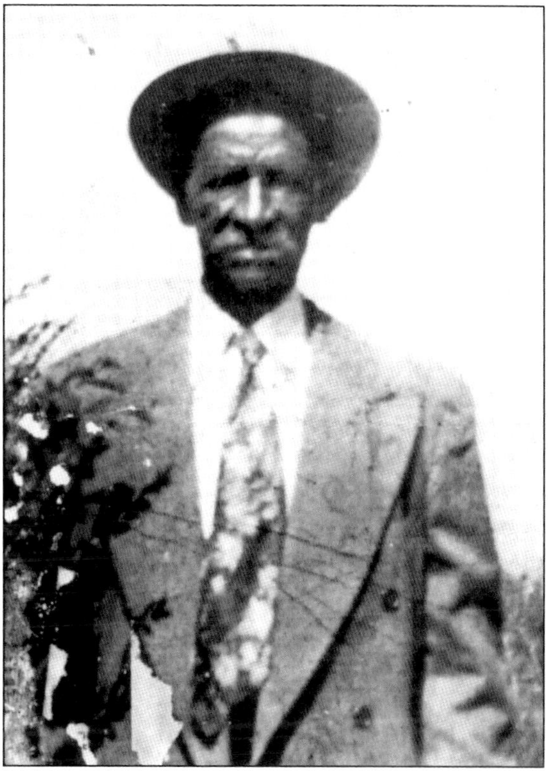

Charlie and Agnes Truss Phillips were the parents of 12 children, 8 of whom finished high school. Four went on to become teachers, and one became a chemist. They had 50 grandchildren including a doctor, an FBI agent, several computer experts, one employee with the State Department of Transportation, three CEOs, and many teachers and other educators. They had over 100 great-grandchildren and great-great grandchildren. (Courtesy of Mildred Phillips Swain.)

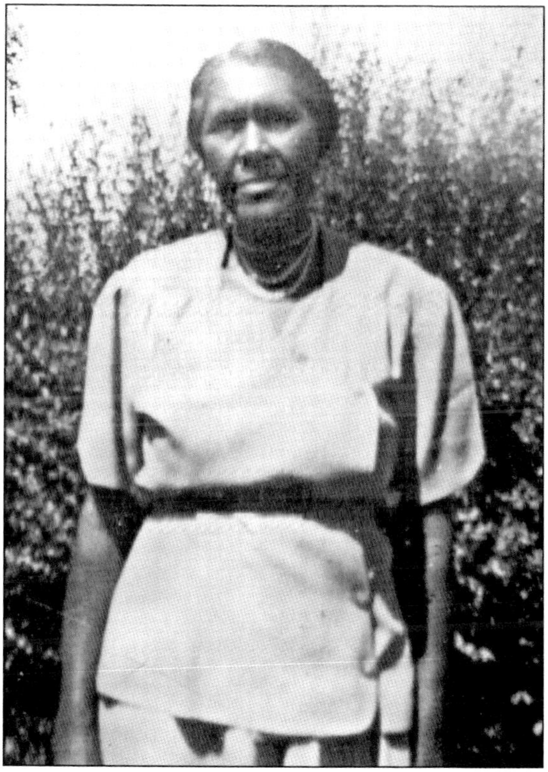

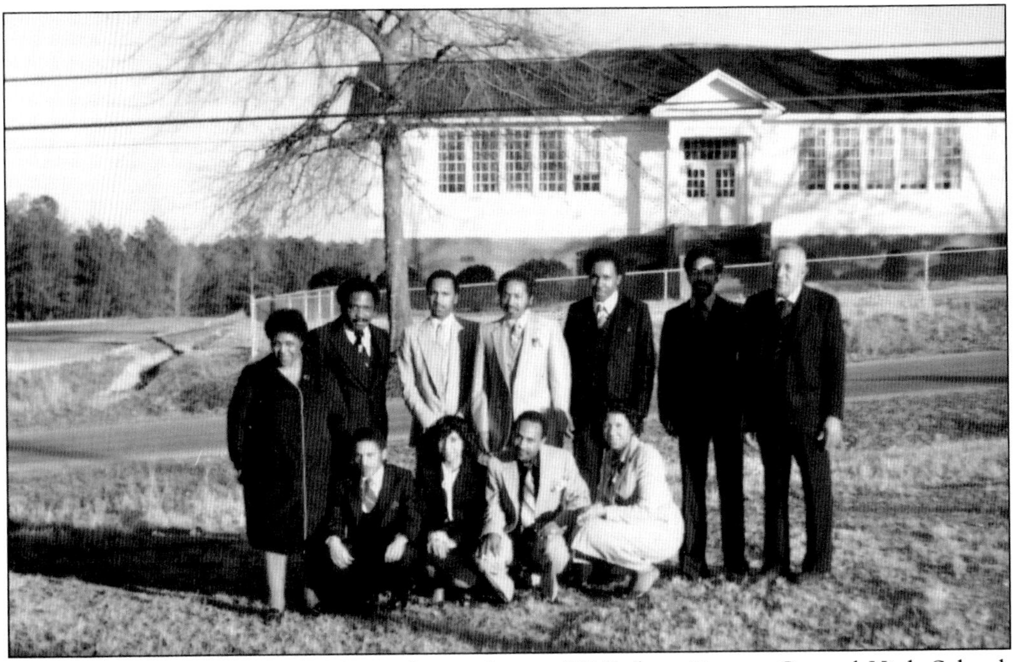

The Cunninghams are pictured together in front of Talladega County Central High School. From left to right are (kneeling) Timmy Cunningham, Gloria Smith, William Cunningham, and Elinor Cunningham; (standing) Velma Cunningham, Thomas Groce, Donald Cunningham, Alphonso Cunningham Jr., Gary Cunningham, Kelvin Cunningham, and Alphonso Cunningham Sr. (Courtesy of Kelvin Cunningham.)

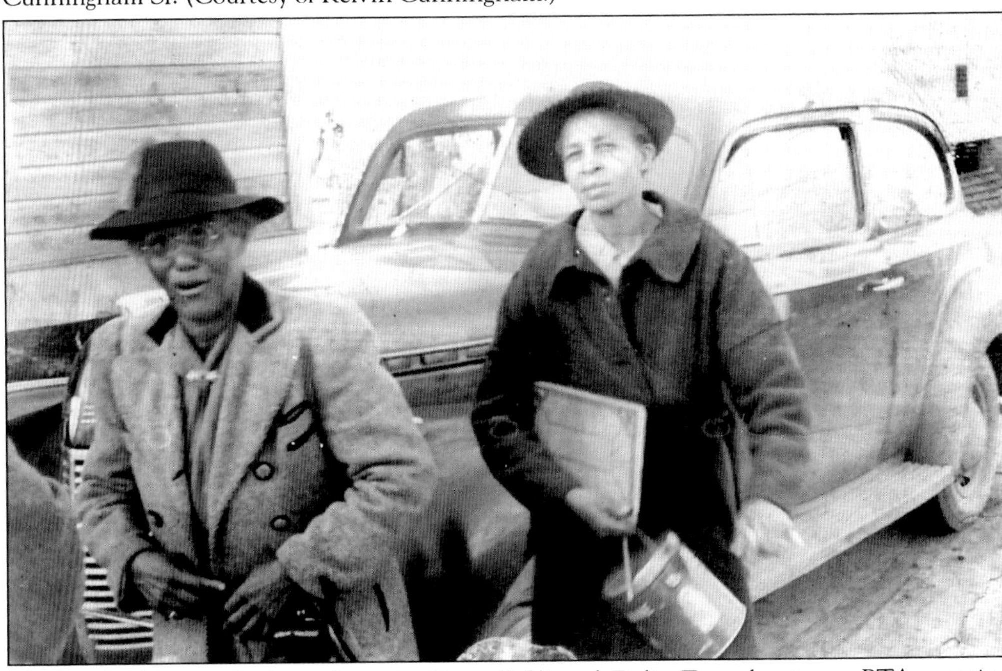

This 1942 photograph shows Jeannie Cross (left) and Delia Truss leaving a PTA meeting at Talladega County Central High School. Delia was secretary of the PTA. Note the 1940 Chevrolet. (Courtesy of Lois Embry.)

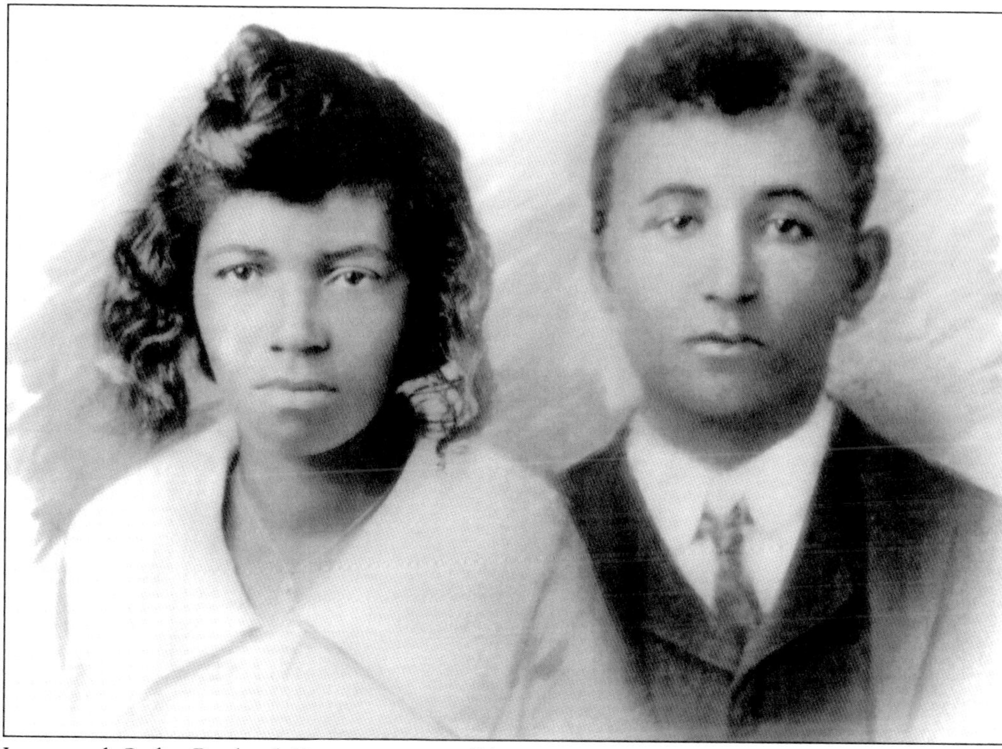

Lune and Sudie Ragland Draper were well-known residents around Stemley Bridge. They owned about 300 acres of land in the Macedonia area, just off Highway 34. In 1919, Lune purchased 900 acres in the Howell's Cove community. He sold land to the Easleys, Turners, Raglands, and Foremans. He built a home on Draper Road that is still standing. They farmed and raised 15 children. Lune died in the early 1930s; Sudie died in 1953. (Courtesy of Jeraldine Draper Reynolds.)

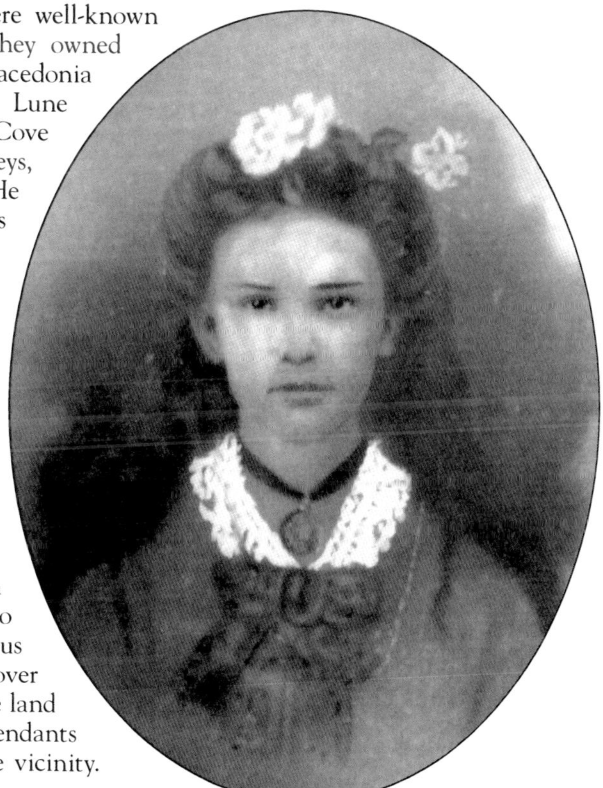

Lavinia Chilton (Morgan) Fulmer (c. 1857–c. 1891) was the granddaughter of Col. George Lipscomb Ragland, an early settler of the Stemley area, who held 75 slaves when the 1860 census was taken. When the Civil War was over and the slaves were freed, George gave land to each of his slave families. Descendants of these slave families still live in the vicinity. (Courtesy of Mike Gurley.)

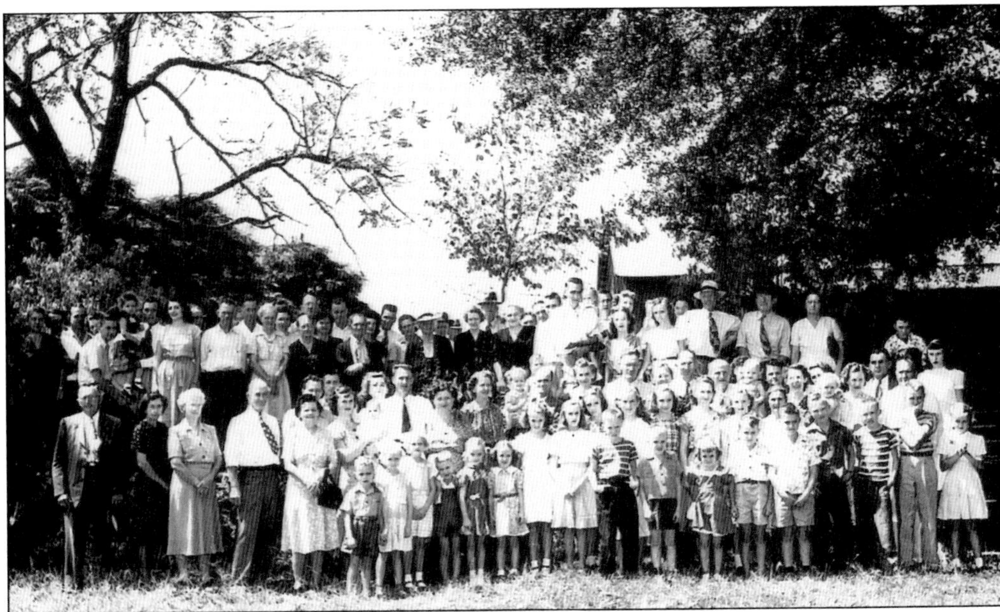

The Sisson family met at the old home place on September 12, 1948, on what is known today as the Marrs farm. The house in the background was probably built before 1850 by James Funderburg's grandfather Sisson. The original part of the house was built from trees felled during the clearing of the land. Built in the "dog trot" style, it consisted of two rooms on one side, a breezeway in the center, and a kitchen on the other side. (Courtesy of James Funderburg.)

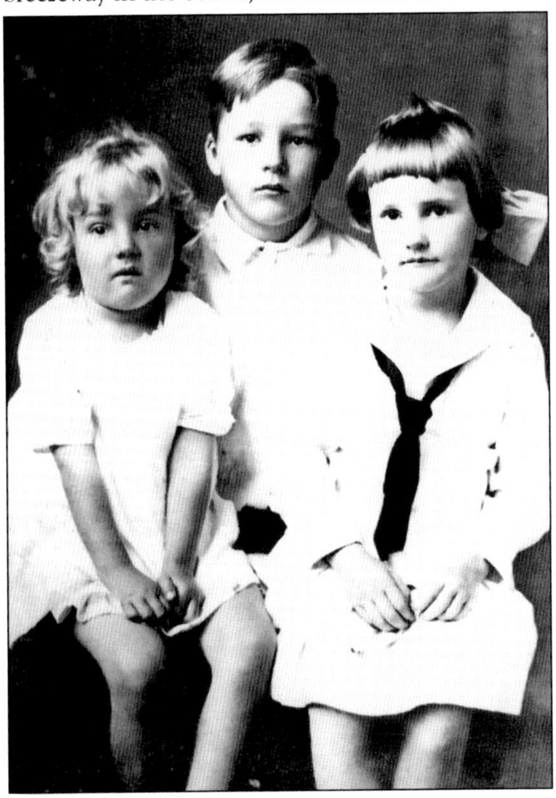

Beatrice (left), Chilton, and Lucille Fulmer, children of Claude and Josie (Bynum) Fulmer, attended Stemley school *c.* 1922–1923 before it combined with Ida Academy to form Idalia Elementary School. Chilton and Lucille had been promoted to the third grade and Beatrice had been promoted to the second grade when they were transferred to Idalia. (Courtesy of Jeanette Zachero.)

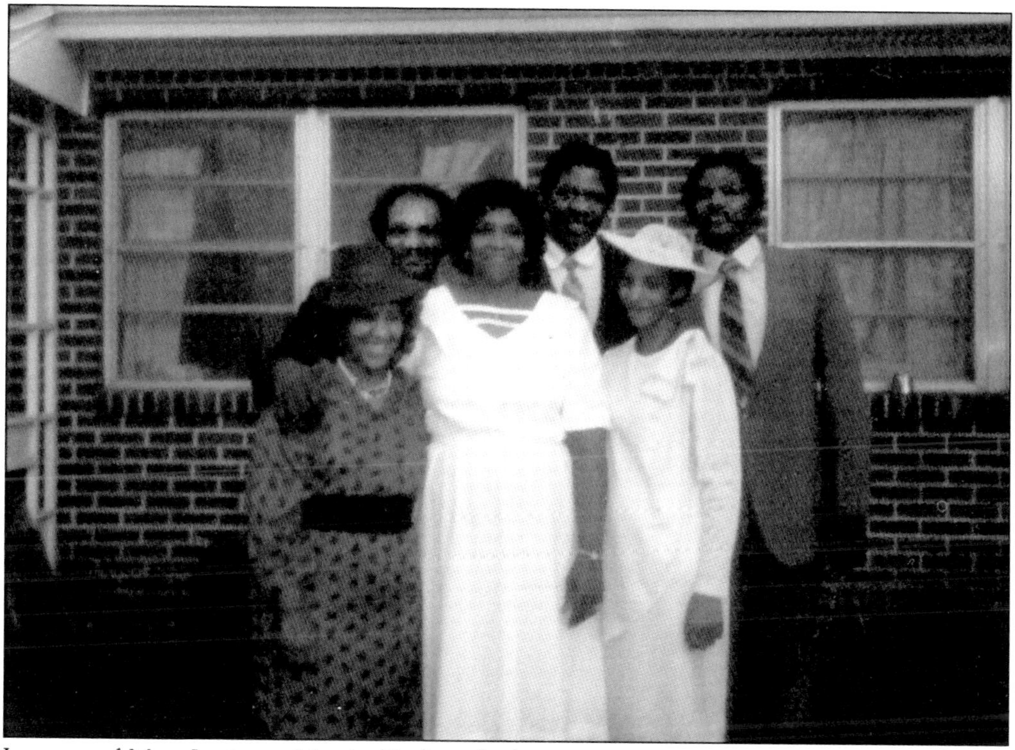

Lonzer and Mary Luzianna Martin Cochran had seven children. This photograph from around 1980 shows six of their children. From left to right are (first row) Helen, Lula, and Mary; (second row) Larry, Robert, and Alonzer Jr. Not pictured is Betty Ann Cochran. (Courtesy of Johnnie Mae Cochran.)

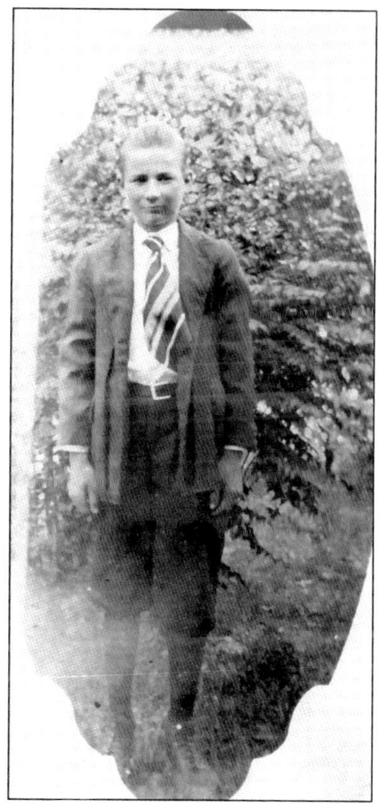

Dewitt Johnson (1903–1979) was a landowner, farmer, and carpenter. At harvest time, he distributed free produce all along Stemley Bridge Road. Notice the stylish knee pants. (Courtesy of the Dewitt Johnson family.)

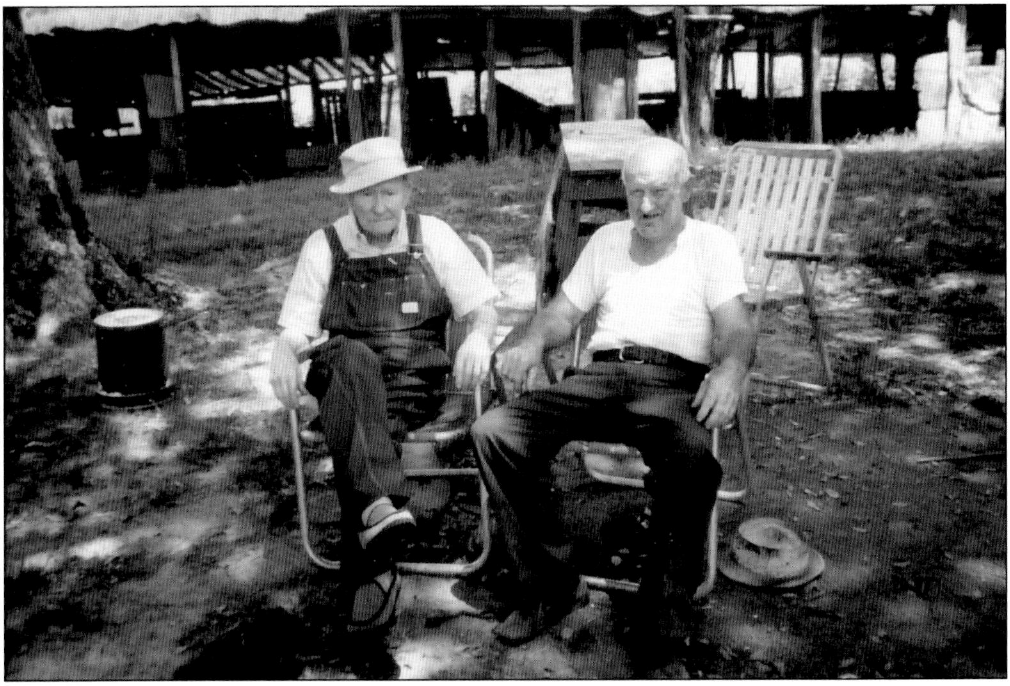

Winston Henderson (left) and Claude Hayes are sitting in Claude's yard in front of his chicken coops. (Courtesy of Charles Henderson.)

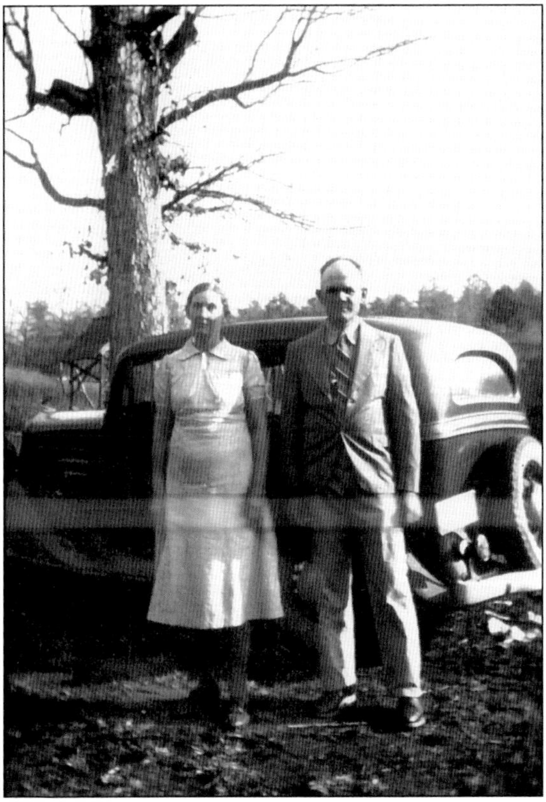

Clifton Harold Daffron and Lois Ethel Hindmon married around 1915. They moved to the Griffitt Bend area in 1928 and later moved to a house on the Old Stemley Bridge Road. Clifton walked to Pell City each weekday to catch a ride to Bynum to work. Clifton and Lois had three children, Clyde, Harold, and Mary. (Courtesy of Thelma Daffron.)

J. C. Ragland, left, and Tom Hanley lived near Talladega County Training School. This photograph was taken c. 1900. (Courtesy of Lois Embry.)

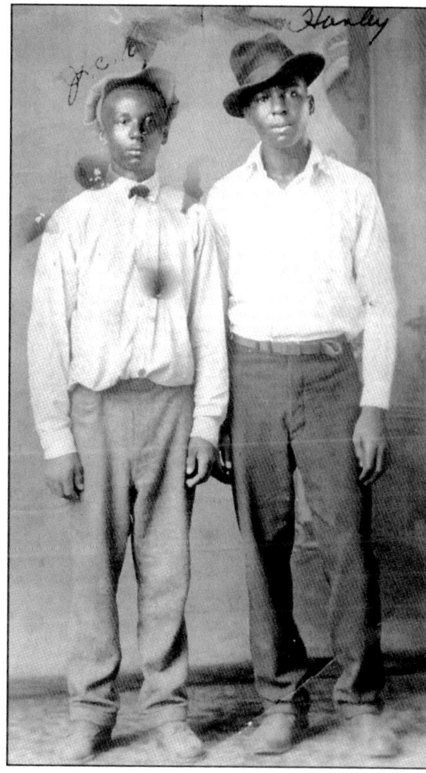

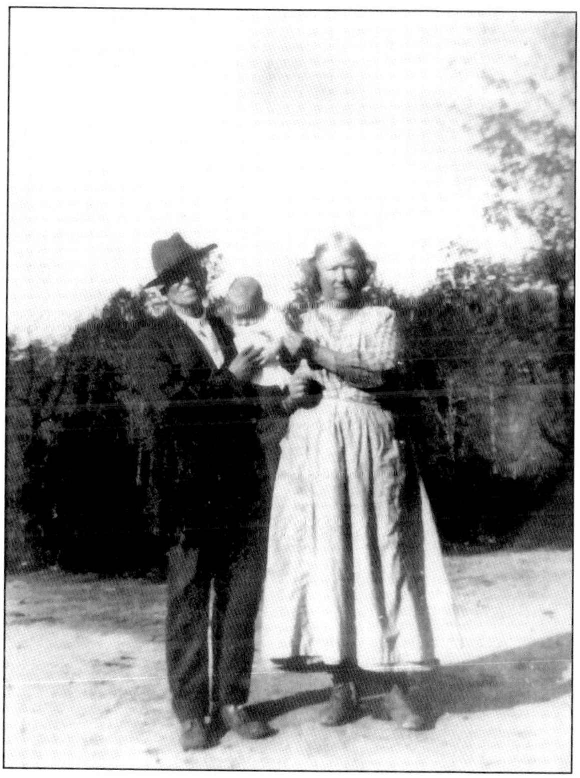

Alex and Mittylene (Fulmer) Henderson are shown here holding their second son, Gerald, around 1910. (Courtesy of Calvin Sanders.)

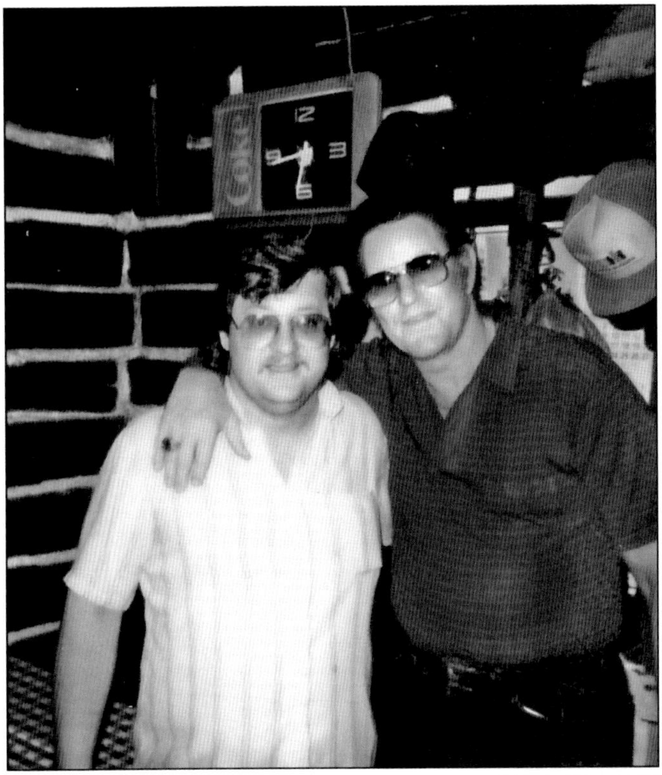

Wayne Hann and Freddie Hart posed for this photograph in the 1980s in the Shack Bar-B-Q. Freddie is a resident of the Renfroe/Alpine area. He earned country music stardom with his hit song "Easy Lovin'." Wayne began playing the guitar and singing as a child. At the age of 13, he made his debut appearance on the *Country Boy Eddie Show* on WBRC-TV, where he starred from 1967 until 1972 when he graduated from high school. Wayne has performed with Freddie Hart along with Ferlin Husky, Tammy Wynette, Freddie Fender, and other well-known country music stars. (Courtesy of Jeffrey Hann.)

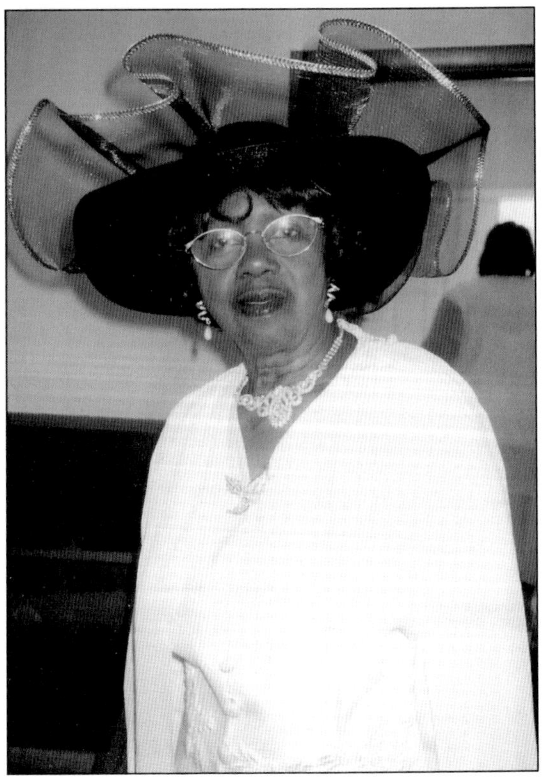

Bessie Lee posed for this photograph at Macedonia Church *c.* 2005. Bessie was the president of Missionary Society at Macedonia Baptist Church. (Courtesy of Rosa Morris.)

Maudie Jane (Johnson) Lawson (1928–1985), daughter of Dewitt and Lucille Johnson, lived in the Stemley area.

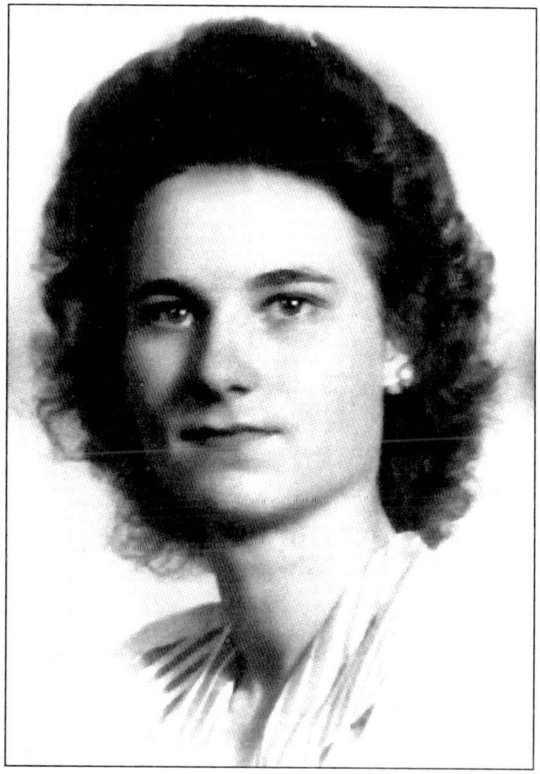

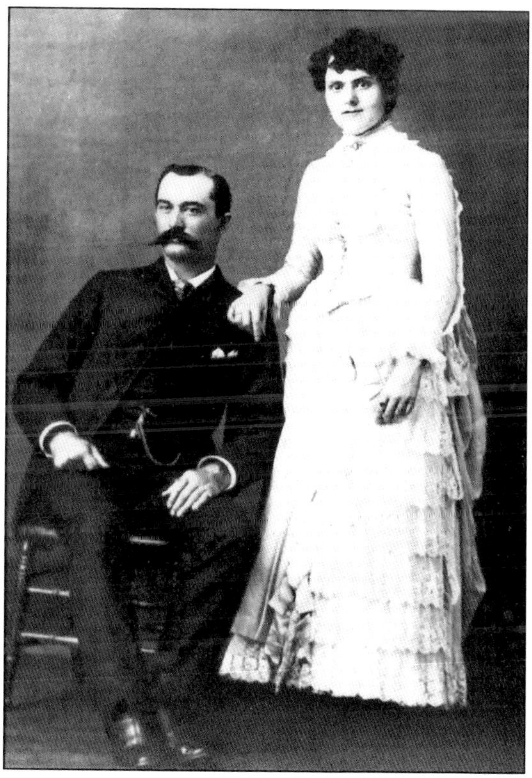

Fred A. Franks (1861–1891) from Georgia married Sallie Nickles. In 1884, Fred and his brother, W. M., were associated with the D. W. Rogers lumber business. After about five years, they located a shingles plant in the Stemley area and employed 30 men. In 1898, a huge fire destroyed the shingles plant. The mill was rebuilt and prospered for several more years. (From Heritage Hall's "Traces of Nearby Past" collection.)

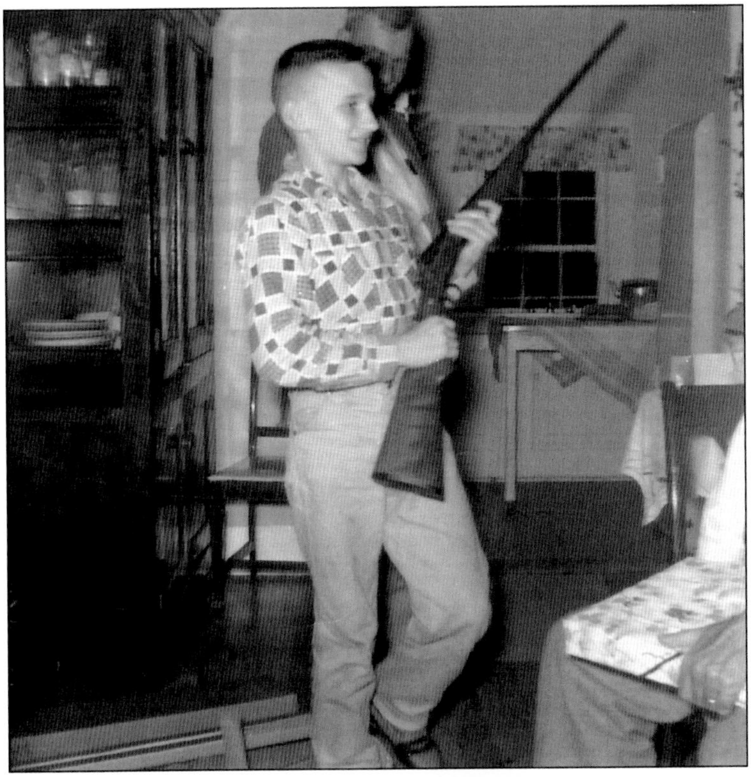

One of the outstanding memories in this country boy's life was the acquisition of his first hunting gun. Larry Johnson, son of Dewitt and Lucille Johnson, was 15 in 1958 when his parents gave him a "410" shotgun for Christmas. (Courtesy of Dot Wesson.)

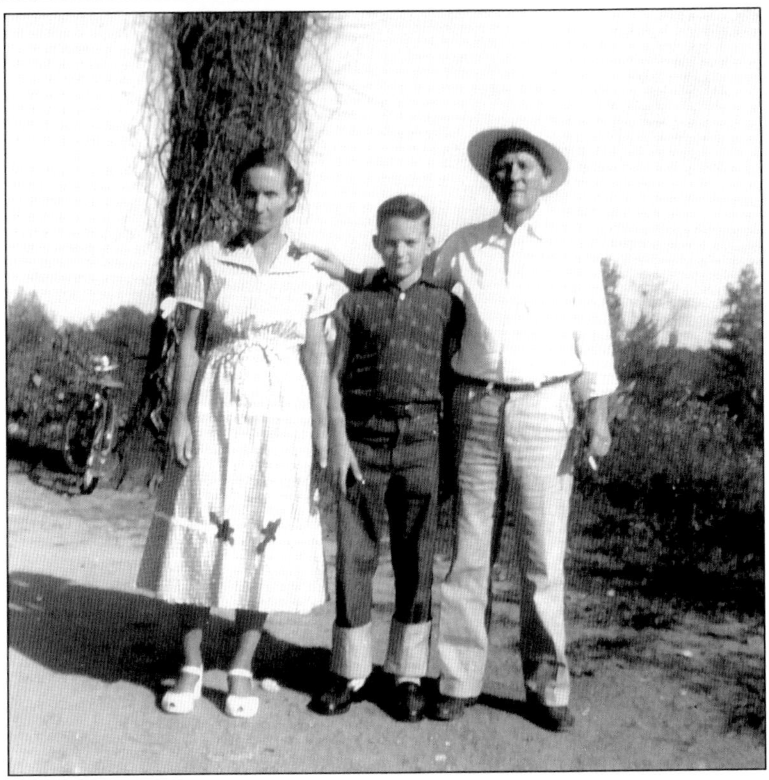

Eva (Burrell) and Winston Henderson, born in 1907, are shown with their son Charles in their front yard. Notice Charles's cuffs. (Courtesy of Charles Henderson.)

This photograph was taken *c.* 1943. From left to right are (first row) Derrell Hann and Haskell Hann; (second row) their sister, Joyce Hann (Wadsworth), and parents, Jewel (Johnson) Hann and Grover Hann. This was taken while Grover was operating the Slab House, where they also lived. (Courtesy of Derrell Hann.)

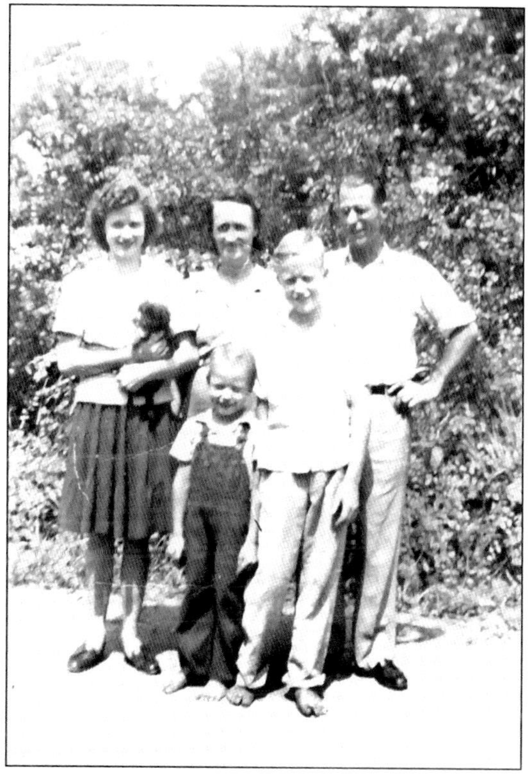

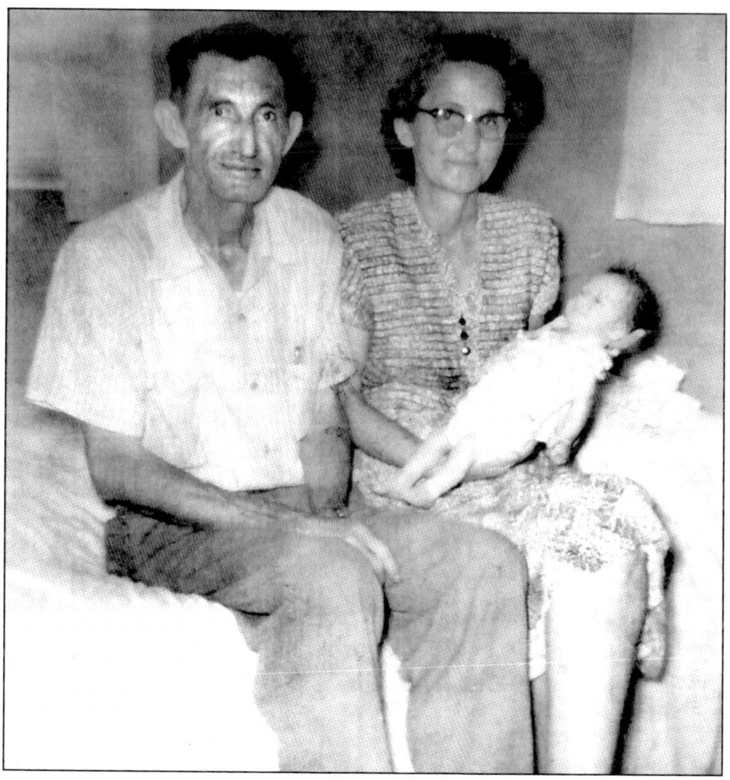

Ernest and Janie Bittle, parents of Dot Bittle Hann, are pictured here holding their granddaughter Sharon Hann (Frieze) in 1956. Ernest served as deputy sheriff for Talladega County for a number of years. (Courtesy of Jeffrey Hann.)

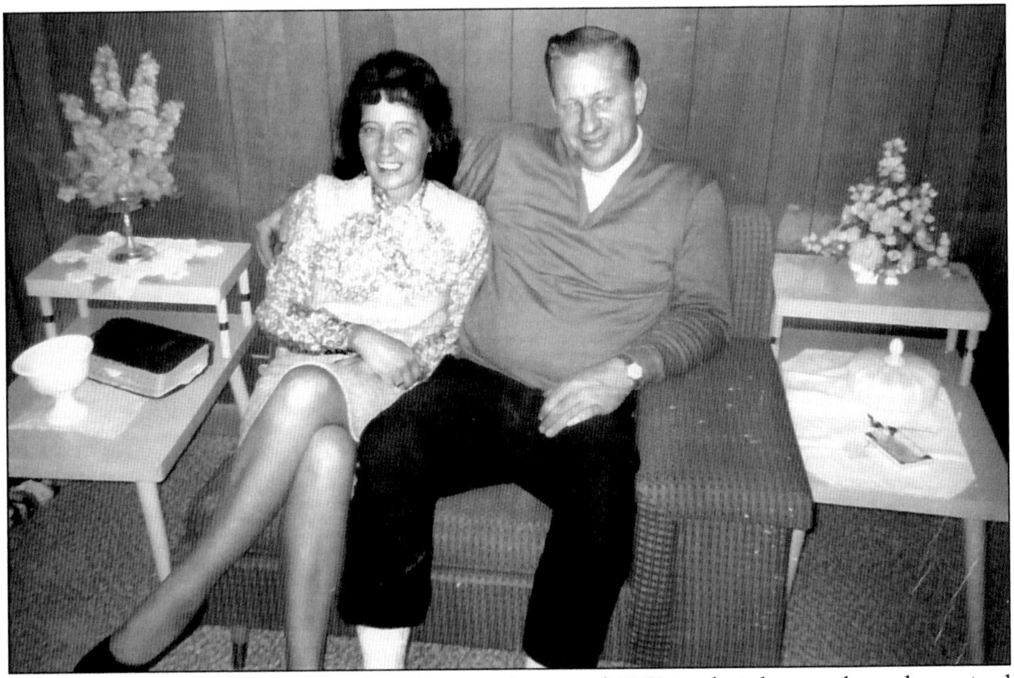

Haskell and Dot Hann posed for this photograph around 1960 in their home where they raised their four children. Haskell was in the army when he and Dot met. They were the owners of Dot's Quick Stop and the Shack Bar-B-Q. (Courtesy of Sharon Frieze.)

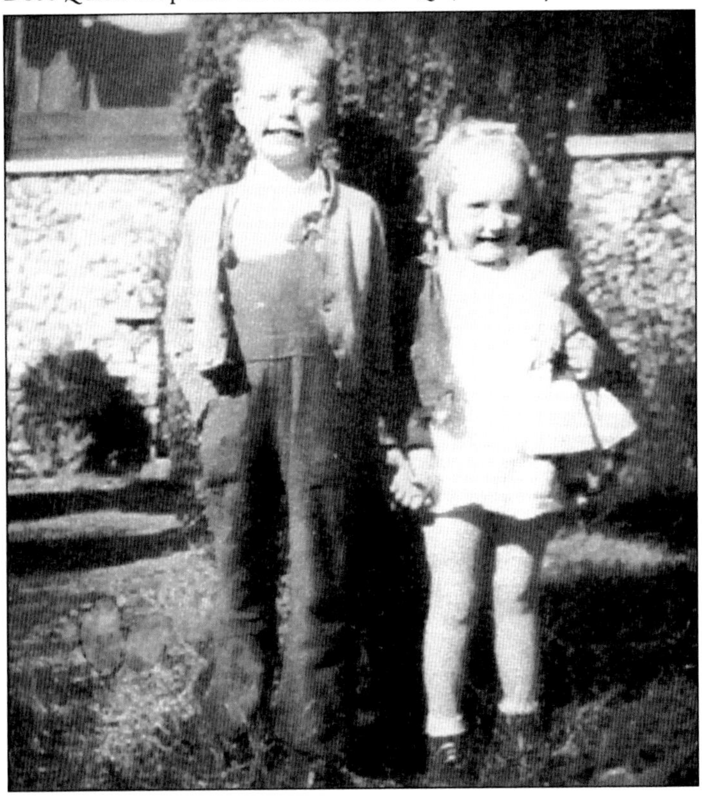

Darrell Hann and JoAnn Daffron were childhood best buddies. Darrell was tax assessor of Talladega County and one of two men from Stemley to be elected judge of probate of Talladega County. He served from 1973 until 1983. JoAnn became a teacher at Stemley Road Elementary School Idalia. (Courtesy of Dot Wesson.)

Donnie Gene Barnes is shown here with his horse, Dixie, in 1946 in front of the family dairy. Donnie rode Dixie to herd the cows. (Courtesy of Belle Hutto.)

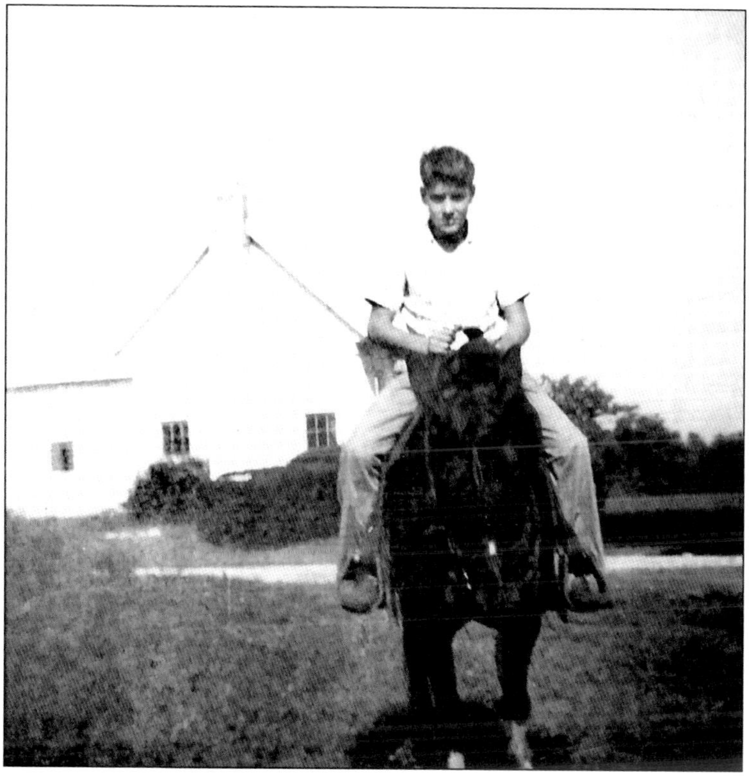

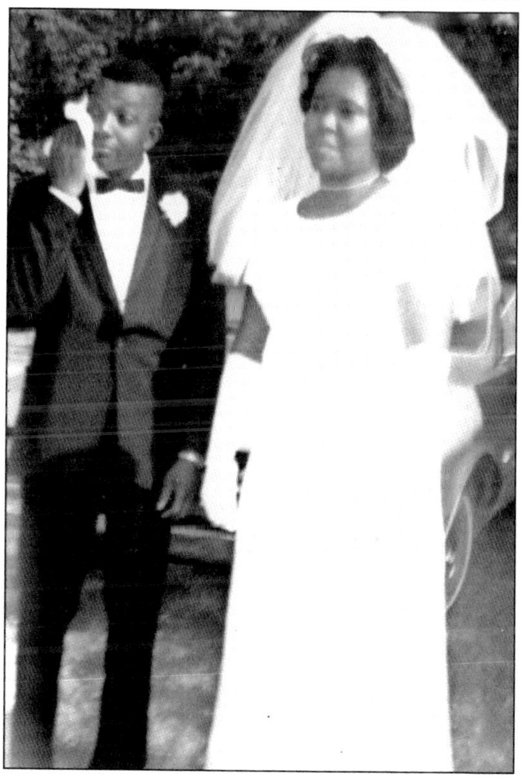

J. C. Heath and Doris Ragland were the first couple to be married by Rev. Moses C. Jones at Macedonia Baptist Church. They were married c. 1949. (Courtesy of Rosa Morris.)

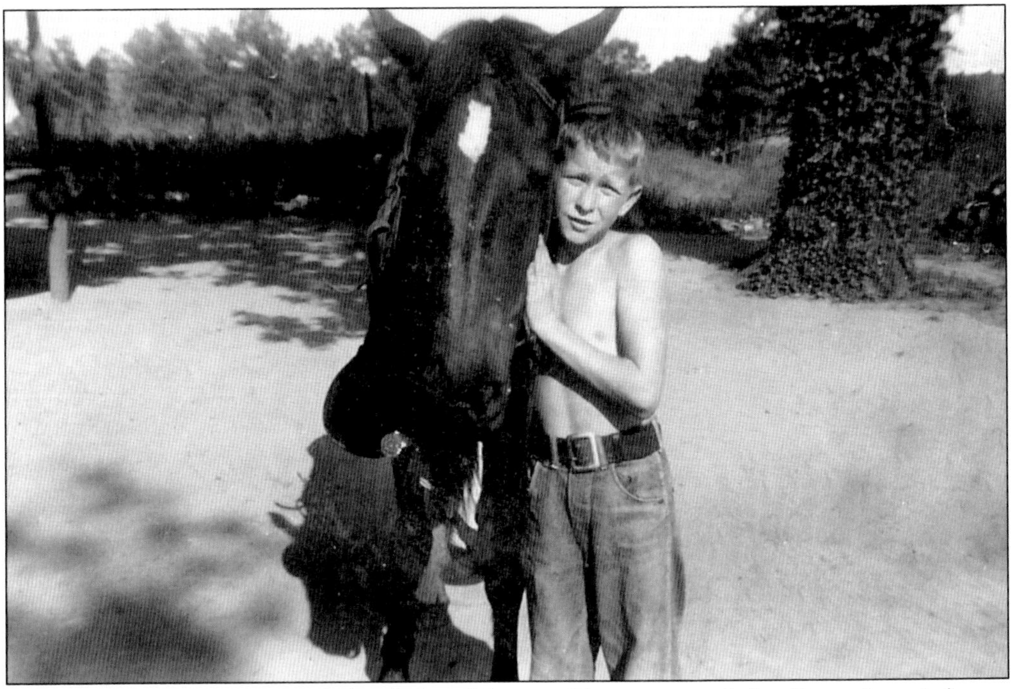

Bill Henderson is posing with his beloved horse, Champ, named for Gene Autry's horse, Champion. (Courtesy of Charles Henderson.)

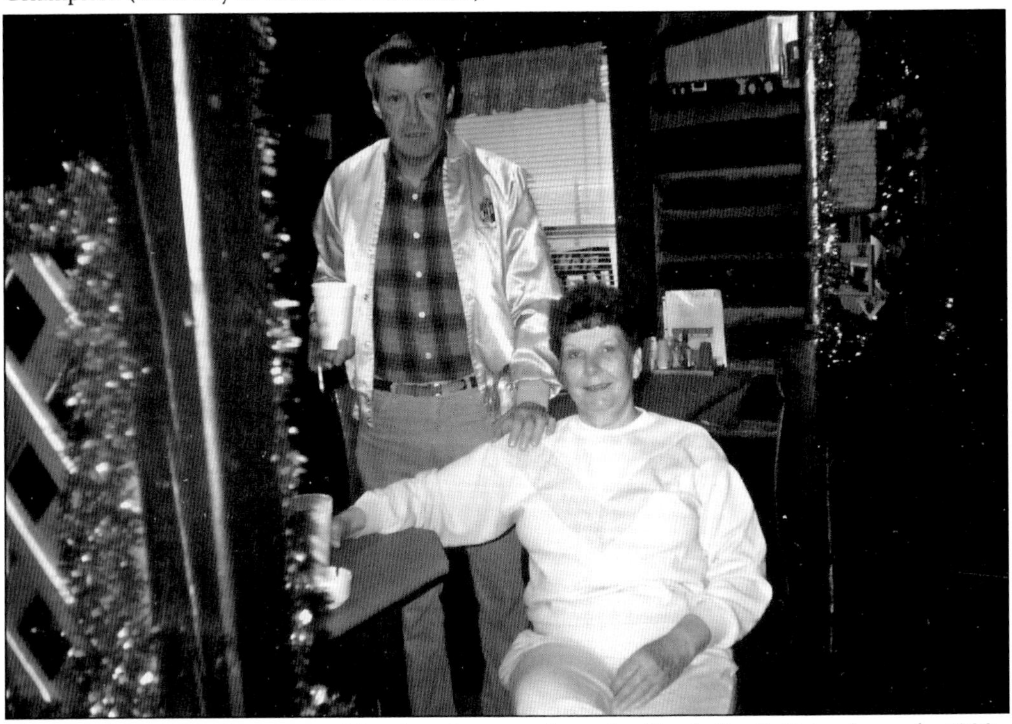

Frank and Ann Hindmon posed for this photograph at the Shack Bar-B-Q in the early 1980s. Frank is the son of Ed and Otha Hindmon, who also had a daughter, Lois. The Hindmons were residents of the Stemley community. (Courtesy of Sharon Frieze.)

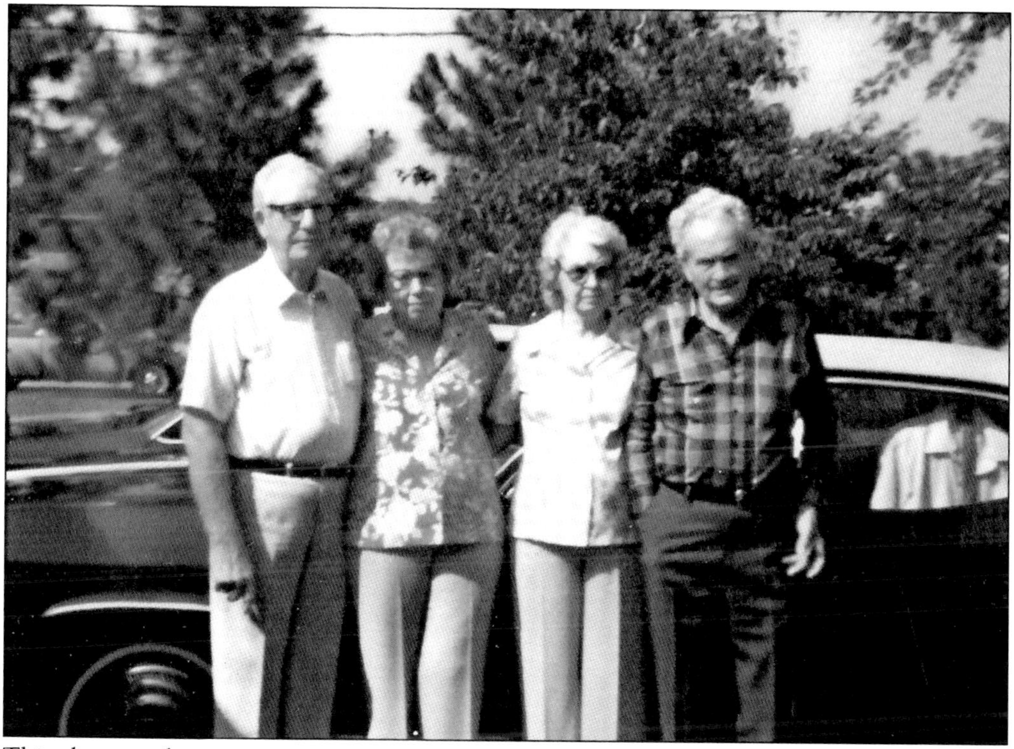

This photograph was taken in 1982. From left to right are Jeff Goray; his wife, Ruth; his sister, Ora Gaither (1912–2005); and her husband, Oscar (1909–2001). Jeff made the military his career. (Courtesy of Ora Gaither.)

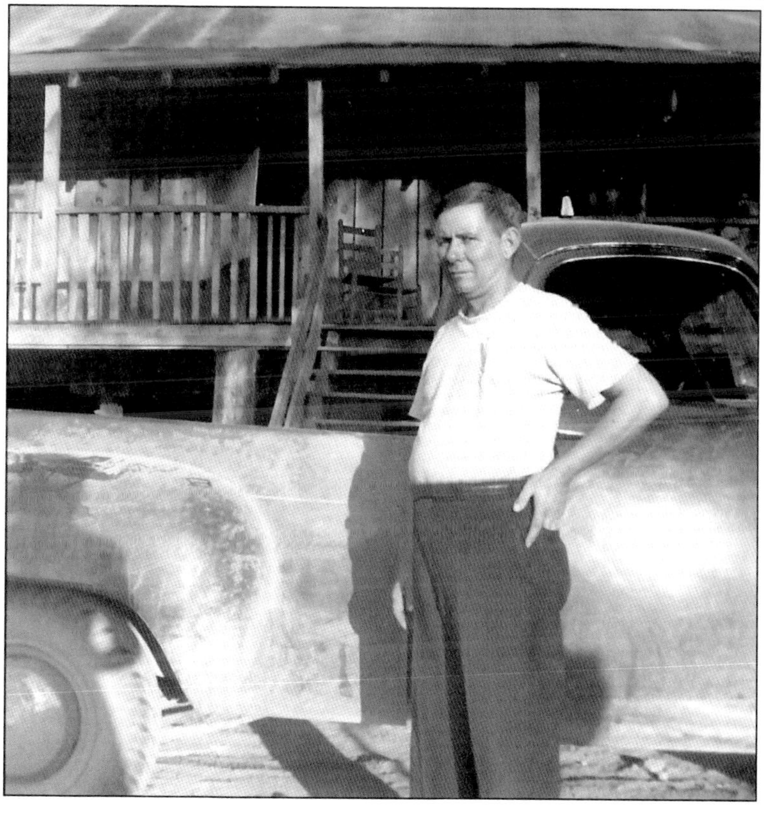

This picture of Henry Endfinger was taken at the old home place of Hendrix and Marie Martin. Henry was the Sunday school teacher at Stemley Baptist Church where the Martin children attended services. (Courtesy of Norman Martin.)

MACEDONIA BAPTIST CHURCH
Talladega, Alabama

Rev. M. C. Jones, Pastor
Rev. E. D. Dye, officiating

OBITUARY

Mrs. Mary Alice Cunningham was born in Talladega County, November 15, 1862. She was the daughter of the late Mr. And Mrs. Alfred Parson.

She attended school at Talladega College when President DeForest was there. At an early age she joined the Congregational Church. When the Congregational no longer existed in this community she became a member of the Macedonia Baptist Church and remained a faithful member until death.

She was married to the late Mr. William Crawford Cunningham and to this happy union ten children (five girls and five boys) were born.

She leaves to mourn her passing after an accident and short illness one daughter, two sons, eight grandchildren, thirty-seven great-grandchildren, and many other relatives and friends.

God's fingers touched her and she fell asleep on January 13, 1963. In truth the common touch she kept on life made her great.

Life is like the leaves of the
mighty oak,
Which only stands for a season;
Then returns to Mother Earth
From whence it came."

Mary Alice Parsons Cunningham (1862–1963) was married to William Crawford Cunningham, and they were the parents of 10 children. She attended school at Talladega College. She was a dedicated midwife who served throughout the community for many years, delivering babies whenever she was called upon and being picked up by mule and wagon. Everyone loved her, and she was known as "Aunt Alice." (Courtesy of Rosa Morris.)

This 1957 photograph is of Tom Wilson, his wife, Ruth (Smith), and two of his daughters, Frances (Kearley), left, and Helen Fay (Taylor), right. Tom owned and operated River View Tavern on old Stemley Bridge Road on the left of Stemley Bridge from 1947 to 1958. Catfish and chicken were served, and the occasional weekend band charged a 50¢ cover charge. The Wilson family lived next door to the tavern. (Courtesy of Frances Wilson Kearley.)

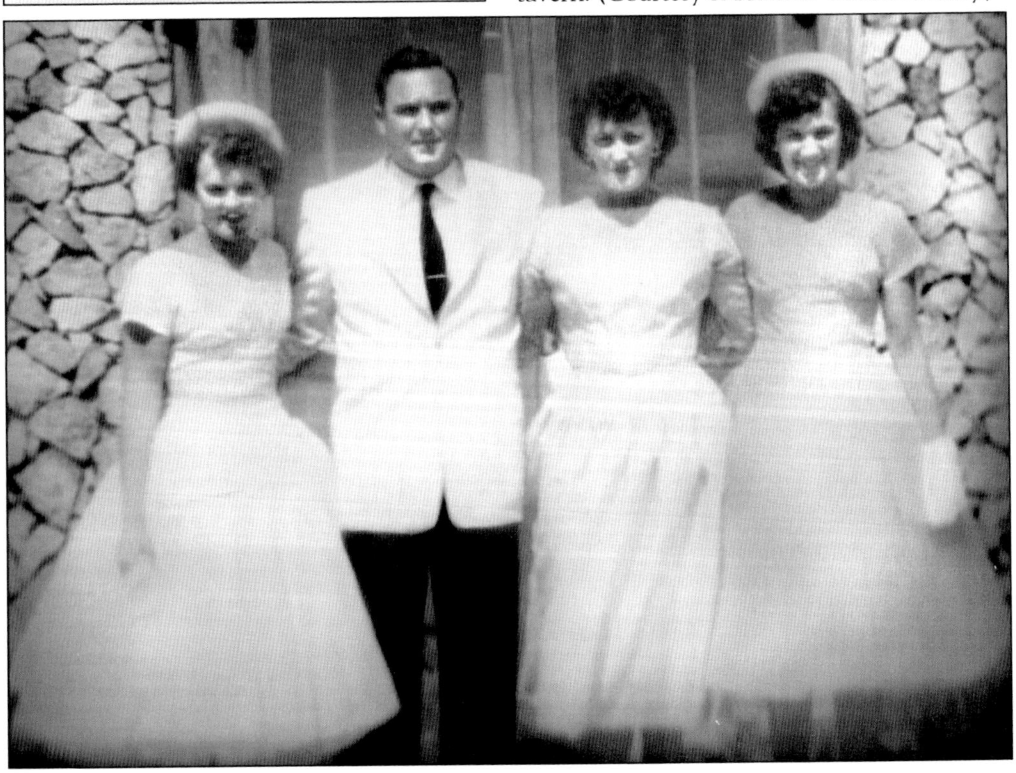

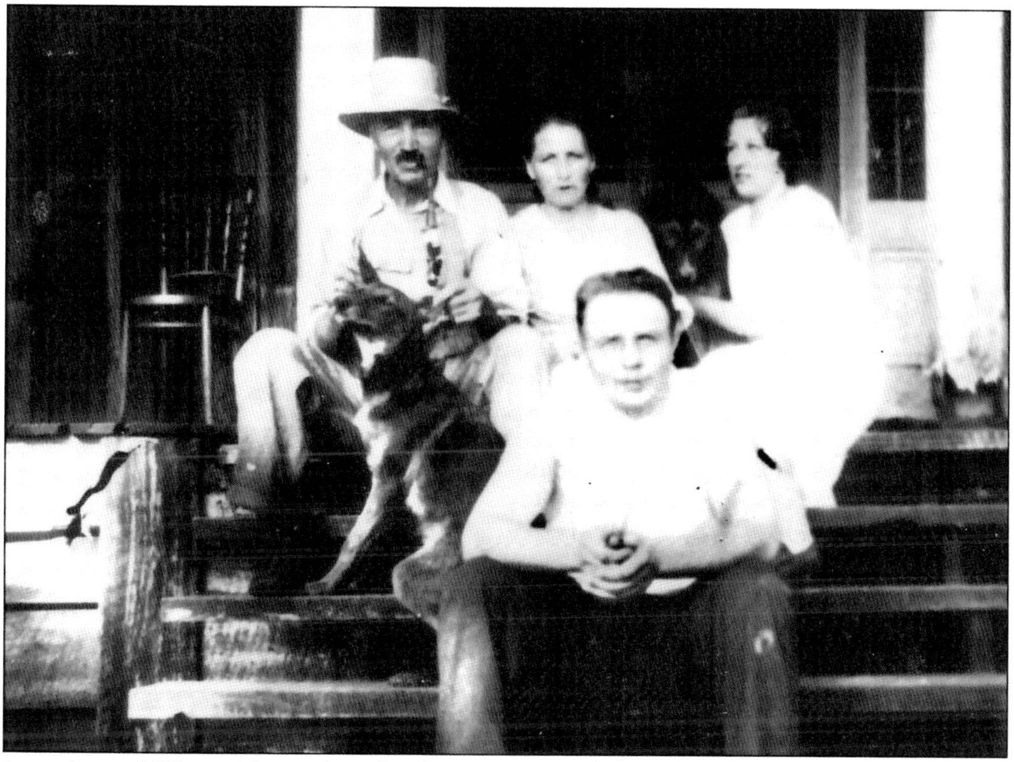

Lauardus and Tibina Ahten, their daughter, Terese, and Lauardus' nephew, George Ahten, are pictured here on the steps of their home on the old Linder Place on Stemley Bridge Road in the early 1930s. The family lived and farmed here until 1936 when they returned to Germany. Terese married Bernard Schmidt in 1937. George settled in Knoxville with his bride, Lena Warfen, where they eventually owned a dairy. (Courtesy of Laura Schmidt.)

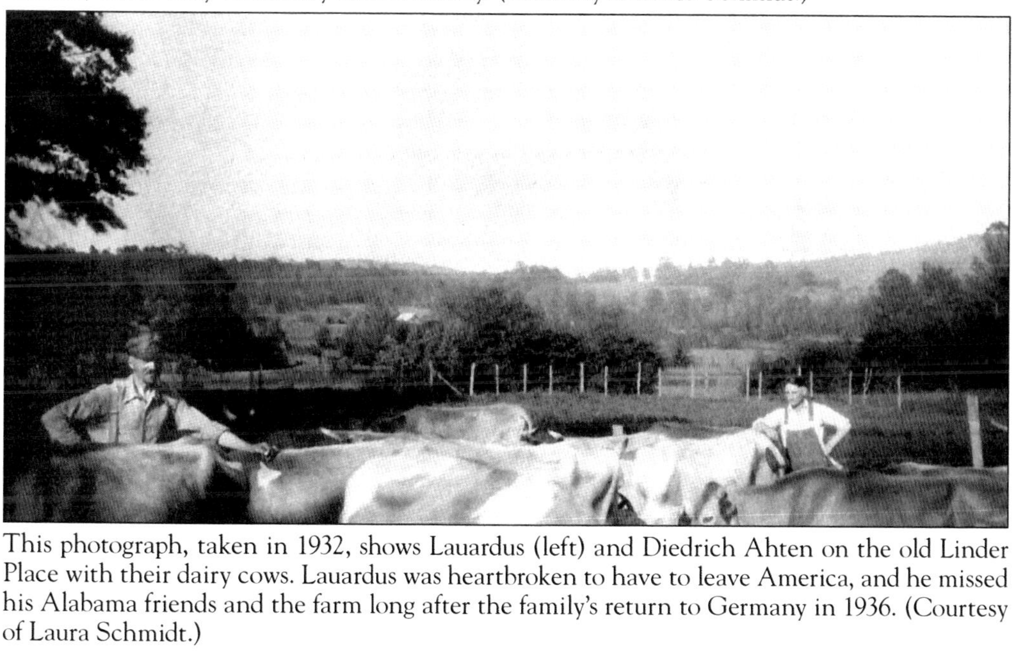

This photograph, taken in 1932, shows Lauardus (left) and Diedrich Ahten on the old Linder Place with their dairy cows. Lauardus was heartbroken to have to leave America, and he missed his Alabama friends and the farm long after the family's return to Germany in 1936. (Courtesy of Laura Schmidt.)

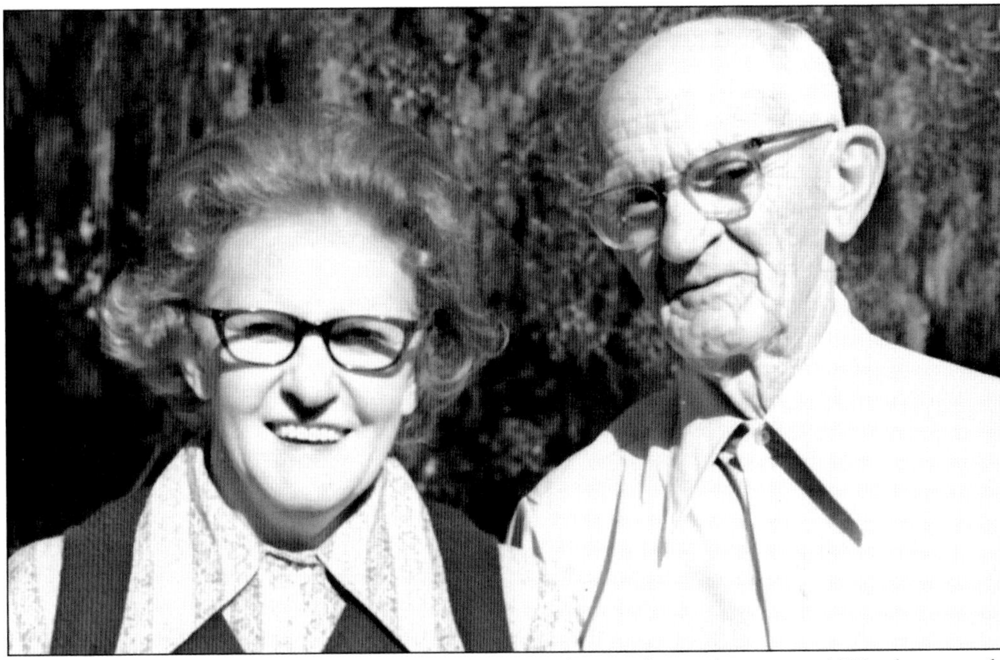

James Polk Burk and his wife, Louise Stephens Burk, are shown here in a 1972 photograph. They both worked at Bemiston. They moved to the Stemley area on the old Lincoln Highway in 1942. (Courtesy of Jean Burk.)

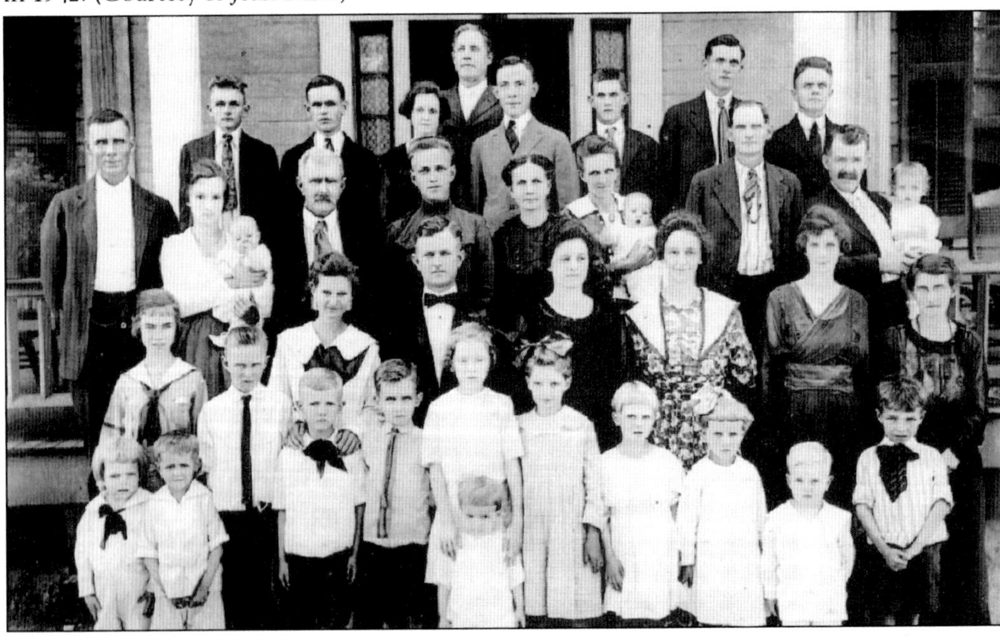

The Henley family from Renfroe is shown here about 70 years ago. Among those shown are, in no particular order, Pat Henley, Billy Jones, Mozelle (Henley) Greene, Agnes (Henley) Hayes, Blanche (Hallman) Henley, Kathleen (Henley) Street, Pauline (Henley) Hallman, Eppy Andrews, Willie (Henley) Hethcox, Monroe and Minnesota (Jones) Henley, Minnesota's parents, Minnie Lou (Henley) Parks, Will Hethcox, A. Finis Henley, Trotter Jones, and Dr. and Mrs. J. M. Thomas. (Courtesy of Lisa Baggett.)

Belle (Barnes) Hutto and her mother, Nannie Lee Barnes, are pictured together in 1948 on Belle's Jeep. Belle's father, Johnnie Barnes, bought her the Jeep to drive to Winterboro where she was attending school. (Courtesy of Belle Hutto.)

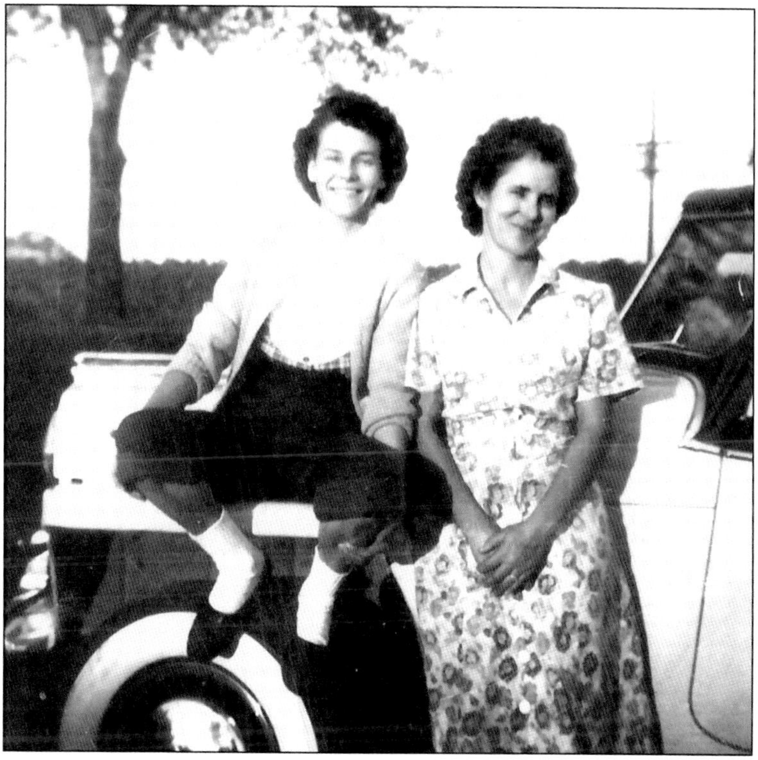

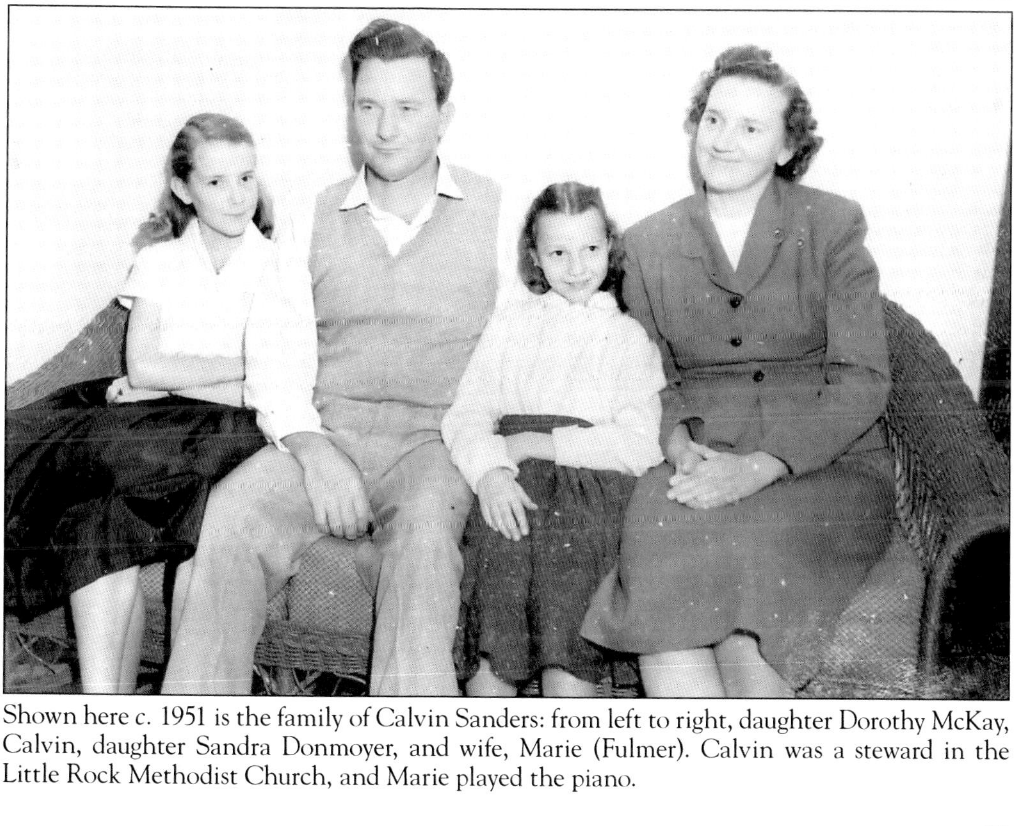

Shown here c. 1951 is the family of Calvin Sanders: from left to right, daughter Dorothy McKay, Calvin, daughter Sandra Donmoyer, and wife, Marie (Fulmer). Calvin was a steward in the Little Rock Methodist Church, and Marie played the piano.

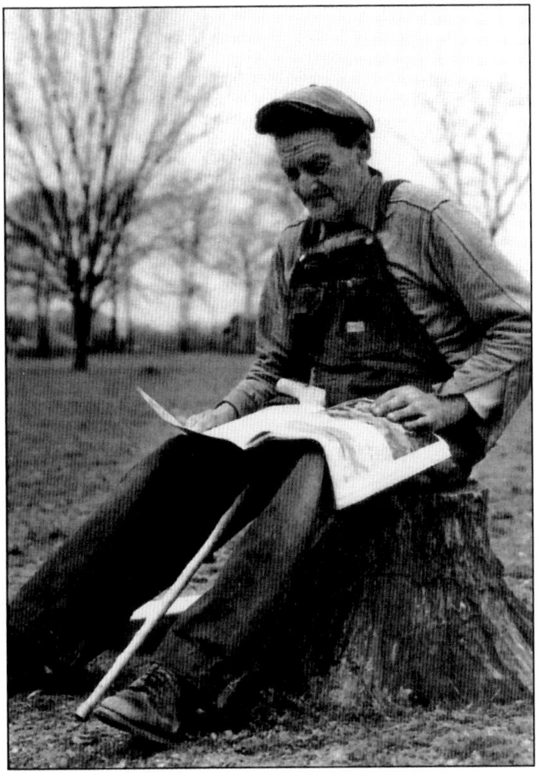

Three generations of the Schmidt family were owners and operators of a gristmill and gin on Choccolocco Creek for almost 100 years. George Ludwig Schmidt (1867–1960), photographed in April 1941, inherited the mill from his father, Bernhard Schmidt, who built it right after the Civil War with his father-in-law, Jacob Harmon.

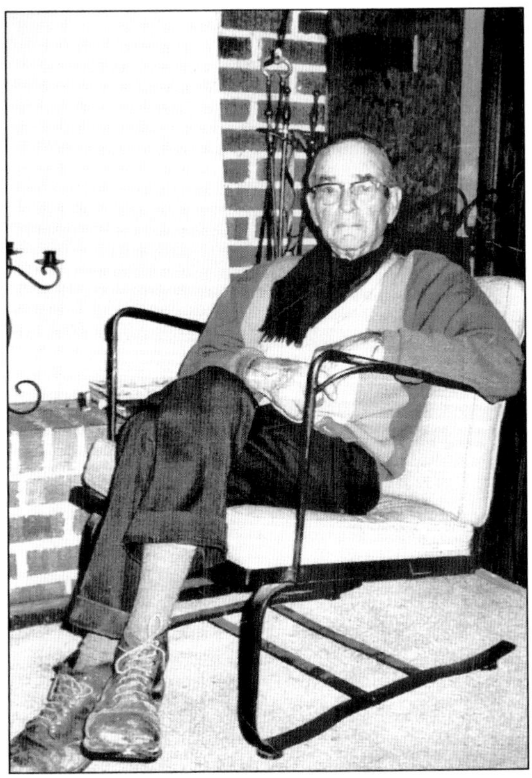

George Ludwig Schmidt rebuilt the mill after it was destroyed in the floods of 1886. He later passed the mill on to his son, Bernard Schmidt (1906–1988), photographed in the fall of 1984, who ran it until the early 1960s, when Logan Martin Dam was built and the area was flooded.

Five

MILITARY

This chapter is dedicated to those who represented the Stemley community serving in the various military branches and political and government offices—from the War of 1812 to the most recent deployed reserves, to the officials who brought about changes in legal and various other systems for the betterment of the Stemley community and society in general.

The history of our men at war begins with Reece Howell, an early settler who served in the War of 1812. Then came the Civil War (1861–1865), which tore our nation apart. Later came World War I (1914–1918) and then World War II, which began for the United States when Japan attacked Pearl Harbor in 1941 and ended in 1945 with the dropping of the atomic bombs on Hiroshima and Nagasaki. Around that time, our involvement in the Vietnam War began and lasted until 1973, after which the cold war began. Our men fought in the Korean War (1950–1953) and the Persian Gulf War (1990–1991). The September 11, 2001, terrorist attacks on U.S. soil have resulted in the current War on Terror, in which men from the Stemley are active.

Alongside our brave militia, in honor stand our leaders, who have made changes while serving in office, bringing about recognition for the area around Stemley Bridge.

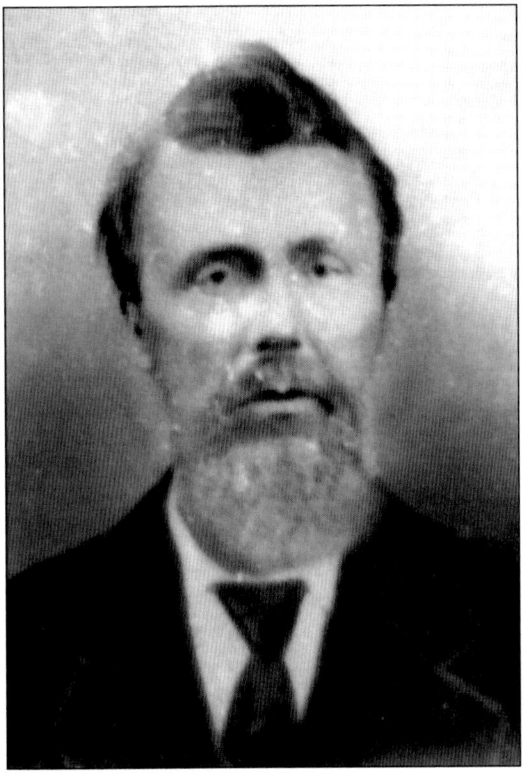

In 1844, John J. Gambrell (1839–1918) moved to Renfroe in Talladega County from South Carolina. He served in the Confederate war as a teamster. In 1866 after the war was over, John married Melvina Lowery. (Courtesy of Sid Gambrell.)

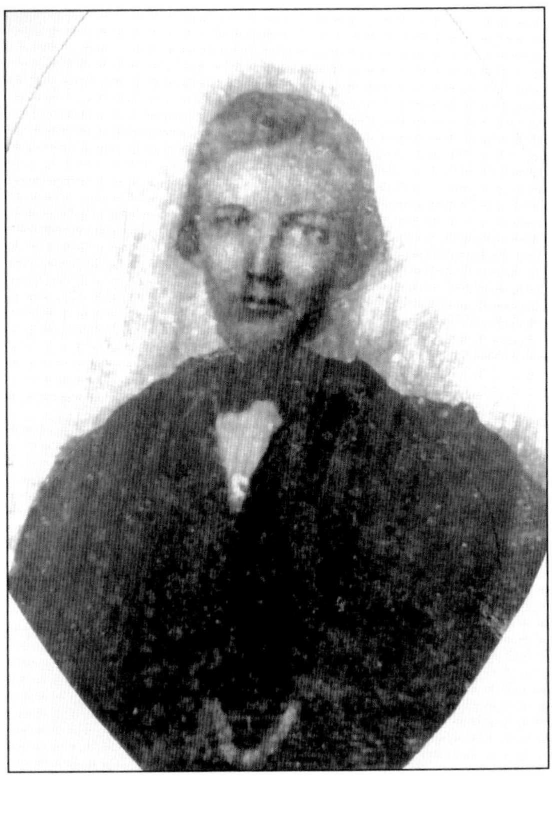

Benjamin R. Hubbard, born around 1841, was the youngest son of John Hubbard. Benjamin was in the Civil War. After the war, he married Mary Josephine Gambrell, and they moved to Texas, only to return to Renfroe before he died. (Courtesy of Sid Gambrell.)

Theodore Nathan Sawyer fought in the Civil War and was killed in battle at Shiloh on April 8, 1862. He was married to Nancy Jane Gambrell, daughter of William and Nancy (Cooley) Gambrell. (Courtesy of Sid Gambrell.)

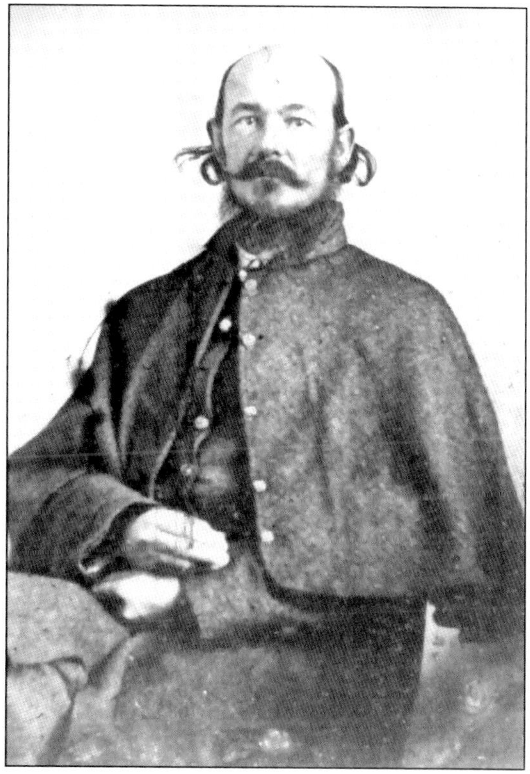

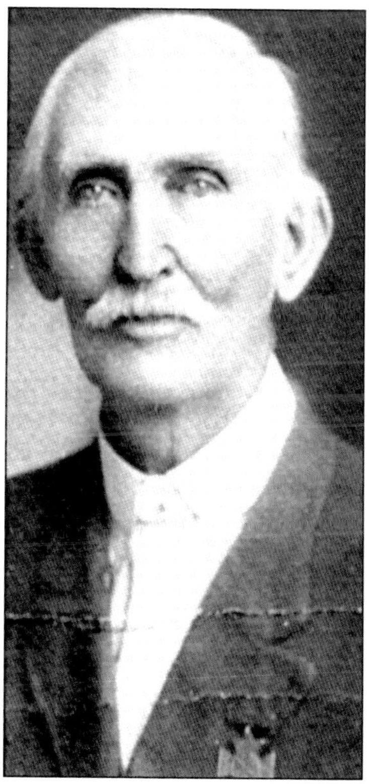

James Thomas Johnson (1846–1943) was known as "One-Arm Jim" after losing his left arm in the Civil War when he was 16 years old. At one time, he was tax assessor of St. Clair County. When this photograph was taken, he was living in Cropwell where the airport is today. Notice his Civil War medal. (Courtesy of Jeanette Zachero.)

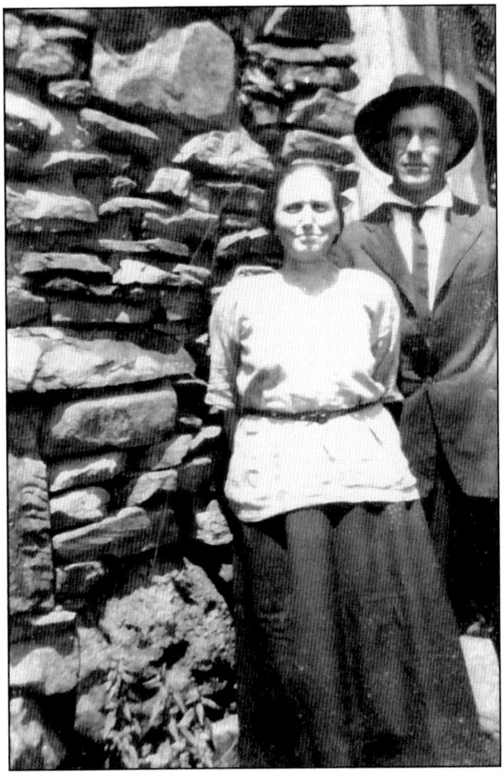

Francis Ann (Floyd) Martin and Melvin Luther Martin were the parents of Hendrix Martin. Melvin Luther was a veteran of World War I. While serving in the military in France during 1918, he was gassed once and wounded twice. He was awarded the French Cross on May 15, 1918. (Courtesy of Norman Martin.)

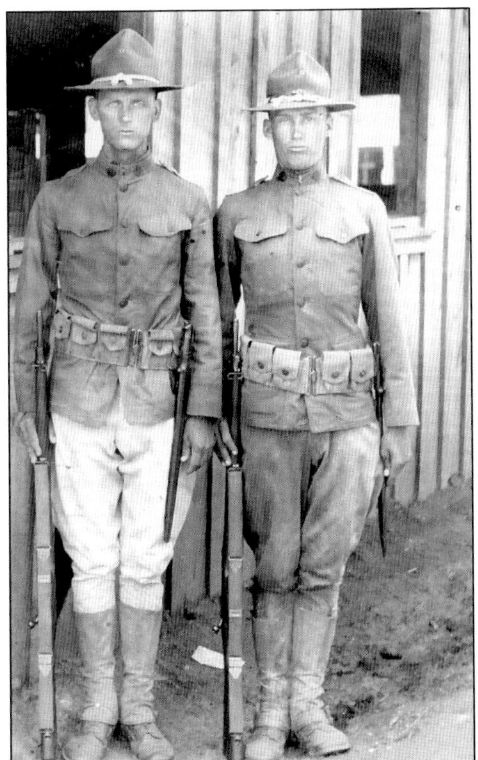

Jack Waits, left, was stationed in Greenville, South Carolina, during World War I. He is pictured here with an unidentified soldier in June 1918. (Courtesy of Rosemary Robinson.)

Paul Hunt George Fulmer was in the army in World War II. He was declared missing in action in the fall of 1944 and sadly was found the following spring when the snow melted. A Dutch lady tended his grave and mailed photographs to his mother, Josie Fulmer. They corresponded for several months. Carolyn Daffron, Paul's niece, met the Dutch lady's son, Math Lask, on a trip to Europe years later. (Courtesy of JoAnn Gauldin.)

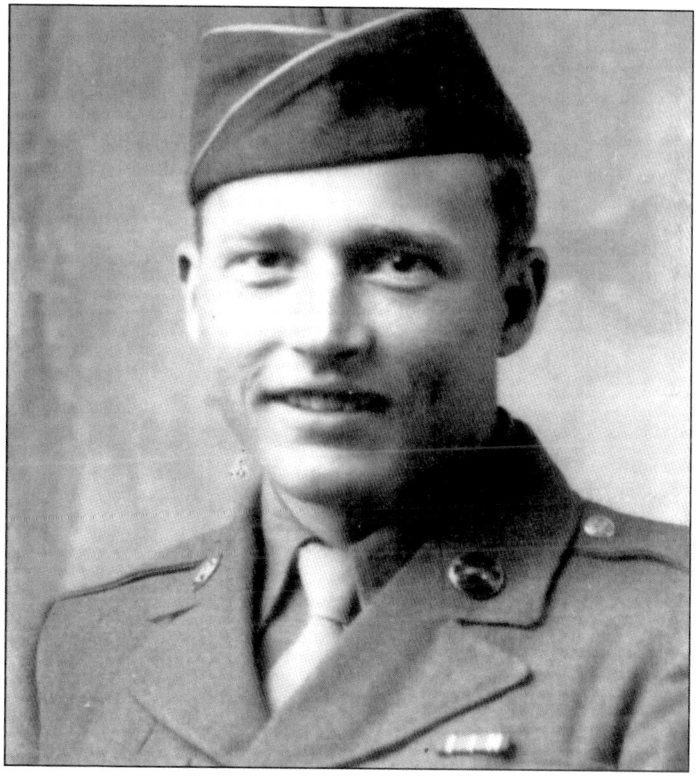

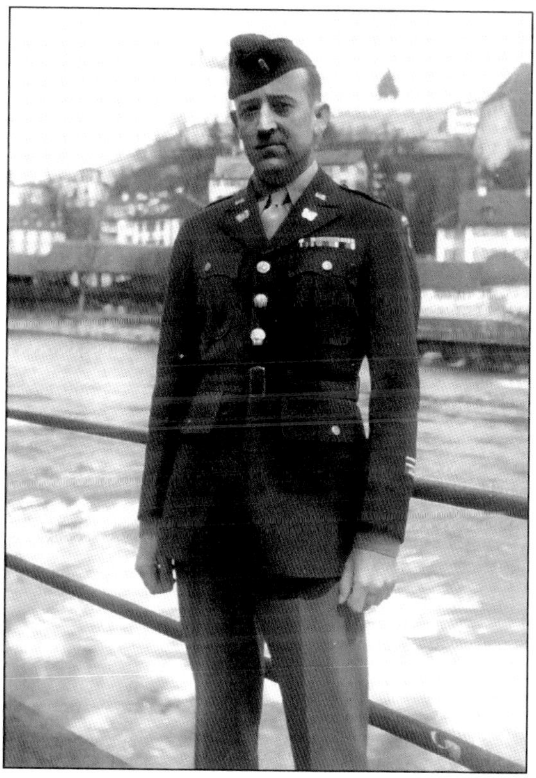

Clyde Daffron, shown here in 1946, was the son of Clifton and Lois Daffron of Stemley. Clyde served in the army in England and France during World War II. He retired as a sergeant after 20 years of service and spent the rest of his life in Leeds. (Courtesy of JoAnn Daffron.)

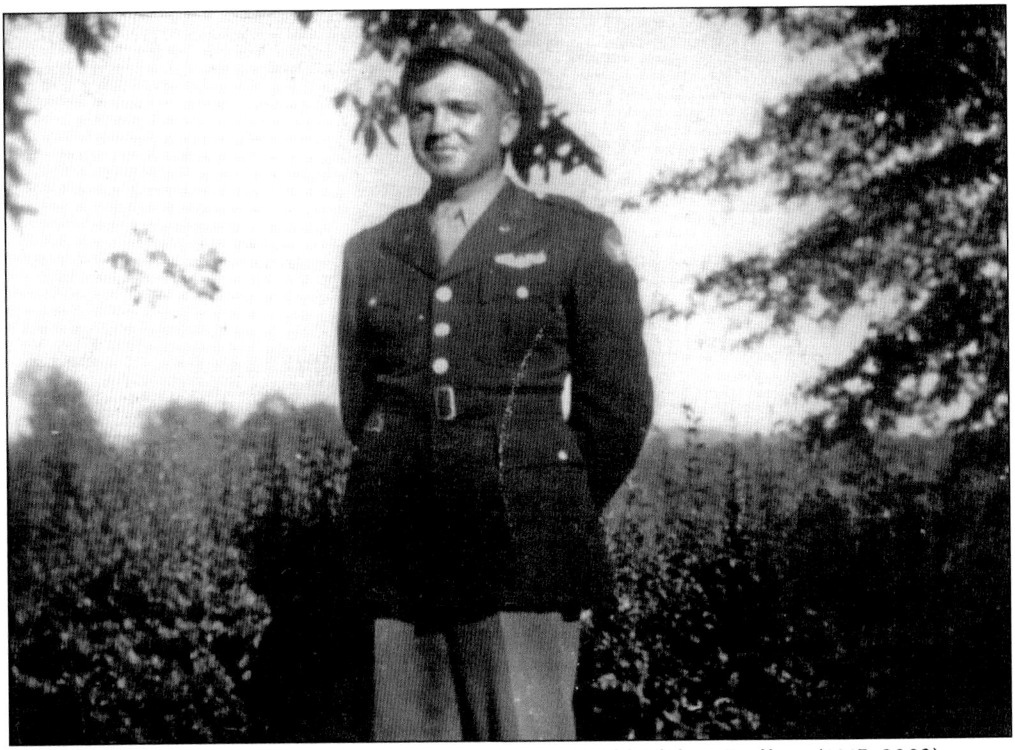

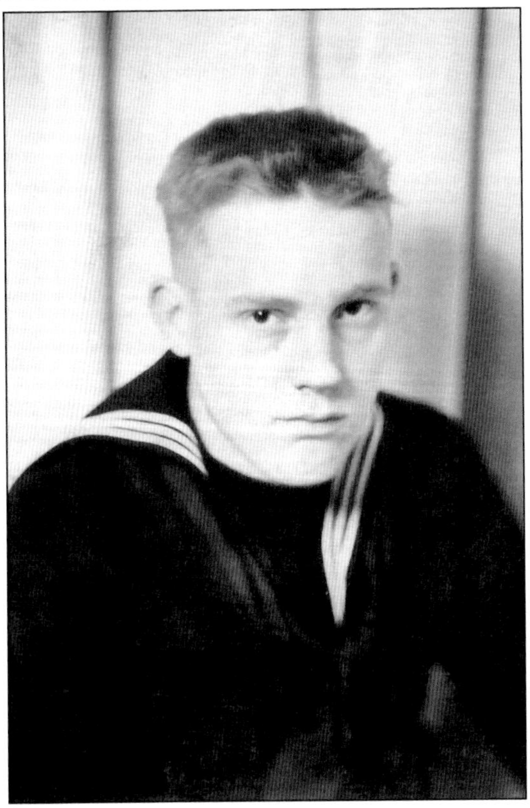

Harold Clifton Daffron (1917–2003) was a native of Ragland but lived most of his life around Stemley Bridge. He served in the 6th Cavalry F Troop from 1937 to 1940 and was a fighter pilot in the Army Air Corps from 1942 to 1946, during World War II. He married Thelma Fulmer from Stemley. (Courtesy of JoAnn Gauldin.)

William Hudson Fulmer (1926–1988), son of Claude and Josie (Bynum) Fulmer, joined the navy c. 1944 and served in Panama. In 1946, he married Lois Hindmon, daughter of Edward and Otha Hindmon. (Courtesy of Jeanette Zachero.)

Thomas Spencer served in the army in World War II. He spent three years in China, Burma, and India in the supply unit. (Courtesy of Mary Frances Spencer.)

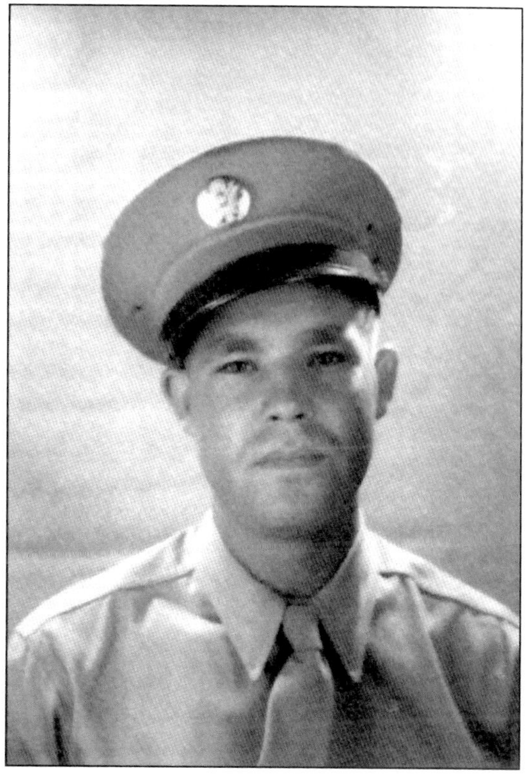

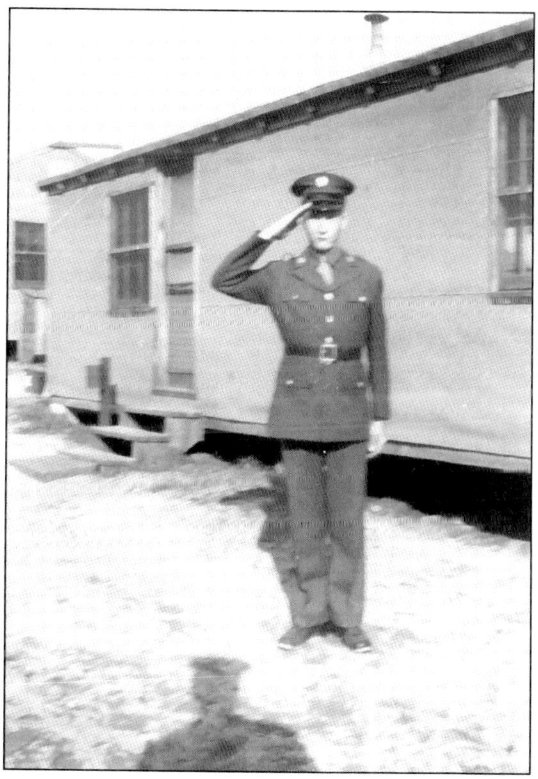

Calvin Sanders is shown here as a new recruit. The blouse, belt, and hat are not standard GI issue. Calvin served in the army during World War II from November 1942 to December 1945 and rose to the rank of artillery sergeant. (Courtesy of the Sanders family.)

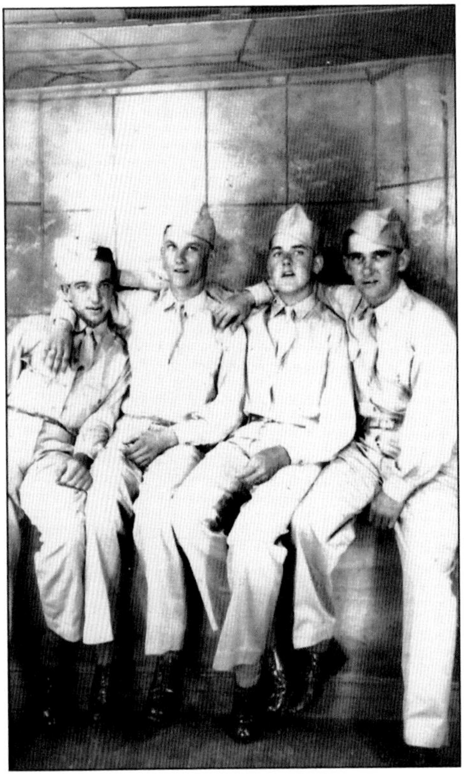

Earl Johnson (1926–1988), second from left, served in the army during World War II. He was the son of Dewitt and Lucille (Hubbard) Johnson. (Courtesy of the Dewitt Johnson family.)

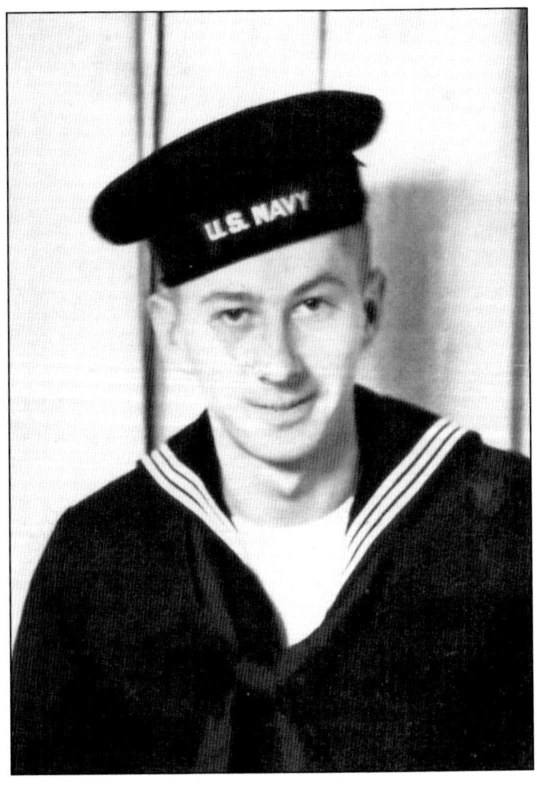

Lowell Fulmer (1923–1997) served in the navy during World War II. He was the son of Eugene and Mable (Smelley) Fulmer, who lived on Stemley Bridge Road. (Courtesy of Peggy Hall.)

David Goray, brother of Sam Goray and Ora Gaither, served in the army during World War II. He was killed in action while serving in Germany. (Courtesy of Ora Gaither.)

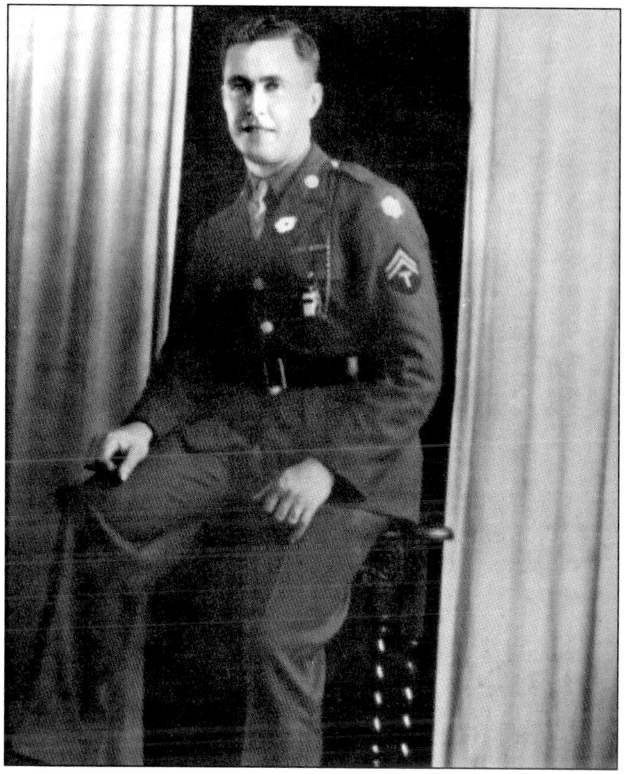

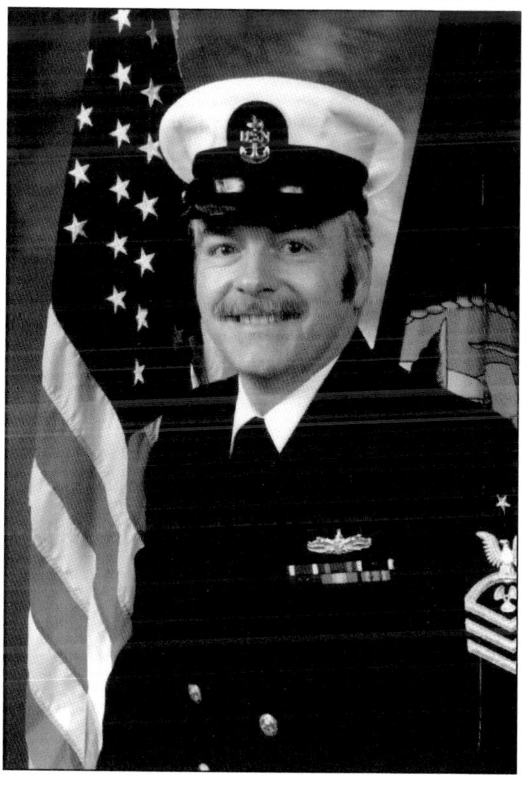

This photograph of Donnie Lee Barnes Jr., grandson of John and Nannie Lee Barnes, was taken in 1990. Donnie Lee served in the U.S. Navy for 20 years, serving during the Vietnam War and Desert Storm. He was a cold war veteran. He retired as chief petty officer in 1998. (Courtesy of Dan and Mary Barnes.)

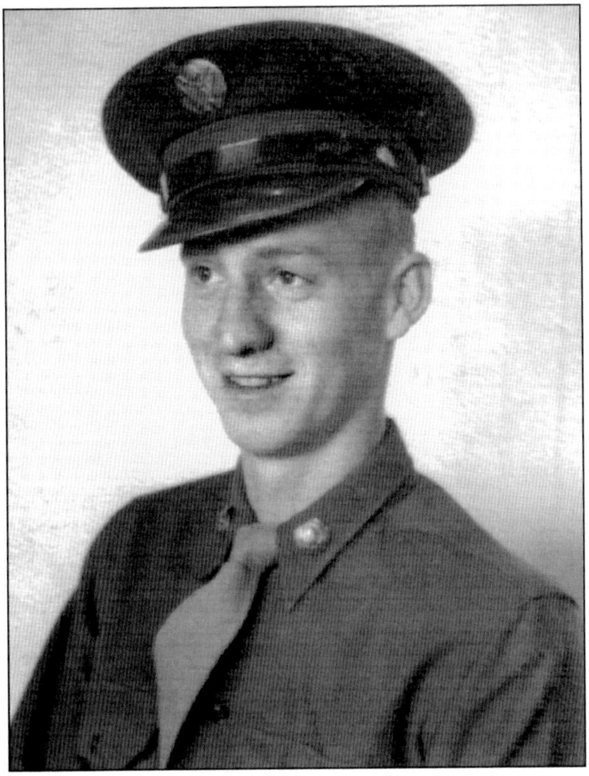

Herbert Fulmer was serving in the army in Germany *c.* 1949 when this photograph was taken. The ship that Herbert was on hit a glacier, and all personnel had to board another ship; fortunately, there were no injuries or casualties during this accident. (Courtesy of Louise Gunter.)

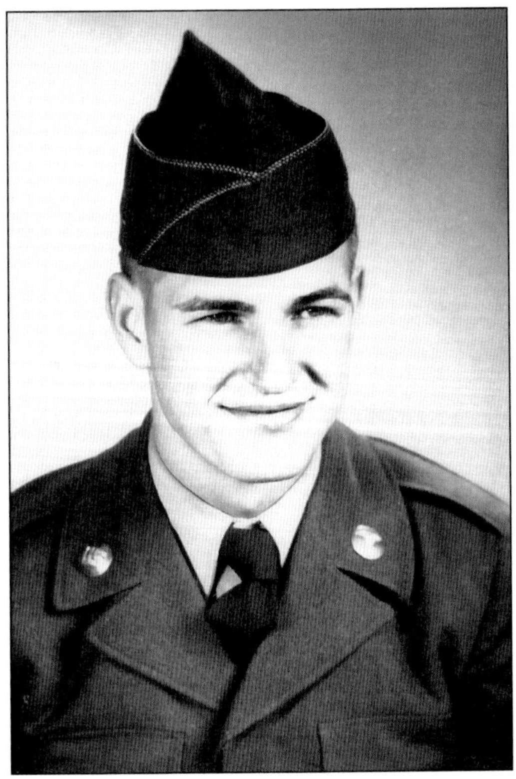

Timmons Hendrix Martin, eldest child of Hendrix and Marie Martin, left home at the age of 17 to join the army. He served in the Korean War for 13 months and was stationed at Fort Jackson, South Carolina, for a short time. (Courtesy of Norman Martin.)

Thomas Johnson (1934–1963) was a private in the army c. 1951–1953. He was the son of James and Beatrice Johnson. (Courtesy of Jeanette Zachero.)

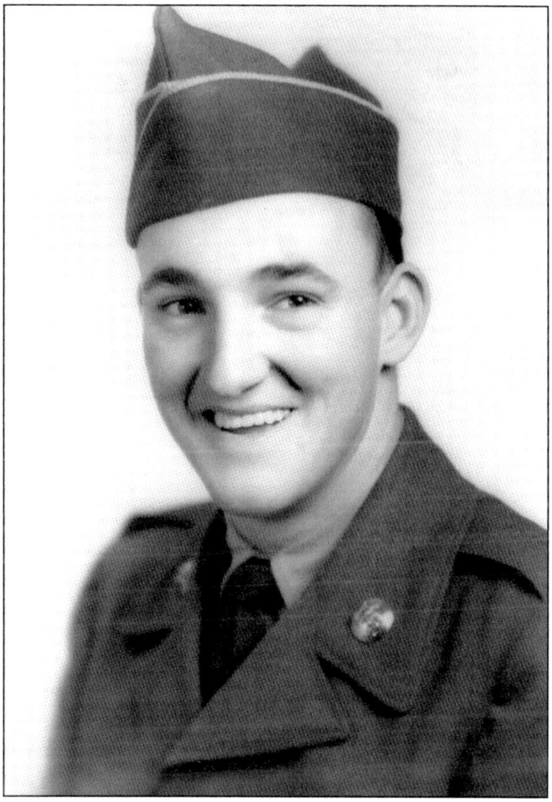

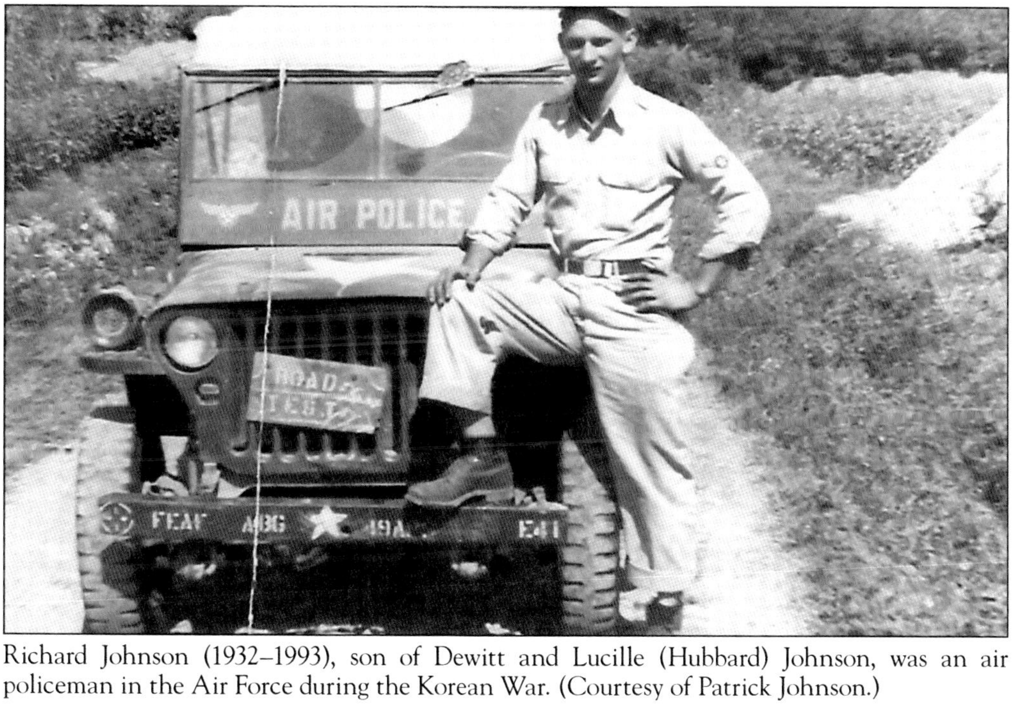

Richard Johnson (1932–1993), son of Dewitt and Lucille (Hubbard) Johnson, was an air policeman in the Air Force during the Korean War. (Courtesy of Patrick Johnson.)

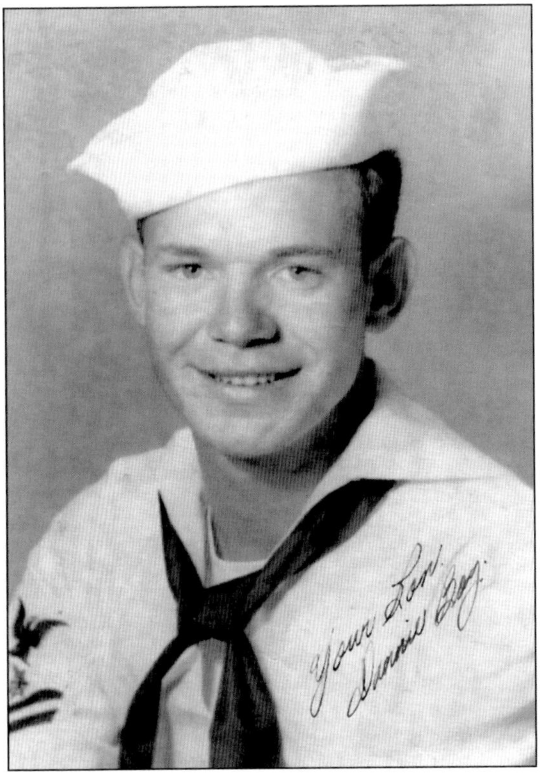

Daniel Barnes at age 17 served in the navy as a navigator. He later went to college, took courses in math and chemistry, ran a service station until midnight, studied with his buddies until 2 a.m., and passed all his courses. He was in the reserves and was recalled to active service during the Korean War. (Courtesy of the Barnes family.)

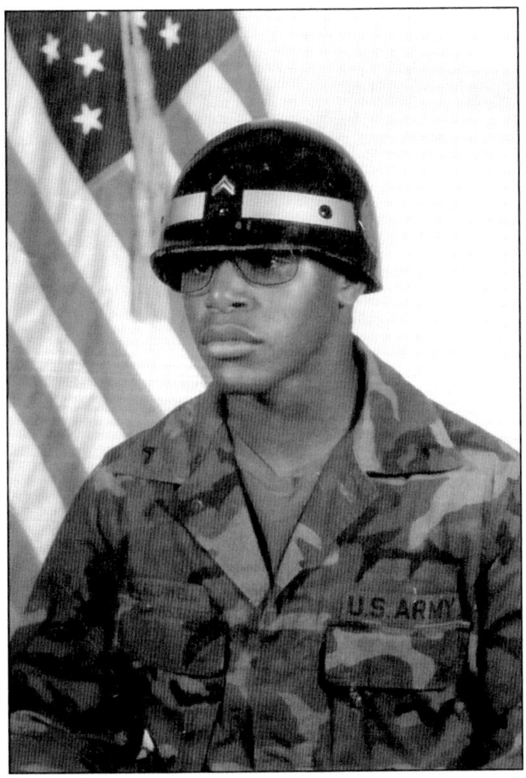

James Earl Caldwell, son of Lonzer Cochran Jr. and Annie Mae (Caldwell) Cochran, joined the army in January 1982 and received an honorable discharge on November 20, 1992. His tour of duties included Fort Dix, New Jersey; Turkey; Bolivia; Honduras; Panama Canal; Fort Story, Virginia; and Germany. He married Arla Jane Stockdale, and they have five sons. (Courtesy of Johnnie Mae Cochran.)

Timothy Dewayne Cochran, son of Robert and Johnnie Mae Cochran, was in the navy from 1987 to 1995. He was accepted into the Hospital Corpsman School, studied field medicine, and worked in an intensive care unit. He served in Turkey and during Desert Storm. He reached the rank of petty officer third class and earned numerous medals and awards. He currently is working as a surgical assistant. (Courtesy of Johnnie Mae Cochran.)

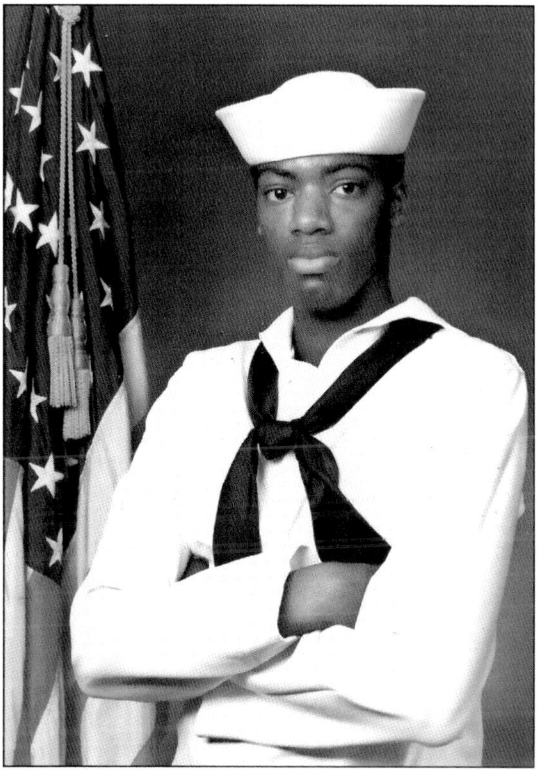

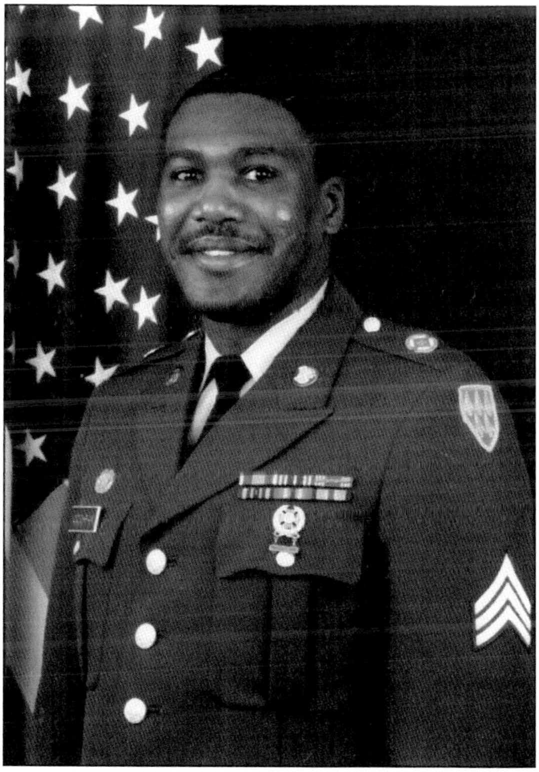

Ricky Cochran, son of Lonzer Cochran Jr. and Annie Mae Cochran, joined the army in April 1980. During his military service, he was stationed in Germany twice and in the Middle East in 1990. He received an honorable discharge in 1992 and went to work at the Anniston Army Depot. In 2002, he was called back to duty after the terrorist attacks of September 11. He married Brenda Cochran, and they have three sons. (Courtesy of Johnnie Mae Cochran.)

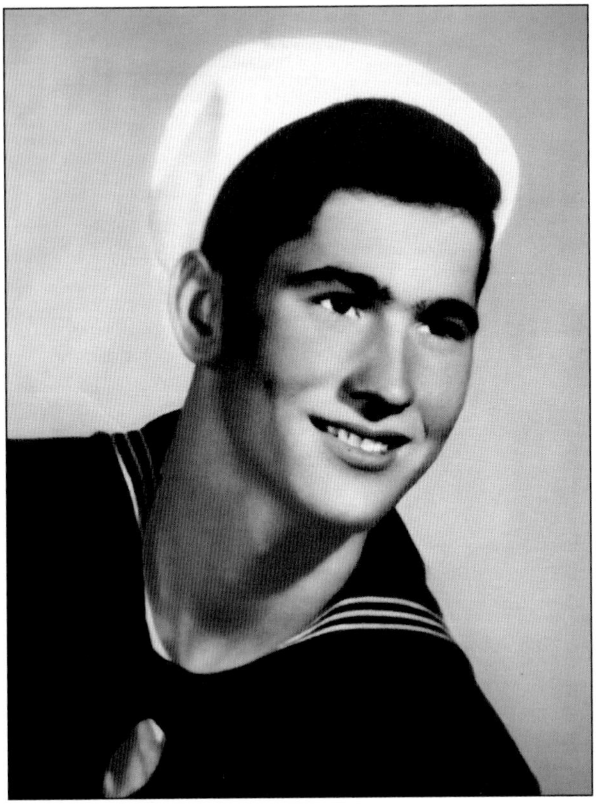

Dwain D. Sanders, born October 31, 1937, is the son of Samuel and Naomi Sanders and the grandson of Y. T. and Myrtle Sanders. Dwain served in the navy from January 1957 until June 1960. He joined the army in May 1961 and retired in May 1981 as a first sergeant in the 24th Infantry Division at Fort Stewart, Georgia. While in the army, his tours of duty included Korea, Germany, Alaska, and Vietnam. After retiring from the army in 1981, he went to Jacksonville State University and became a state trooper with certification as a driver license examiner. He worked with the Department of Public Safety in Talladega from 1991 until 2002. Dwain is married to Mary (Carroll) Sanders. (Courtesy of Dwain D. Sanders.)

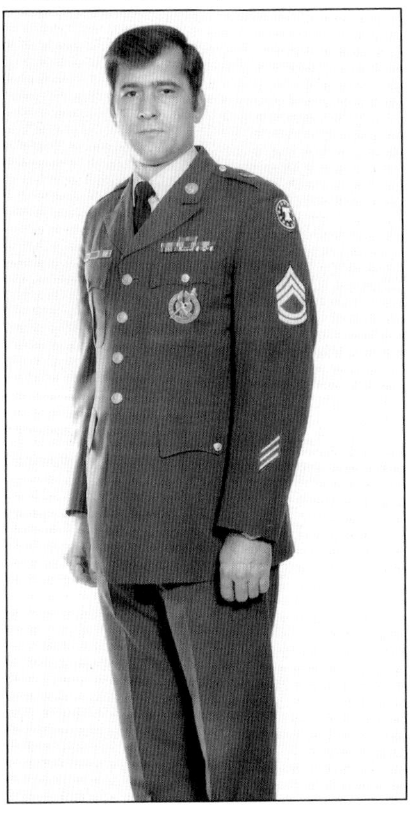

Jerry Studdard attended Idalia Elementary School when he was in the fourth grade. He became a deputy sheriff soon after graduating from high school. He was working on the ABC Liquor Board when he was elected sheriff of Talladega County in 1979. Studdard has held that office for seven terms, longer than any sheriff of Talladega County. In 1994, during his administration, a new jail was built. (Courtesy of Peggy Hall.)

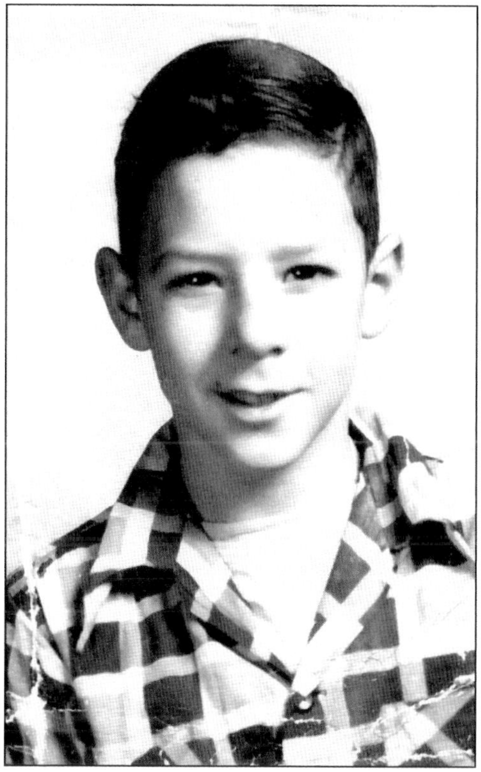

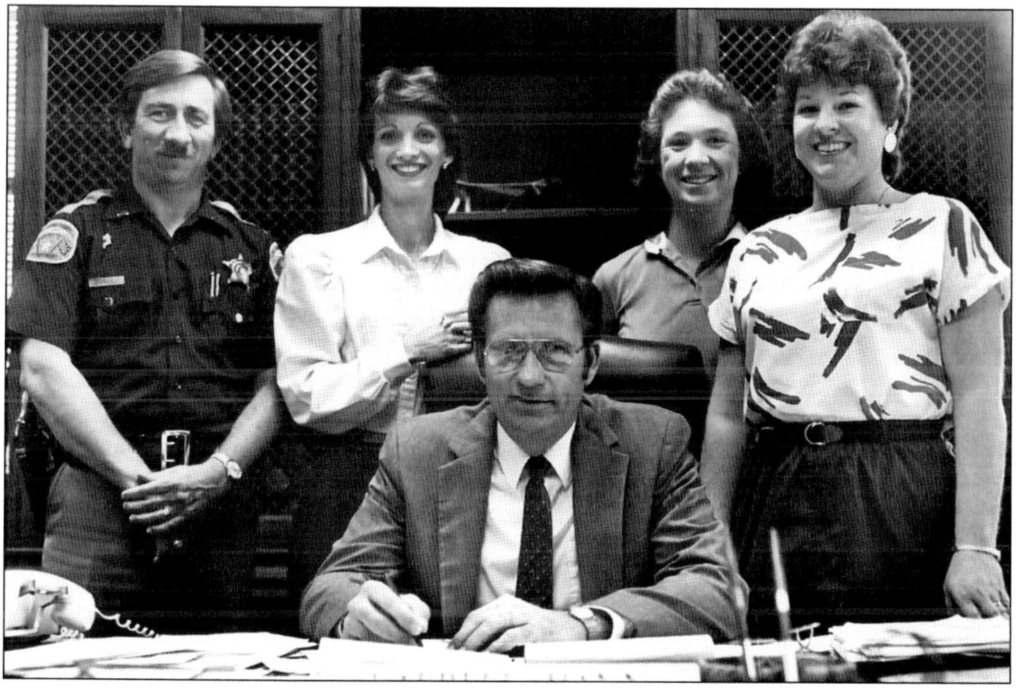

Derrell Hann, probate judge of Talladega County, is shown here signing a peace officers proclamation on May 11, 1984. Standing behind Derrell from left to right are Deputy Bailiff Charles Bonner, Donna Smith, Pam Canada, and Lynn Martin. (Courtesy of Peggy Hall.)

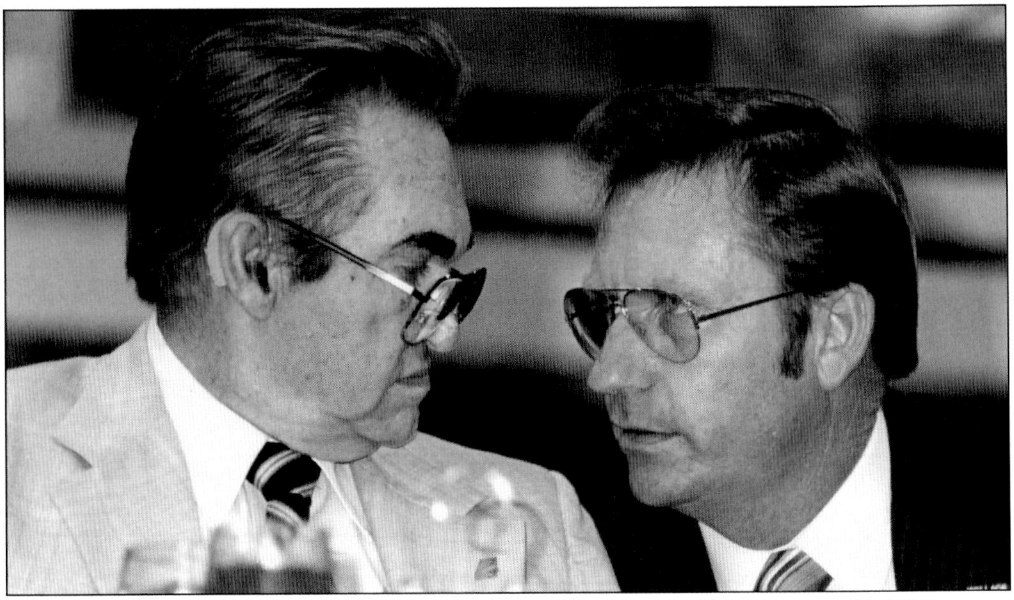

Probate Judge Derrell Ray Hann, right, is pictured here with Gov. George C. Wallace on Wallace's visit to Talladega. Derrell was born near Stemley Bridge in 1939 to Grover and Jewel Hann. He contributes his success to his roots in the Stemley area. He served as tax assessor from 1973 to 1983 when he was elected probate judge. While in office, Hann's achievements focused on organization and accountability, including implementing an inventory system, updating equipment, and refinancing loans and bonds. He turned to Wallace for help with the county water system, resulting in the county having one of the largest water filtration plants in the state. (Courtesy of Derrell Hann.)

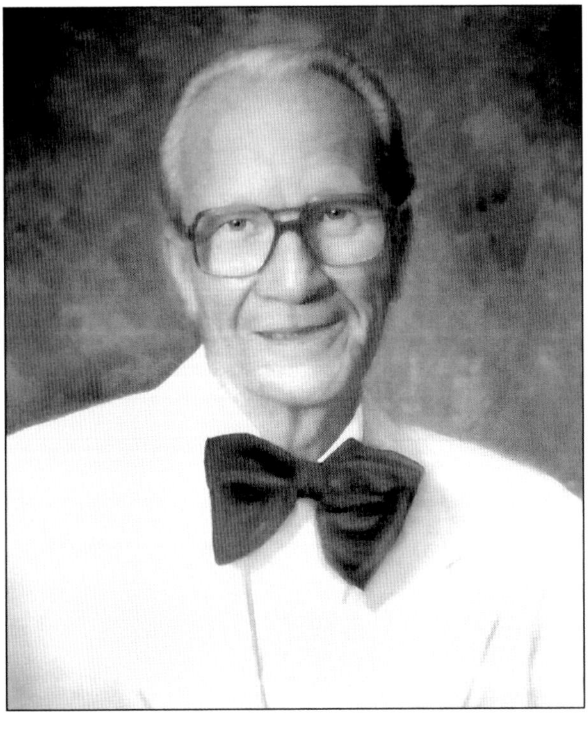

Probate Judge G. Kyser Leonard was born, raised, and resided in Renfroe. Kyser was an undertaker and operated Usrey Funeral Home for 40 years, the last two years as a partner. For nine years, he was coroner of Talladega County. He served eight years in the Alabama House of Representatives and in the Alabama State Senate. In 1970, he was elected probate judge of Talladega County. Kyser retired from politics in January 1977. (Courtesy of Probate Judge Billy Atkinson.)

Six

BUSINESS

Legend has it that the Creeks mined tin along the Coosa River during dry seasons when the water was low. They refused to tell white settlers the location of the mines. There are many caves or tunnels up and down the Coosa River, from Choccolocco Creek to Logan Martin Dam. If any of these housed tin mines, it has not been determined.

Besides farming, early businesses in the Stemley area included water-powered gristmills and gins, a carding plant, and a shingle manufacturing plant along Choccolocco Creek and the Coosa River. As the area became more populated, general stores were opened to supply needed commodities and services. The Stemley area remained mainly an agriculture community until the mid-1960s, when Lake Logan Martin provided financial and recreational opportunities.

People around Stemley Bridge whose entrepreneurship played a dominant role in the community set a foundation for future businesses to come. Early settlers who took a chance with business here were the founders of what has become a flourishing community with many businesses in successful operation today. With roulette odds and using life savings, the early inhabitants brought about financial opportunities that led to economic growth for individuals and the community alike.

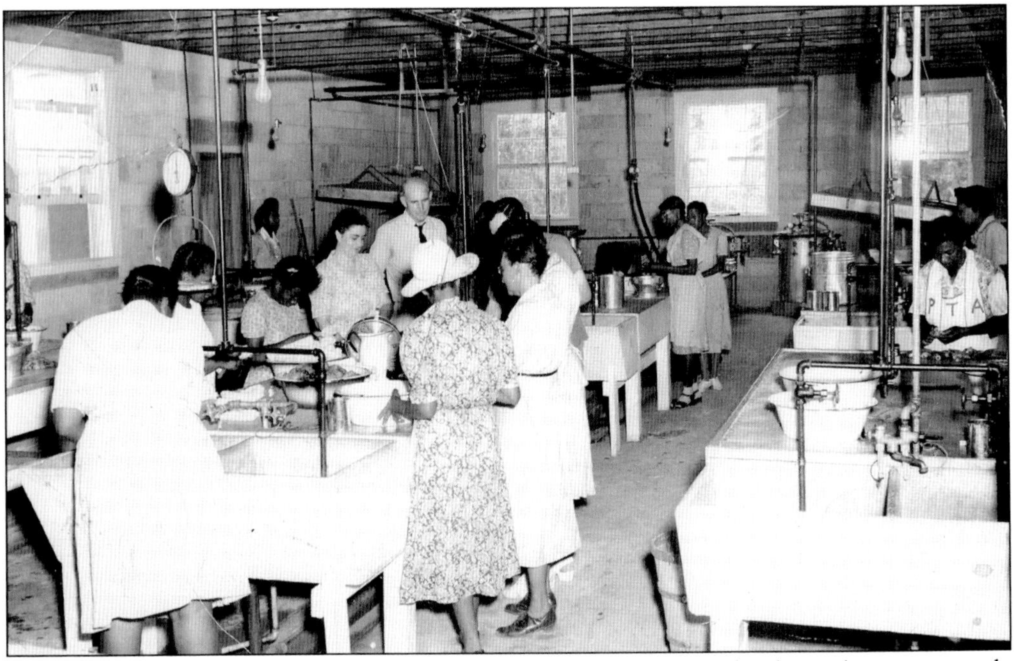

The Canning Plant was located in Talladega County Training School in what is currently the Talladega County Central High School band room. It was the only one of its kind in the Talladega County area. The plant was available to the general public to use for canning fruits and vegetables around 1940. Mr. Armstrong was the vocation agriculture teacher, and the students worked the plant as one of their projects. (Courtesy of Barbara Dunn.)

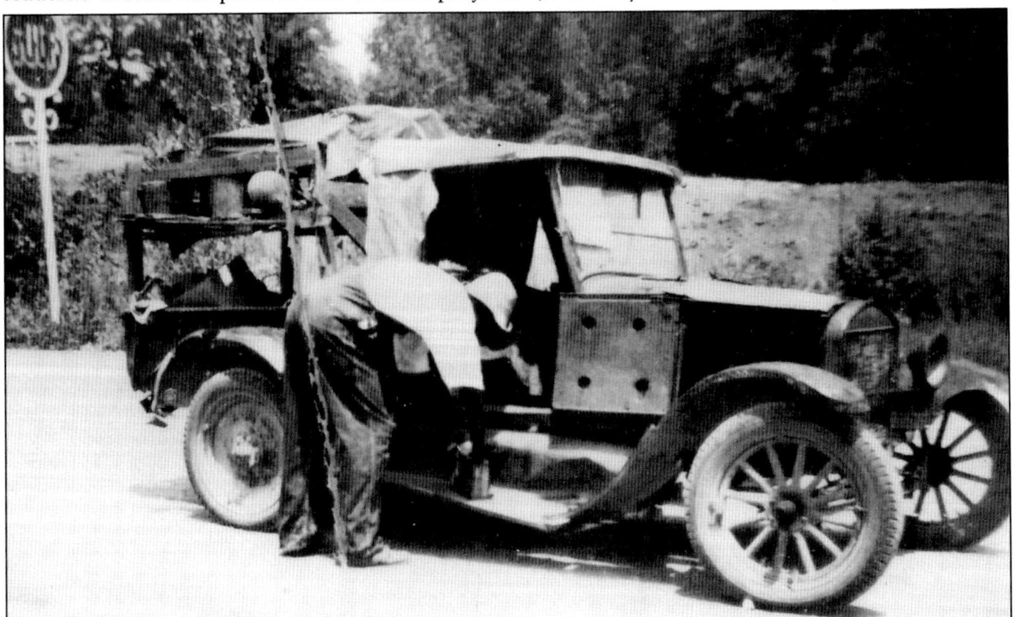

Charlie Phillips made a good living as a peddler around Stemley Bridge in the mid-1900s. Having retired his mule and wagon, he is pictured here with his Model T Ford, parked at Williamson's Store and loaded with vegetables and other items that he sold on his route into town. (Courtesy of Mildred Phillips Swain.)

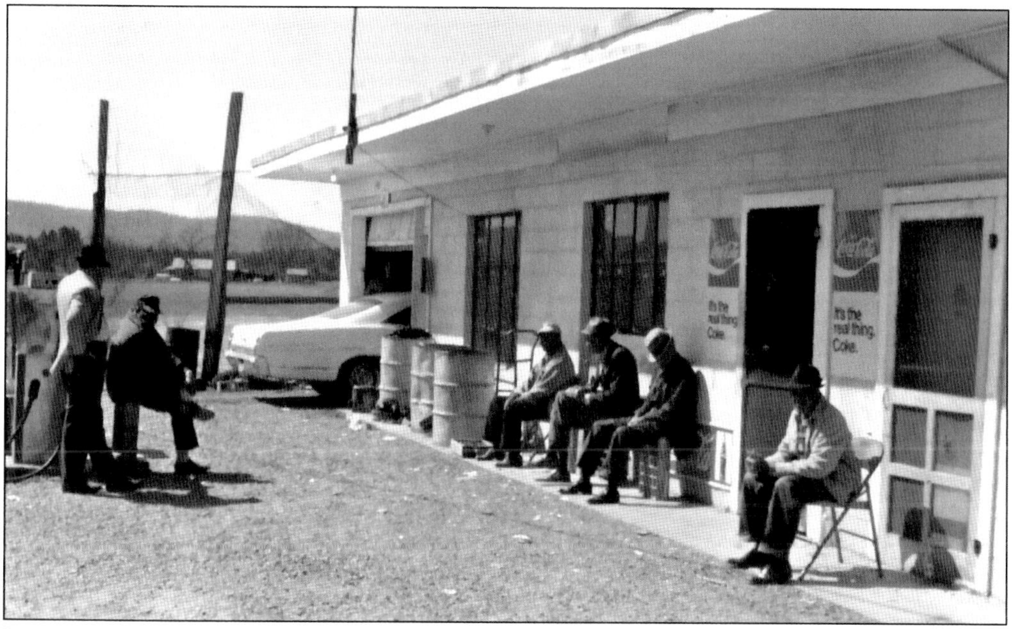

Lawson's Grocery, near Talladega County Training School, was a place where customers could sit and talk or even take a nap in the 1940s and 1950s. Standing at the gas pump is Alphonso Cunningham. J. B. Truss is sitting next to the gas pump. Sitting alongside the building from left to right are J. C. Ragland, Burt Lawson, Robert Cunningham, and Archie Cunningham. (Courtesy of Kelvin Cunningham.)

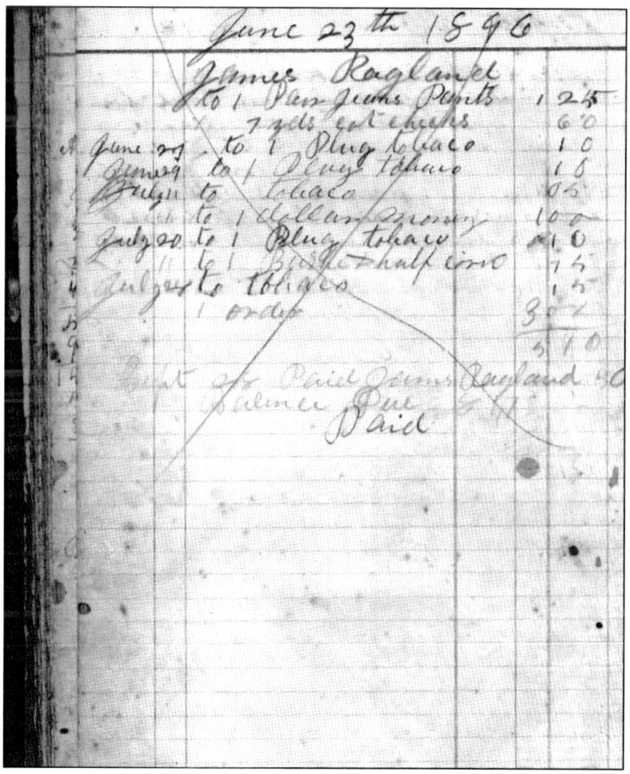
June 23th 1896
James Ragland
to 1 Pair Jeans Pants 1 25
7 yds cot checks 60
June 27 to 1 Plug tobaco 10
to 1 Plug tobaco 10
to tobaco 05
to 1 dollar money 100
July 20 to 1 Plug tobaco 10
to 1 Bushel half corn 75
to tobaco 15
1 order
Paid

George A. Fulmer ran a general store on the Fulmer home place for several years. Shown here is a page from his account book of 1896. James Ragland is a descendant of a slave held by George L. Ragland in the 1860s. The "X" drawn across the sheet indicates the account was paid in full. (Courtesy of the Claude Fulmer family.)

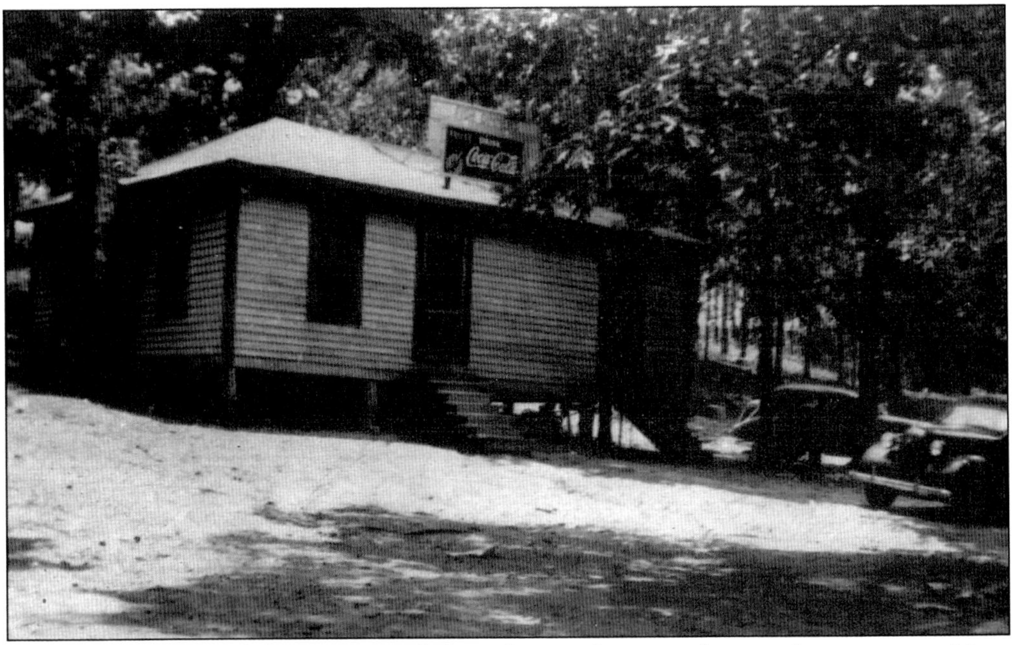

Camp Pleasure was a fishing resort with log cabins, a dance pavilion, and a restaurant. Many people came here in the 1930s and 1940s in chaperoned groups to camp outdoors. They slept in tents and went swimming in the river. They were allowed to help pay for their stay with garden vegetables. (Courtesy of Derrell Hann and Mildred Morriss.)

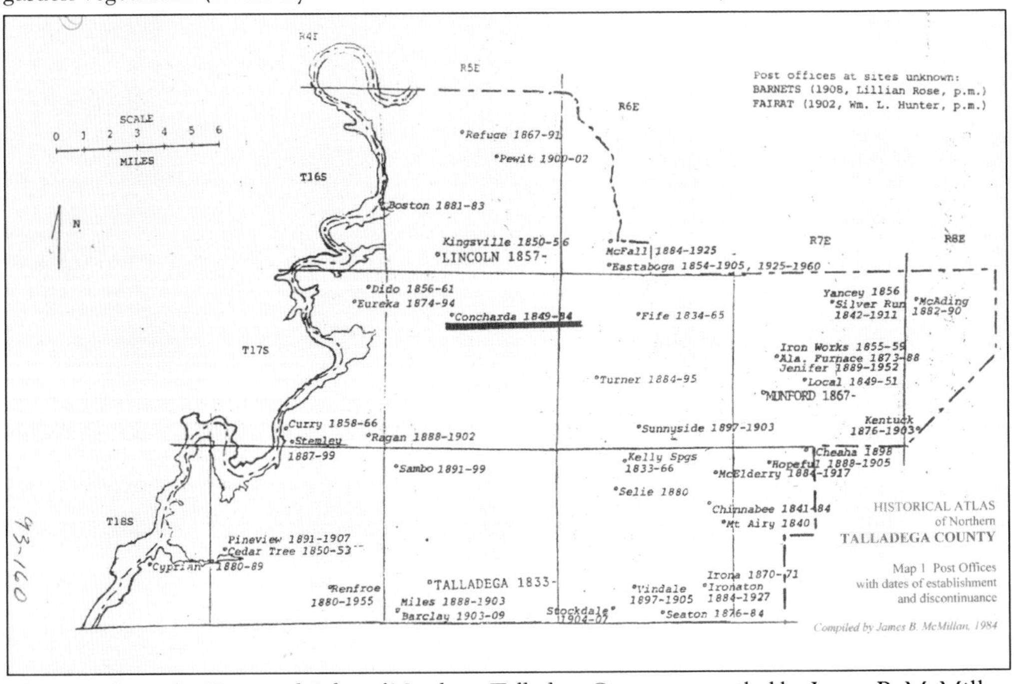

This map from the *Historical Atlas of Northern Talladega County*, compiled by James B. McMillan in 1984, shows the post offices in that area with dates of establishment and discontinuance for each. Not included are Barnets (1908, Lillian Rose, postmaster) and Fairat (1902, William L. Hunter, postmaster), as their locations are unknown.

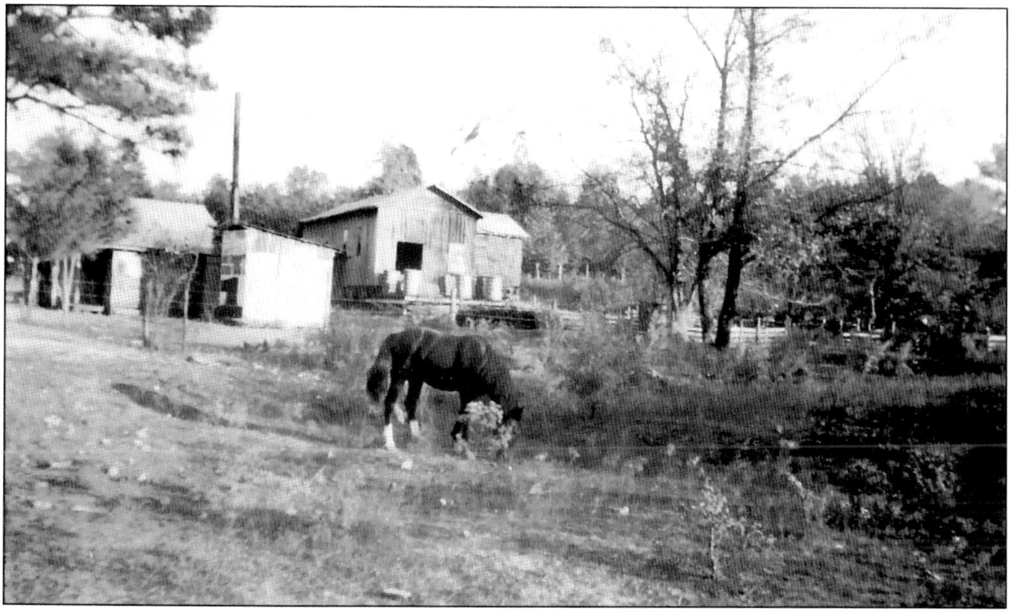

Nearly everyone around Stemley Bridge raised cotton and took it to Stemley Bridge Cotton Gin, owned by Johnny Williamson. The cotton gin was located on Stemley Bridge Road at the "Double Bridges." (Courtesy of Joe Williams.)

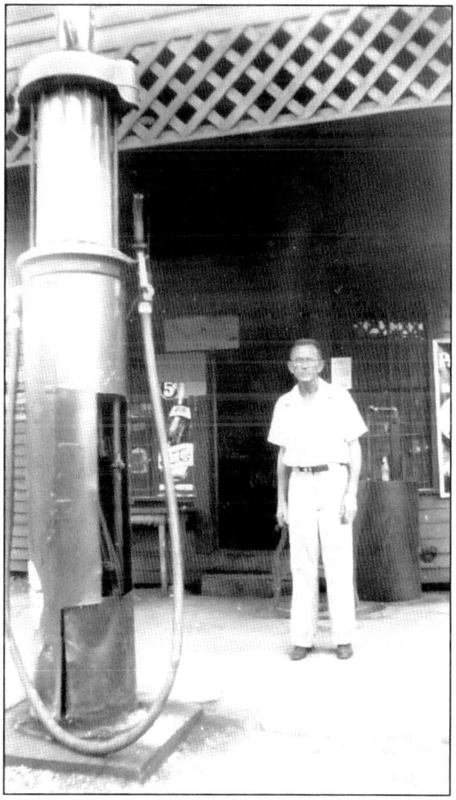

This country store located at the "Double Bridges" on Stemley Bridge Road was owned by Johnny Williamson. Note the old-fashioned gas and kerosene tanks. (Courtesy of Joe Williams.)

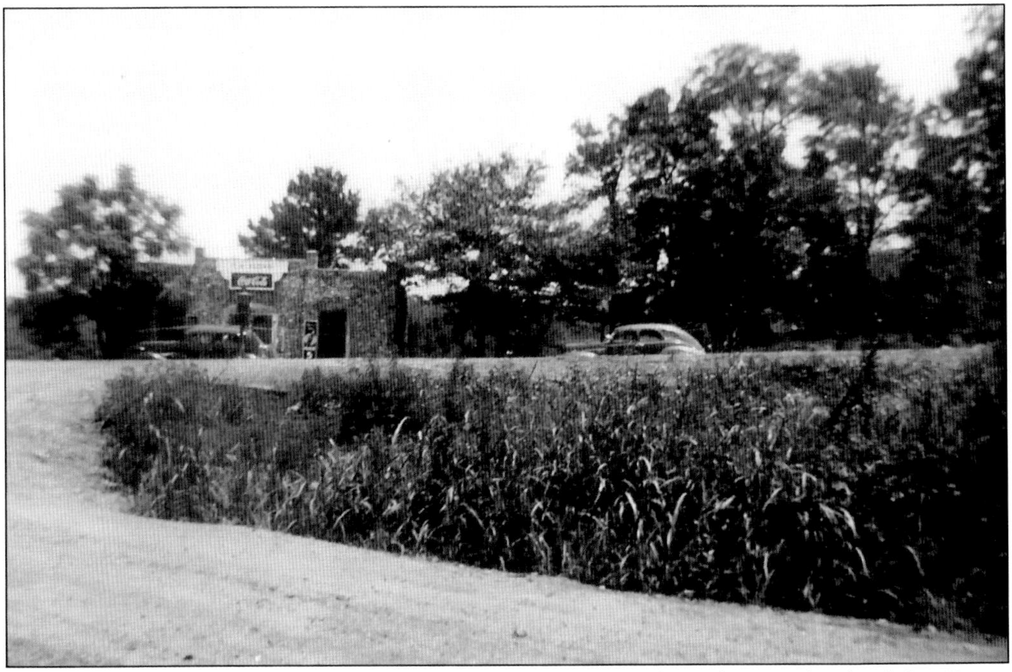

Timmons Floyd's Little Rock Store, shown here, was located on the east bank of the Coosa River at the old Stemley Bridge. Directly across from it was River View Tavern, nicknamed "The Slab House." If you turned right, you would be at another one of the area's remembered places, Camp Pleasure. (Courtesy of Charles Henderson.)

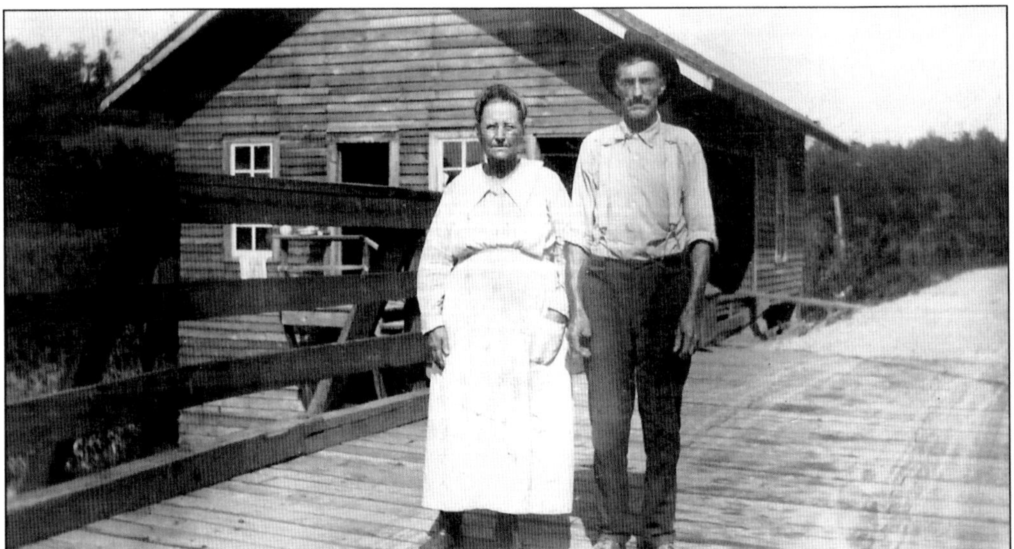

General Woods and his wife are pictured here on the old Stemley Toll Bridge where they worked collecting tolls during the early 1900s. (Courtesy of Rosemary Robinson.)

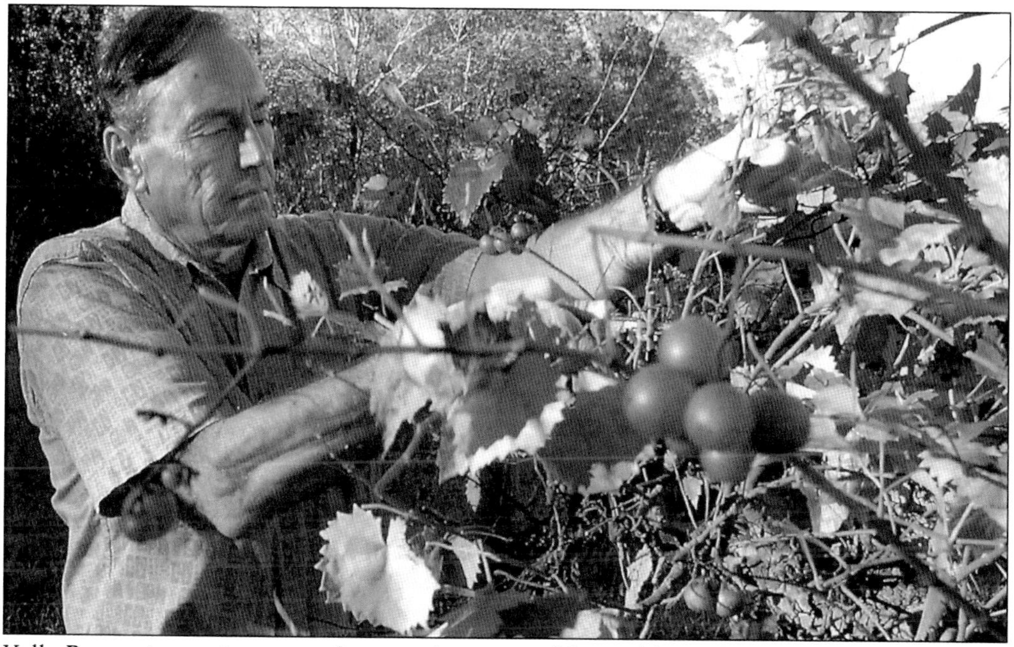

Kelly Bryant is pruning muscadines in the vineyard he and his wife, Susan, own overlooking Lake Logan Martin in Griffitt Bend. Bryant Vineyard is on land that has been in the family since the late 1800s. For years, the farm was owned and operated by Joseph S. Armbrester, grandfather of the Bryants, who found the Coosa Valley ideal for raising a family and growing cotton. (Courtesy of the Bryant family.)

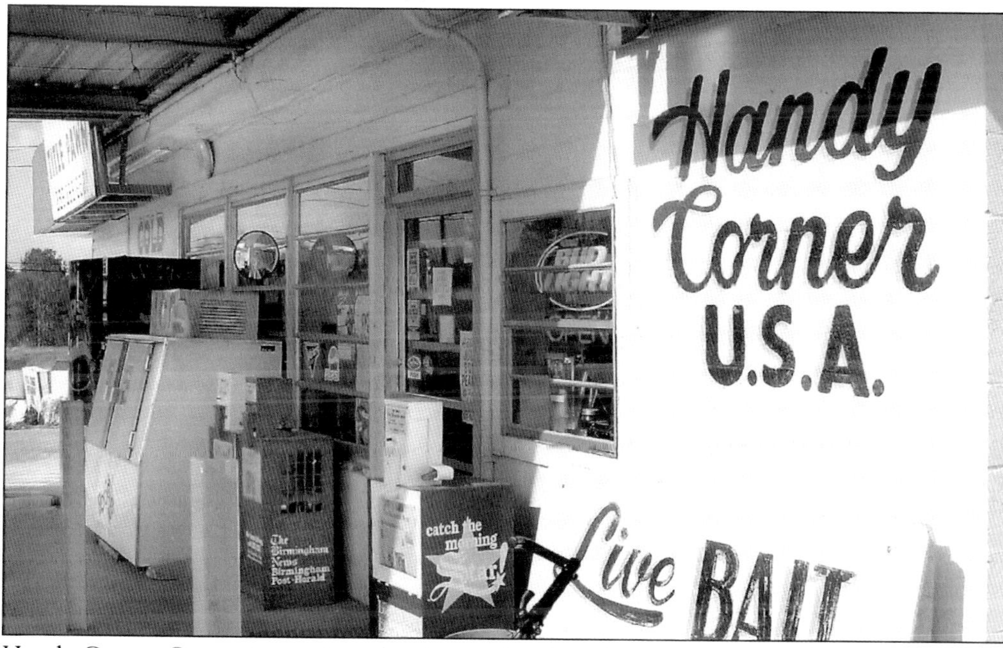

Handy Corner Convenience Store has been a local landmark for 30 years. It is located in the heart of the community at the intersection of Stemley Bridge Road and Stemley Road, at the only blinking traffic light in the area. Handy Corner is currently operated by Tony and Tara Zachero. (Courtesy of Coosa Valley Electric Cooperative.)

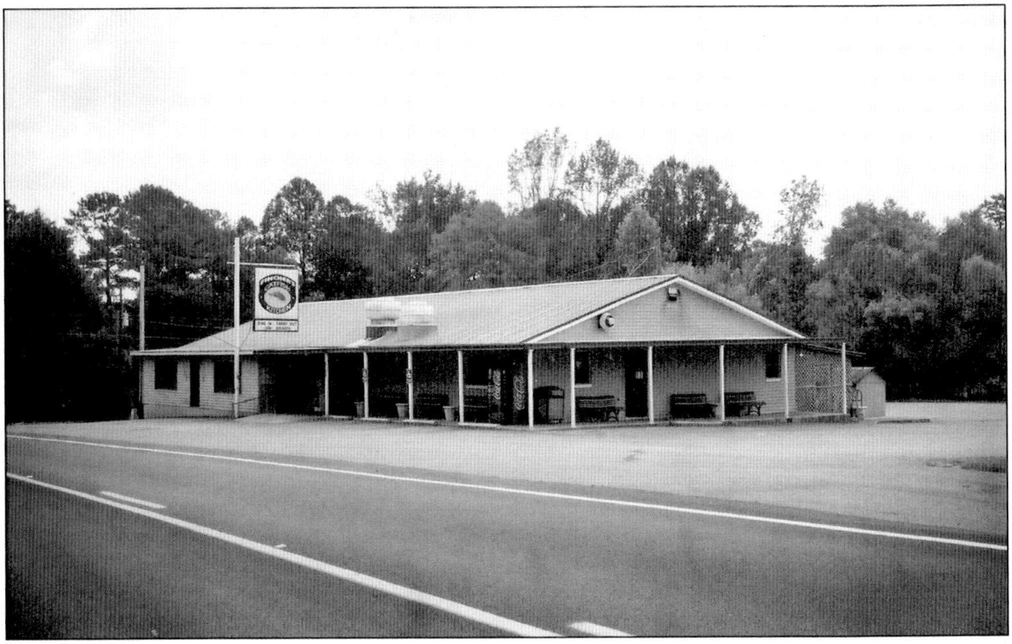

Finchers Catfish Kitchen, a popular seafood restaurant, is located on Renfroe Road. It opened around 1989 and is owned and operated by Doug and Kim Fincher. (Courtesy of Laura Schmidt.)

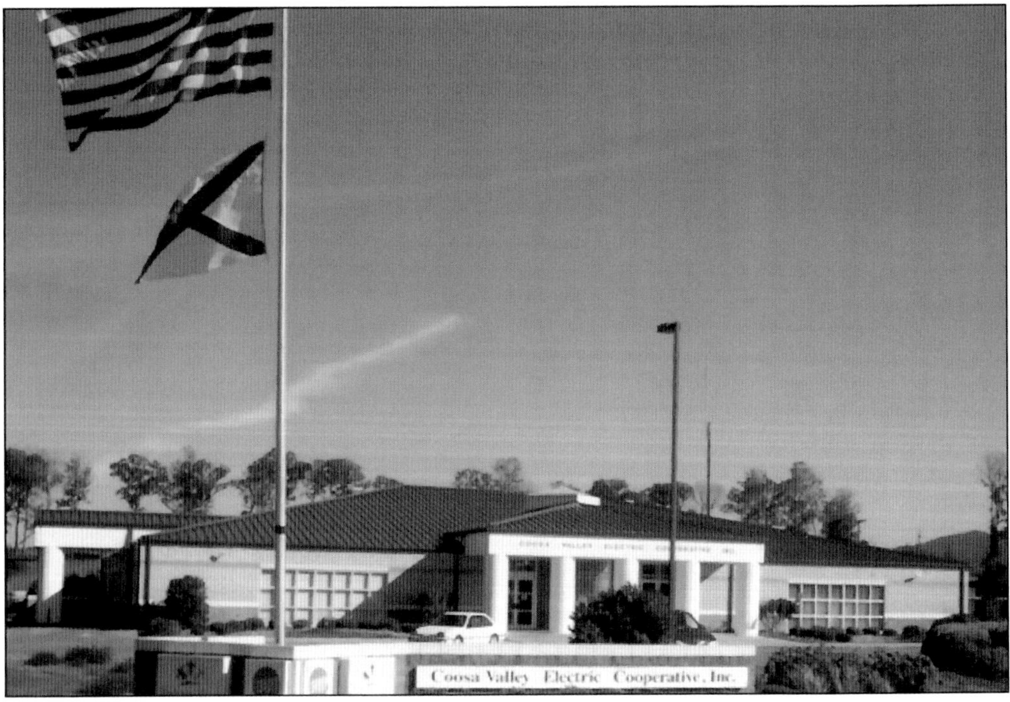

Coosa Valley Electric Cooperative was founded by a group of farmers in 1939 to bring power to a few hundred rural customers in Calhoun, St. Clair, and Talladega Counties. Today the cooperative serves some 16,000 members in six counties. Unlike investor-owned utilities such as Alabama Power, CVEC is governed by a board of trustees elected by the consumers. (Courtesy of Coosa Valley Electric Cooperative.)

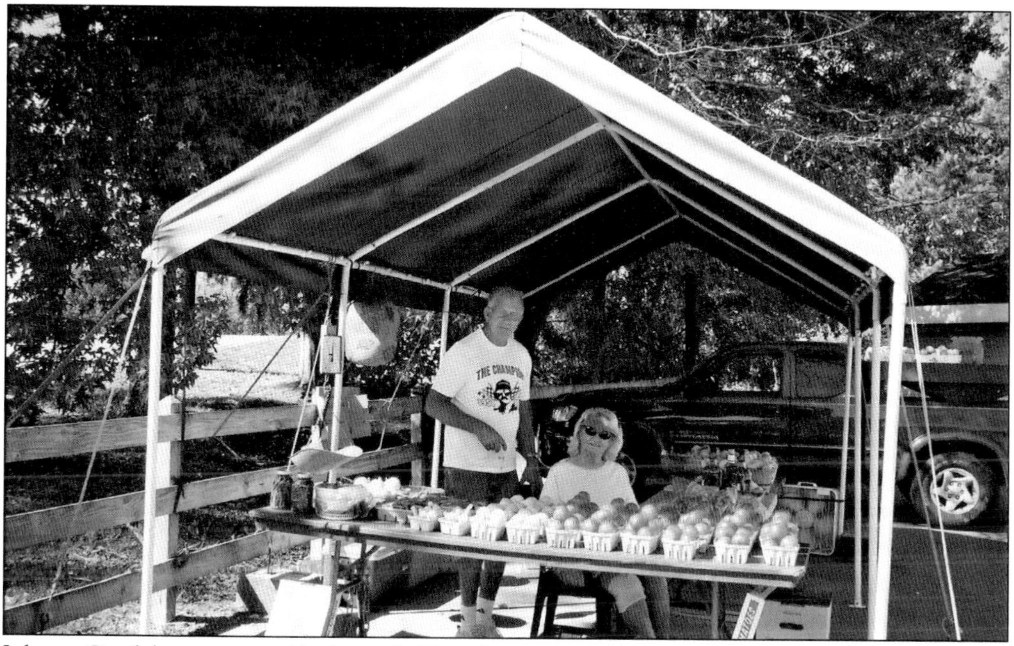

Johnny Castleberry, assisted by his wife, Faye, has operated his popular produce stand on Stemley Bridge Road West for five years. Johnny is up at 3:45 a.m. every Tuesday through Saturday during the summer months to make the trip to the Birmingham Farmer's Market and be back at his stand by 8:30 a.m. Peaches and tomatoes are customer favorites, but his display includes a variety of vegetables and fruits. (Courtesy of Laura Schmidt.)

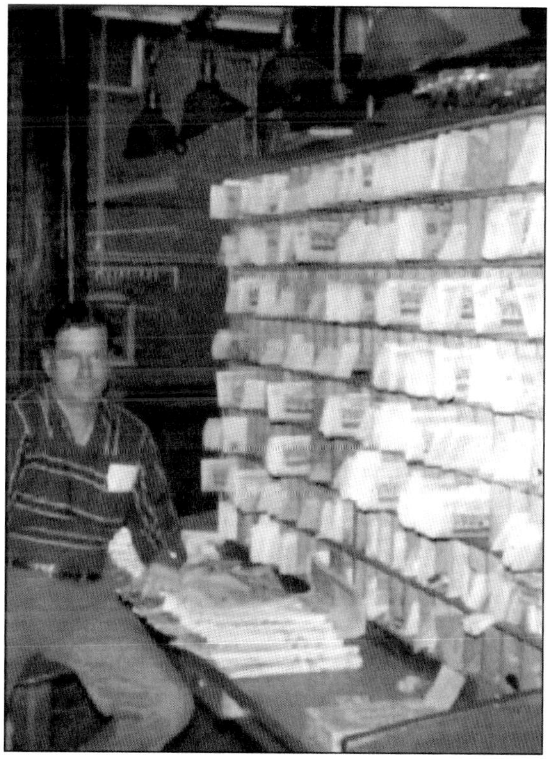

W. Hugh Sims, shown here around 1943, was Renfroe's mail carrier beginning in 1918 and spanning 39 years. He was one of the earliest mail carriers for the area. He had two horses and rode them on alternate days. Hugh was very active in the Renfroe community: he was a 50-year Mason, served in various capacities at Hepzibah Baptist Church, and was a director of Talladega County Farm Bureau. (Courtesy of Lisa Baggett.)

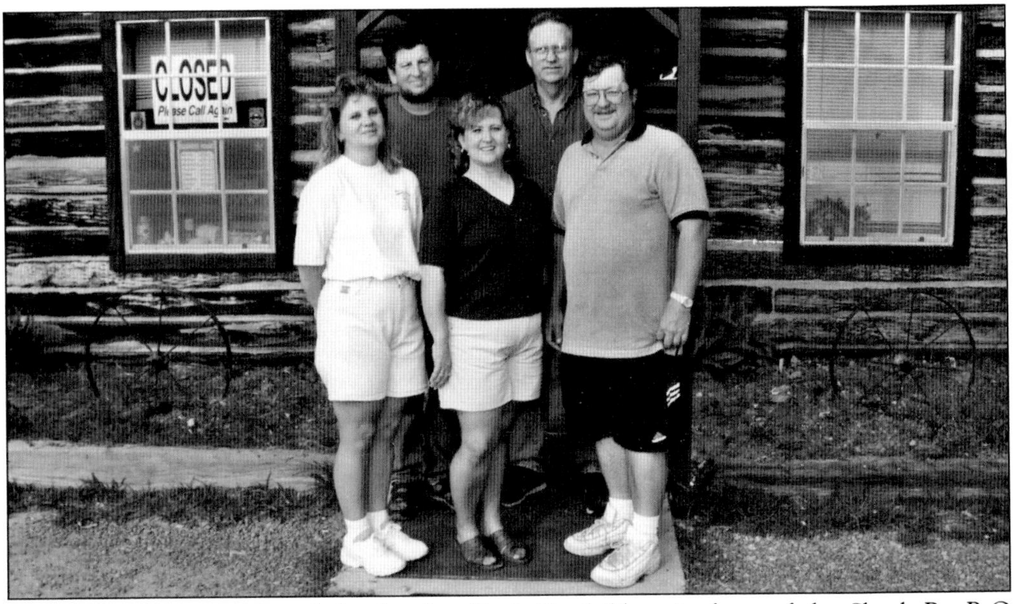

Darrell Ray Hann poses with his brother Haskell's children in front of the Shack Bar-B-Q c. 1990. From left to right, are (first row) Shane Hann (Haney), Sharon Hann (Frieze), and Wayne Hann; (second row) Jeffrey Hann and Darrell Ray Hann. Sharon is the current owner of the Shack, which is operated by her siblings, her children, and her nieces and nephews. The Shack has become a historical landmark of the Stemley community. Jeffrey Hann is the main cook who tends to the fire pit where all the meat is cooked. (Courtesy of Sharon Frieze.)

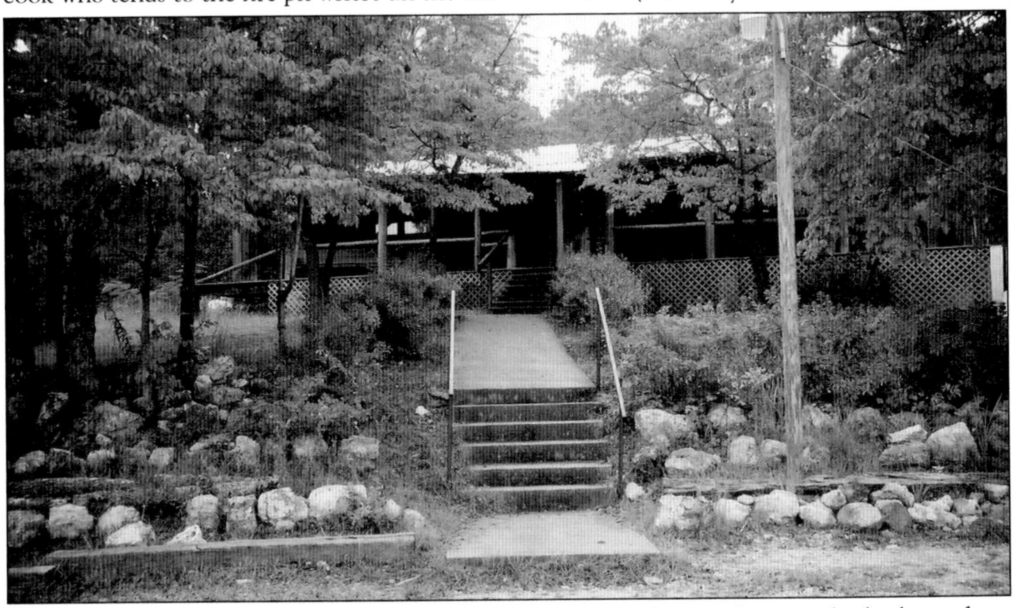

Stemley Station, a family restaurant located on Stemley Bridge Road across the highway from Handy Corner, has been serving the Stemley community for 20 years. The Bill and Kay Huffaker family and friends cleared the property and used the wood to build a hand-hewn log structure. The restaurant burned down in 1999, but within five months, the Huffakers, with the help of their customers and church friends, built the present building, which is about twice the size of the original. (Courtesy of Dot Wesson.)

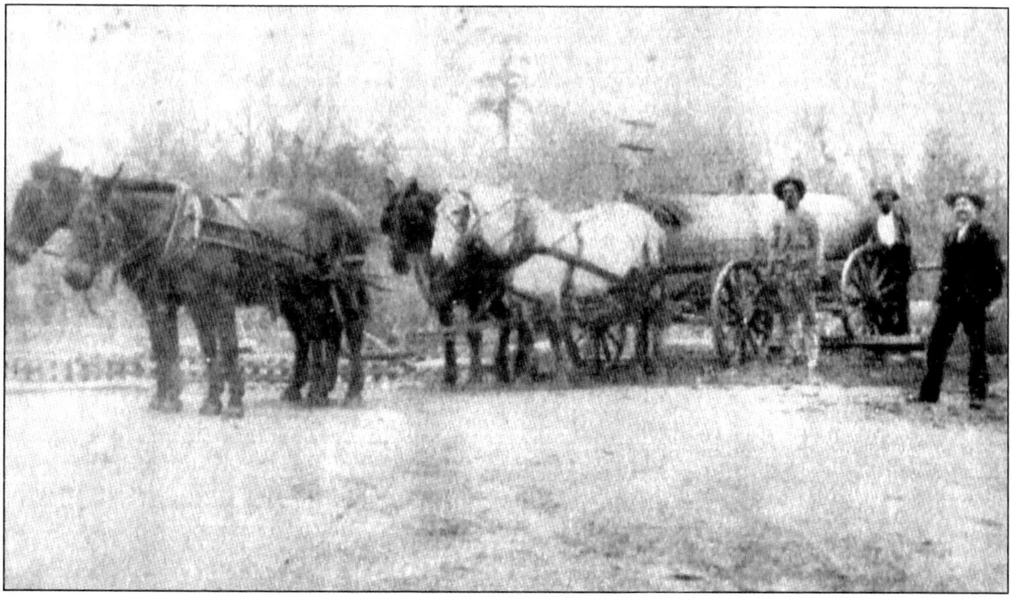

At Schmidt's Mill, a wagon loaded with cotton was driven onto the scales and weighed. The cotton bolls were then sucked upstairs to the gins where the seeds were removed and the loose cotton was dropped back down for bailing. Some customers took their cottonseed back with them to be planted or used for fertilizer or feed. Others sold their seeds to the mill, which processed them to get the oil. Teams of oxen or mules and horses, as shown here, were used to haul barrels of cottonseed oil to Talladega for further processing or to the train station to be taken to New York. (Courtesy of Laura Schmidt.)

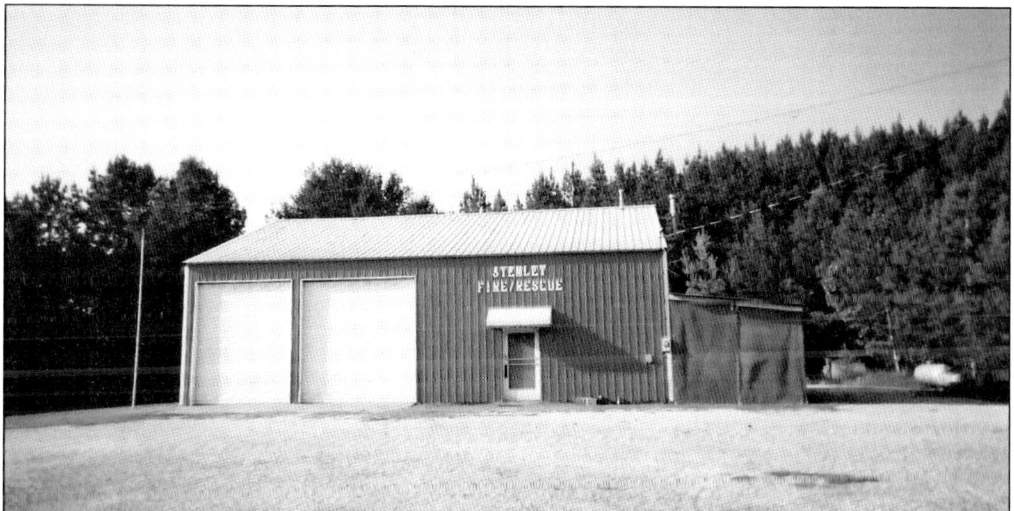

The original location of the Stemley Volunteer Fire Department was on Highway 34 at the double bridges. The chief was Charles Watts. Among the members were Marvin Williams, Glenn Williams, A. C. Beck, Charles Watts, James Beck, Roy Hill, Johnny Paul Hutto, Johnny Wiggins, Leslie Hutto, Dude Garrett, Richard Johnson, Haskell Hann, Clay Williams, and Pete Pilkington. In 1984, the fire department moved to the present location of Fire Station No. 2 on Old Lincoln Highway. Station No. 1 on Old Stemley Bridge Road began operation in 2003. (Courtesy of Pete Gaither.)

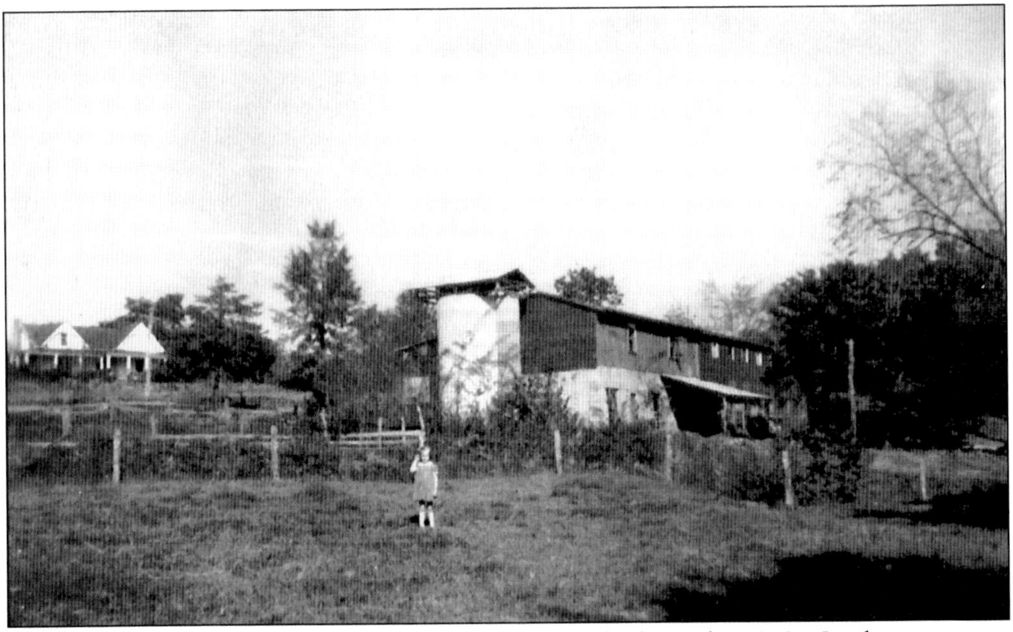

Above is the home of Bernhard Schmidt, which was built in the 1880s. In the center are Schmidt's oil mill, store, and silo. Built in 1883, the mill was in operation until 1913 and could process five tons of cottonseed per day. Previously used only for planting, seeds could now be processed to make nylon, cooking oil, paints, and cattle feed. Bernhard's great-granddaughter, Laura, is standing in the pasture *c.* 1944. (Courtesy of Laura Schmidt.)

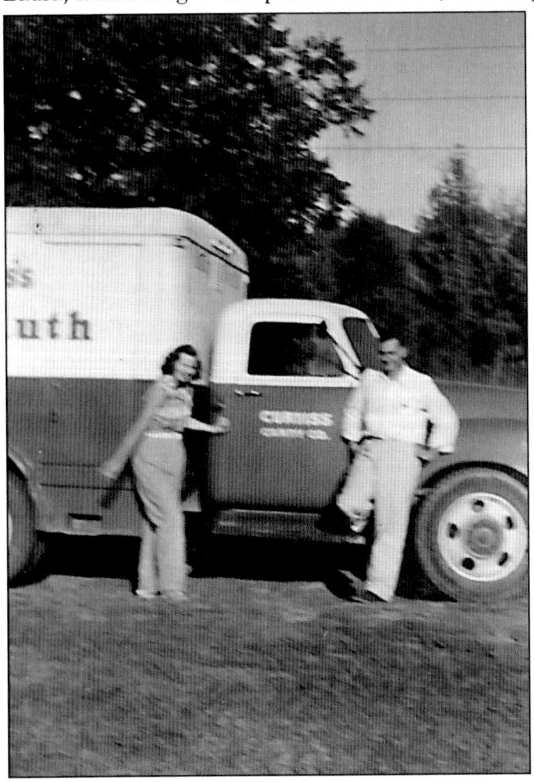

Herbert Sims and his sister, Annie Laura (Sims) Porter, are standing beside the Curtiss Candy Company truck Herbert drove on his daily routes in 1952. His Wednesday route left Talladega, went by the county training school, up to Glen Williamson's store, down the Stemley Bridge Road, past Floyd's store and across the river to Cropwell, down the Florida Short Route 231, through Vincent and Harpersville, then crossed over to Renfroe and back to Talladega. (Courtesy of Herbert Sims.)

Bob Nabors is pictured here around 1938 beside the general store he owned next to Stemley Bridge on the St. Clair County side. (Courtesy of Rosemary Robinson.)

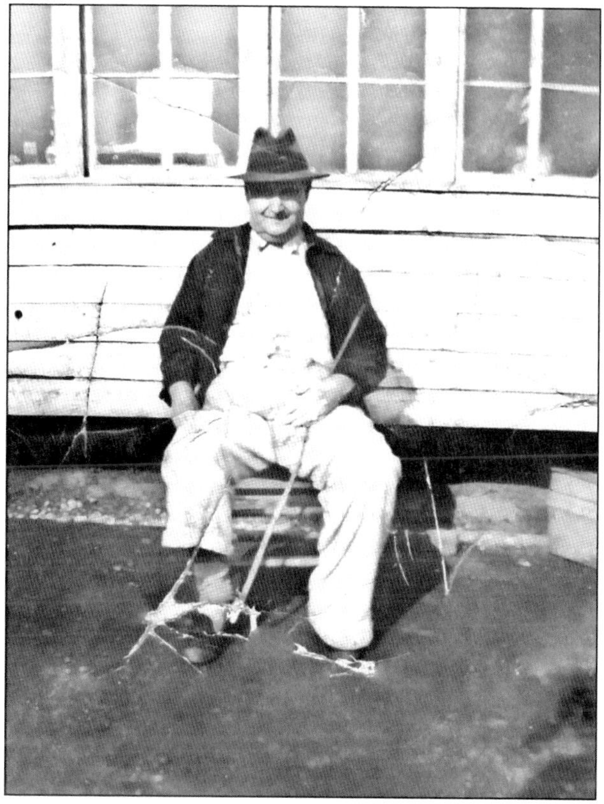

Stemley Metal Working Company (1965–2002) was operated by Harold and Thelma Daffron. Thelma was the office manager and Harold's number one supporter. Harold fabricated, sandblasted, welded, and refinished metal. The storm of 1993 collapsed the roof "beyond repair," yet he repaired it. He had the mind of an engineer, skill of a machinist, and heart of an entrepreneur. Harold Daffron was Stemley Metal Working Company. After he reached retirement age, friends would drop by the shop for the "serious work" of solving world problems or reminiscing. (Courtesy of JoAnn Gauldin.)

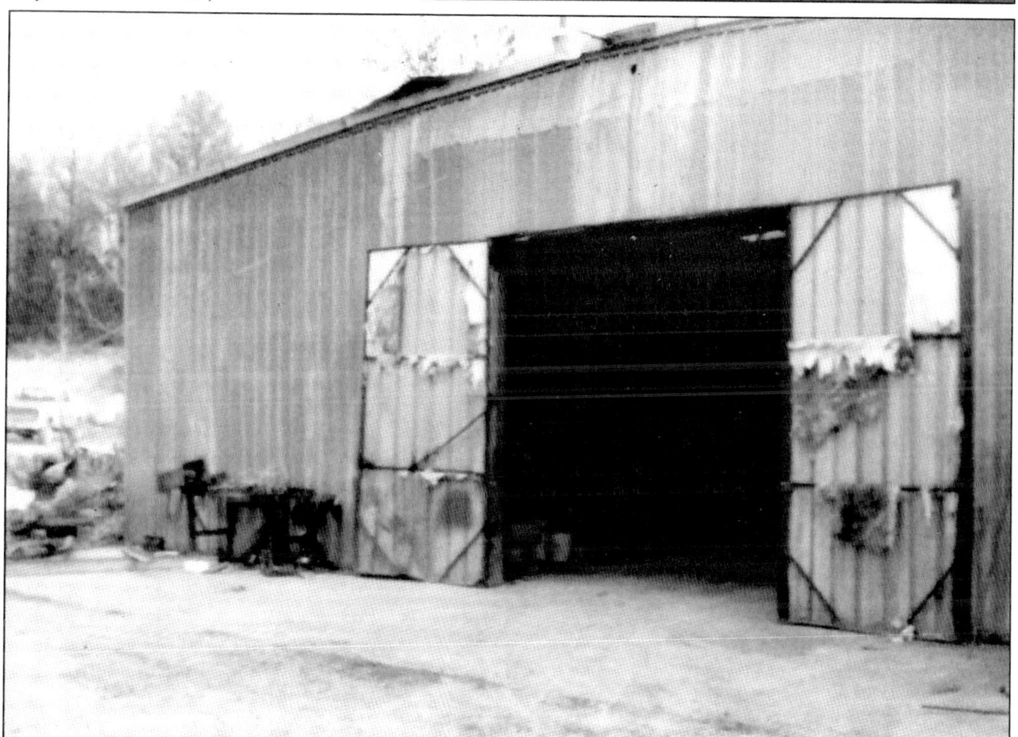

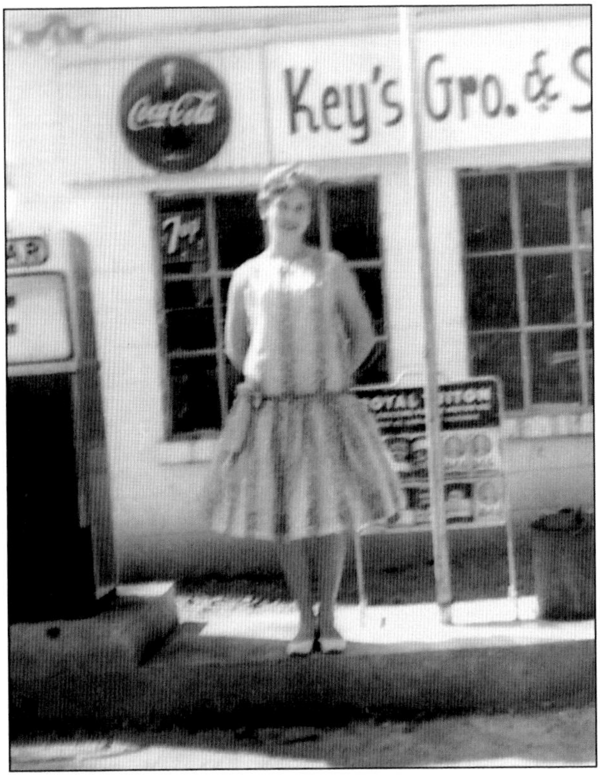

Thurston and Ruby Key, the owners and operators of Key's Grocery on Stemley Bridge Road, built the store in 1958. Dorothy Kay Key (Huffaker), daughter of Thurston and Ruby, posed for this photograph c. 1960 in front of the family store. Thurston and Ruby also had a son, Ricky Key. (Courtesy of Ruby Key.)

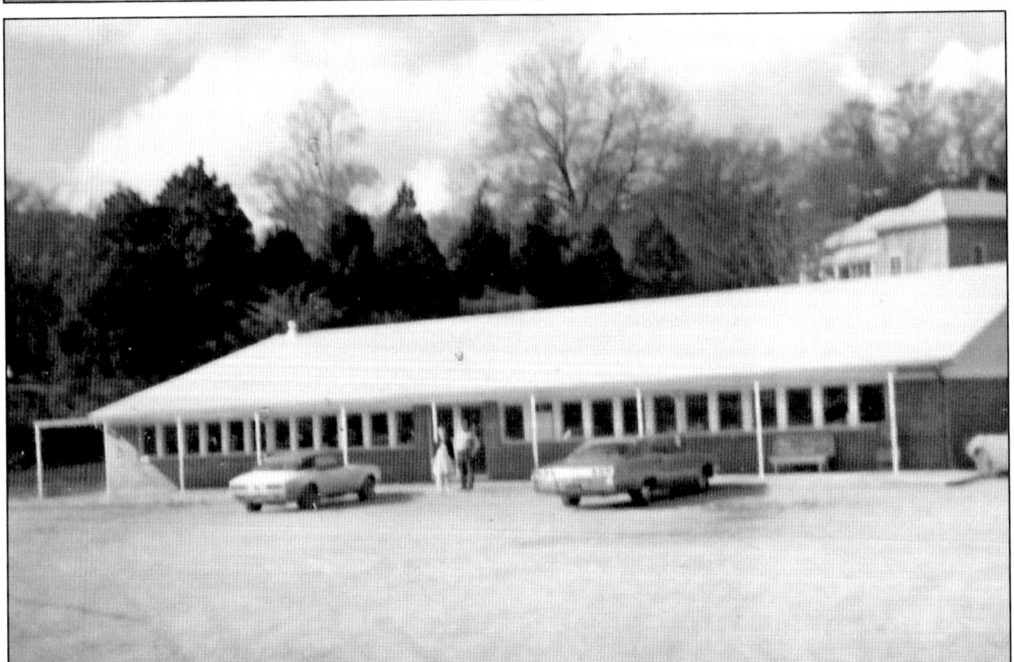

Grover and Ethel Heath owned and operated the Fort Lashley Curb Market from 1971 until 1985. Today Grover maintains three gardens, and Ethel cans and preserves the vegetables. (Courtesy of the Heath family.)

Seven

Lower Logan Martin Lake

Construction began on Logan Martin Dam on the Coosa River in July 1960, and it went into operation in August 1964, flooding 100-year-old businesses and homes in its path. The dam is 612 feet wide, 97 feet tall at its highest point, and is constructed of 180,000 cubic yards of concrete. Its three alternating current generators are capable of producing about 400 million kilowatt hours of electricity annually.

Logan Martin Lake is located on the Coosa River between Logan Martin and Henry Neeley Dams; it is almost 50 miles long, approximately 275 miles around, and has an average depth of 18 feet. The lake is almost equally divided at Riverside. The upper half is fed by the Alligator, Blue Eye, Broken Arrow, Cane, and Ohatchee Creeks. The 17-mile upper end changes very little from the original river channel. Choccolocco, Clear, and Cropwell Creeks, Poorhouse Branch, Rabbit Branch, and Seddon feed the lower half of Logan Martin Lake. Sloughs and these incoming streams widen the lake dramatically from Riverside to Logan Martin Dam.

Logan Martin Lake offers some of the best fishing in the state, including bass, catfish, crappie, carp, and gar. There are thousands of visitors each summer who enjoy water sports, sailing, picnicking, and fishing.

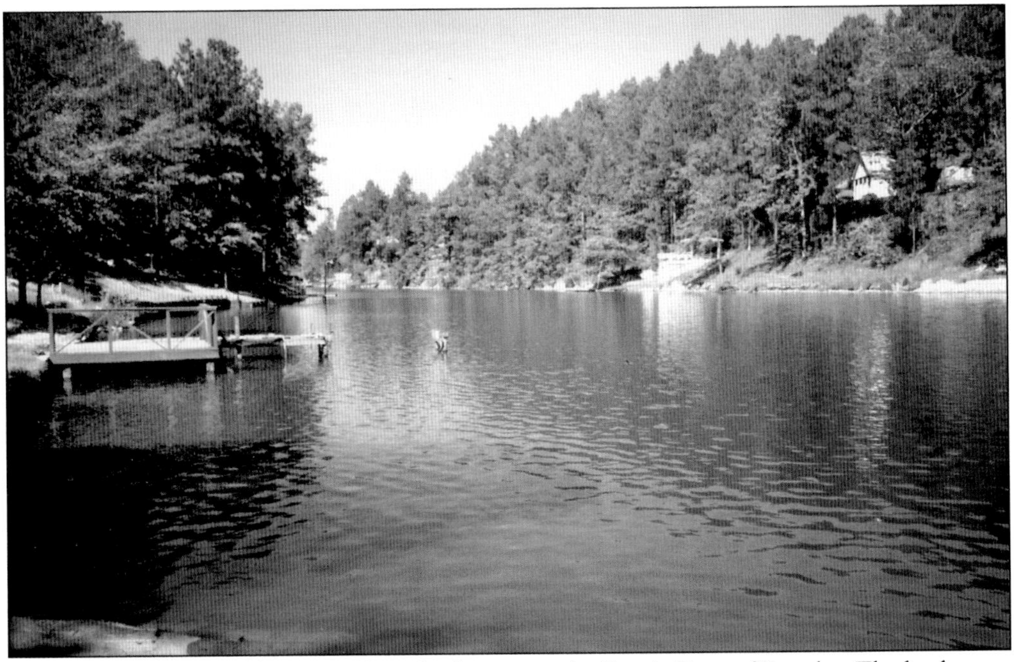

This slough was formed by Coosa River backwater in the South Cove of Stemley. The backwater submerged fields and an old railroad bed in 1964 when Logan Martin Dam was built. (Courtesy of Evelyn Roach.)

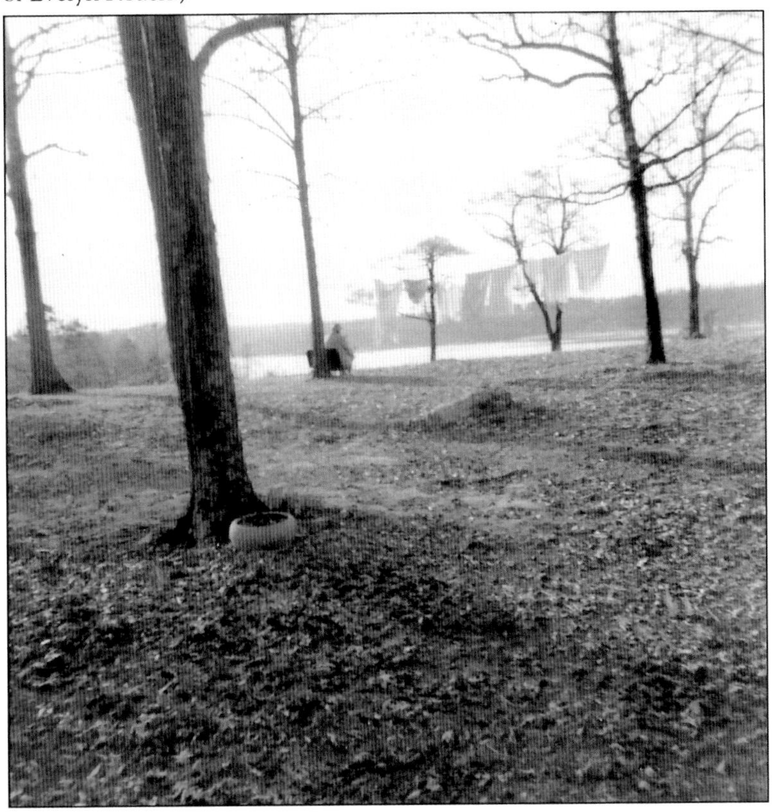

Josie Fulmer is sitting on an old school bench on the backwater of Coosa River in 1965 after Logan Martin Dam had been in partial operation for several months. (Courtesy of Calvin Sanders.)

Steve Stathelson was baptized in June 1969 by Elder Armond Ritch, who was pastor of New Mt. Carmel Primitive Baptist Church. The baptism took place in the backwater of the Logan Martin Dam that covered the old roadbed about one mile north of Stemley Bridge. (Courtesy of Donna Cordes.)

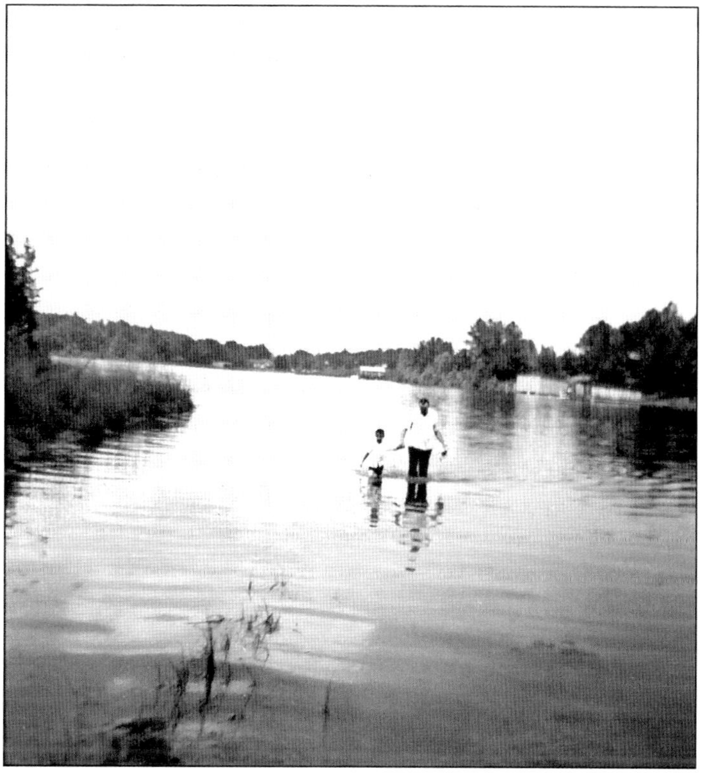

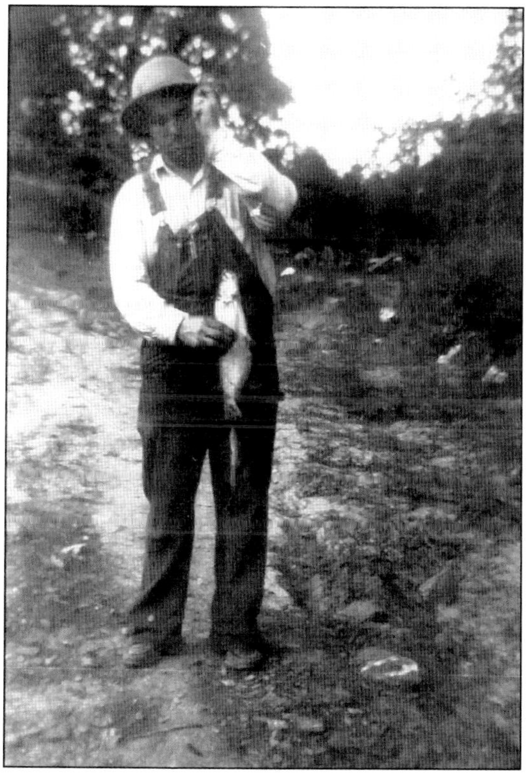

James Fuller is shown leaving Logan Martin Lake with his "catch of the day." James was born in 1917, lived close to the Talladega County water tower, and worked at Bemiston for 32 years. (Courtesy of Adrienne Fuller.)

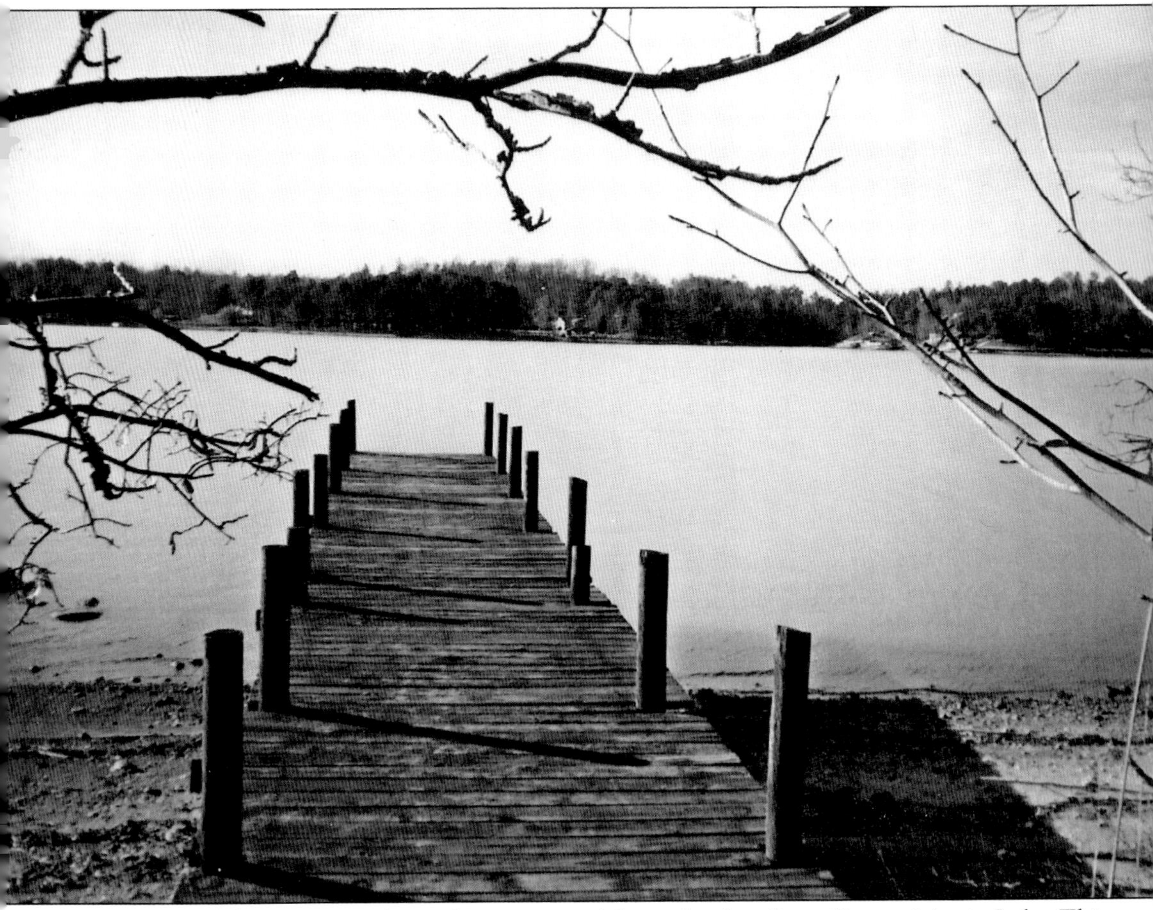

There are fishing piers similar to this one up and down the shoreline of Logan Martin Lake. This one is about three-fourths of a mile north of Stemley Bridge. (Courtesy of Nikolaus Cordes.)